GOODBYE
RHODESIA

CHRIS MEARS

*This book has been printed digitally and produced in a standard specification
in order to ensure its continuing availability*

Published by Antony Rowe Publishing Services in 2005
2 Whittle Drive
Highfield Industrial Estate
Eastbourne
East Sussex
BN23 6QT
England

Map by permission of HarperCollins

ISBN 1-905200-44-7

Cover photo by Jan Teede
Typesetting by Freddy Gilles and Tony Leighton

Printed and bound by Antony Rowe Ltd, Eastbourne

Introduction

We had lived in Rhodesia for 25 years, and returned to England in 1977. We had thought to live in Africa forever. This was not a land where immigrants talked of 'home', but a place to make a living and a home out of a hot, rough, in turns arid and tempestuous, largely uninhabited and uncultivated *bundu*.

Martin and I left near the end of the "war" for black independence, three years before Ian Smith and the white government was brought down more by pressure from the rest of the world than by terrorism from within.

We loved this country, which was first called Southern Rhodesia, then just Rhodesia (after Northern Rhodesia became Zambia) and is now Zimbabwe. It was time to leave because we could see nothing but trouble in the future under a black government. In southern Africa we all watched the "wind of change" sweep down from Kenya, the Congo, Nyasaland, Northern Rhodesia, Mozambique, Angola, bringing with each stride, with each state of independence, black-against-black wars and consequent ruin and mayhem.

We were in our late forties, our two daughters were independent and established and there was half a hope they would follow us once we had made a foothold. Now or never we had to make the break. The tobacco and maize farm that was to have been our life's work and our pension was to yield neither. Everything we possessed was packed in crates, our dog was flown to English quarantine kennels, and with £900 that we were allowed to bring out, returned to the land of our birth. Rhodesians told us there was standing room only in England, and apprehensive English relatives warned us we'd be too old to find work in a country with labour problems.

Within two days of arriving at Heathrow we each found jobs, and somewhere to lay our heads (not standing). It was the wisest thing we've ever done. It could be said that displaced white farmers only got their just desserts: that they had stolen the land from the Africans who lived there and now it was time to give it back.

Rhodesia's history had all started in 1890, when Cecil Rhodes and the Pioneer Column, lured by gold, first hoisted the Union flag near what was to become Salisbury. Nobody questioned if it was right to make deals with the black tribes that lived there - adding the country to the British Empire was bringing civilisation, carving up the land into farms and giving or selling acreages to white men to grow food and tobacco was progress. It was being done throughout the world: nineteenth- and twentieth-century Europeans thought that way.

I often wonder what this land we called Rhodesia would have been like if left in the hands of the mainly Shona and Ndebele tribesmen. The influence of the West and East could not have been ignored entirely. We were told it was right to help the deprived native to a better life - the term "black man" wasn't considered polite then.

At school in England on Empire Day we had stood at Assembly and sung patriotic songs, and the Vicar, or some other worthy gentleman, would come and give us a talk about heathens and pygmies and evil slave traders. We'd sing with the good Bishop Heber:
"In vain with lavish kindness
The gifts of God are strown,
The heathen in his blindness
Bows down to blood and stone."

When we grew older, Anthony Eden told us the strength of the Empire was the way out of our post-world-war economic crisis and that it was impossible to exaggerate the significance of Empire trade. We were urged to go out and help build up this Empire. It was our bounden duty to civilise Africa. People emigrate today with much less noble aspirations.

I didn't go for this reason. I went for the excitement.

But now in 1980 in Rhodesia, three years after we had left, there was a black government, a new name. Zimbabwe started to sort

4

itself out and life settled down and became enjoyable again for the whites, relieved at last of any army or police call-up duties. Tobacco-farming friends again enjoyed life by the swimming pool and sundowners and braaivleis on the stoep (drinks and barbecues on the verandah).

With the end of sanctions, Britain was again buying their tobacco (best in the world), South Africa their maize, the world their minerals and flowers.

Old Rhodesian friends visited us in our tiny house while we beavered away in the cold and wet, scraping ice off the car windscreen. They showed us their snaps of blond children in beautiful, flowering gardens with swimming pools in the sun, and on holiday on Natal beaches. For twenty years their dream lasted. Even though we had to work hard, we reckoned life was fuller in England and particularly with the chance of world travel, easy and without too much expense. We had never been too good at the restricted social life of the bush.

But just sometimes, the odd thoughts: "Had we done the wrong thing?"

During these early days of independence, farms in Rhodesia were actually bought by the Marxist government for the resettlement of former guerrillas and refugees. These "veterans" presumably found life on isolated farms less to their liking than roaming in bands terrorising blacks and whites, so after a few years, when the plots had been stripped of their trees and the wells and boreholes silted up, the lands were abandoned.

Twice we visited the new Zimbabwe in the 1980s. All was friendly, black and white all alike, all forgiven. A fence was erected round Victoria Falls to stop it being overrun and we were charged to go in, surprisingly on three scales - overseas visitors extortionately (unless they paid in US dollars, pounds, marks or whatever), South Africans moderately, and locals cheap. After a while you got used to this.

Although white faces prevailed among the visitors in the hotels (which were, however, far from busy), there was a different face on the country, particularly in First Street, Harare. Now black babies were breast-fed by *umfazis* under the jacaranda and flame trees in the avenues and Cecil Square. In the past Africans sitting on the benches or lounging on the grass were frowned upon, even though the fable had been that there was no apartheid in Rhodesia. Cecil Square had been where "Europeans" took lunchtime strolls in the shade and bought bunches of sweet-smelling flowers from eager stallholders.

Now the veneer of fraternity was too forced. I felt uneasy. No-one else appeared to be.

Let me first tell you my story of Rhodesia from 1952.

One

The house by the dam was made of wood, and the day the fire swept down the vlei I thought we would lose everything. I had my daughters by either hand, and Fuji, our Alsatian dog was standing beside us. We were preparing ourselves to wade into the dam if we had to. The doors and windows of the house were shut against the wind that blows before the fire.

I had lived on a Mashonaland farm for nine years, where the grass grows higher than anywhere I know, but I had never seen a fire like it. Now, at the end of an exceptionally dry winter, after a defeatingly wet summer, the grass stood two metres high in the valley. The strong, coarse stems had turned from yellow to drab grey in the excess of their dryness.

The great wind came relentlessly as fast as a man can run, bringing charred flakes of grass and soot from the sky.

My husband, Martin, had gone with his African labourers to start a back fire from the road to the top of the valley, but I could see the fire was so close it had already jumped the road. There was nothing now between us and the fire but the dry grass.

Susie and Paula were not particularly scared. For nearly all their eight and seven years of life, this was the sort of thing that life comprised.

The year before we had deliberately chosen to return to Rhodesia. We had re-emigrated to Europe after ten years in Rhodesia, but found ourselves unable to settle there again.

Martin felt that Rhodesia had at least fifteen years before any revolution came. I thought he was pessimistic in his assessment. So we returned to Rhodesia - the best place we knew to bring up our children. If, later, the country no longer offered a reasonable life to a white population, the children would be old enough to emigrate independently when they wished, as we had done when we were twenty-one.

Our last night in London we had gone to see Anthony Newley in "Stop the World - I Want to Get Off!" We came back determined we were "gonna build a heaven".

The hose running near at hand was ready to combat odd sparks that might land on the tarred felt roof. The garden lawn stood short and green to keep the fire from the walls, while the hard sticks of orange and grapefruit trees we had planted last year were now bent double in the tremendous wind. Above the indigenous trees of the surrounding bush the smoke billowed yellow and grey, so that there was no longer earth and sky, but an enshrouding hell.

Helpless grasshoppers with dry-grass bodies leapt into the small garden trying to flee the raging heat, and above, the circling buzzards and eagles climbed higher and higher, swept in the surge of hot currents.

The drongos (European blackbird sized) were busy wheeling at the edge of the flames - they loved a fire, and the insects it flushed out. The dull brown edges of their wings looked scorched in contrast to their all-black bodies. It was almost as if they had evolved this way.

Martin arrived in a cloud of road dust in the Land Rover with two African labourers and our old gardener, and started to burn back along the edge of the garden. I was tremendously relieved to see them, but it was surely too puny an effort, and I trusted the sanctuary of the muddy dam more. The fire was racing faster down the vlei with flames now four metres high, livid, crackling, roaring, all-powerful, all-consuming. The noise was deafening.

A beautiful great white egret at the last moment abandoned its tree sanctuary in the garden. He was borne along in the terrible draught of the fire, now bearing him down. But with a tremendous effort, using the amazing strength of his wings, he reached an up-current and was swept up free above the smoke and flames and the horror of the valley, to regain the tree perch in the garden. Seconds later the fire passed. Now around the house the smoke was blinding and choking and all I could see were the children's faces, black and stained with smoke tears, but not grief.

We stood on the small verandah and watched the fire die, immediately, as it met the small back-burning fire. The house was safe. Though all around was a holocaust, we stood in the middle untouched.

We watched as out of the blackness the great white bird opened its huge wings and flew across the dam where the fire had now passed through.

A steenbok, a small antelope we often saw nearby, struggled on the edge of the dam. Standing 50cm high at the shoulder, ears spotted and long, and dwarfing a small face, it was too fine a creature, its pointed feet too delicate for the exercise of dragging itself up the bank. But it made it - alive for now, it ran and jumped, hopelessly bewildered, over the blackened earth. Two wild creatures were safe - three, for a speckled quail scuttled from under a flowering shrub across the path under my feet into the burnt-out bush. Martin drove away to his parents' homestead and the compound and barns at the main farm, a mile away on the other side of the hill and in the path of the fire.

Now we stood on the dam wall and watched the fire rushing away from us down the valley. And not ten metres away stood a serval cat, scared to death and staring, standing as high as Fuji, with large pointed ears missing nothing. He looked for all the world like a small leopard, never normally out in daylight, he hunted small buck, hares and rats by night. (Steenbok beware!) Fuji gave a surprised growl then sat on my feet, though she would normally chase anything no matter how large. The cat loped off, slowly, confused.

And everywhere were hares. They had lost their sense of direction and were scampering zig-zag on the hot earth, as though searching for familiar landmarks in the strange land.

We walked back to the house again. The children fought over who should have first bath and then got in together. I swept up the soot and filth through the house, and I could hear Susie complaining through the thin walls that Paula's feet were black.

We loved our little wooden house, though it could be described as primitive. You could say it was two large garden sheds set at right angles with a small verandah in the arc between. It smelt of creosote, and the dark walls were brightened with copper and bamboo ornaments we had brought back from holidays for many years, each one with a memory of Beira sands, the hot lowveld, other countries, other times.

Among the souvenirs were dishes made from seedpods of Philippine trees we'd acquired in our attempt to "escape" Rhodesia the year before. It had been possible when Martin had found a job with a tobacco merchant and was sent to Manila for four months to buy tobacco. He expected to be transferred permanently to Italy where we were all to join him. The Italian tobacco crop failed that year because of white mould, so he was told to go to Mexico for a short season, and then - where?

The children and I were meanwhile living in England with my parents, and Fuji was in six-months' quarantine. The girls needed to go to school (they were having to suffer my tuition) and it looked as though Martin was destined to travel round the world indefinitely overseeing tobacco grading and sales in different regions. Perhaps we should have seen it through - for the first time in our lives we had money.

Martin applied unsuccessfully for other jobs in England. Perhaps he aimed too high and our hearts weren't in it any more. So we returned to Rhodesia (with the bonus he received from his work in Manila) by Union Castle liner through the Mediterranean and Suez Canal and down the east coast of Africa, calling at many ports. I got to see the pyramids on a day trip when the ship went through the Canal, while Martin baby-sat Susie and Paula on the boat. Then we spent a week on gorgeous sandy beaches near Mombasa while the ship was delayed by dock strikes. On the whole not a bad way to travel.

Fuji made the return trip from England by air. I wonder what she made of it all, poor dog. At least she was able to get out of the plane and jump right back into our car at Salisbury airport, no quarantine this way.

Instead of world trips we opened up a new section on our old farm, "Doondo", which means the same as *bundu,* the bush.

And now here we were, the five of us, the day after the fire, in a world that resembled a black carcase surrounding the small faded green garden. The wind blew bits of burnt grass and charred leaves through the windows and doors.

Soon the bush became a battleground. The armistice of shared trouble was over and gave way to slaughter and tragedy.

Killers moved in - a thin whippet-like dog from the compound chased a small antelope, a duiker, across the bare vlei and caught it as it hesitated, lost and confused without its favourite hiding places. We heard its screams, and were unable to reach it in time.

The African labourers from the compound arrived and hurled stones at the hares that had lost their cover, with their pale coats easily visible against the black, and the women and children dug out the rats' holes that yawned like mouths in the open ground. The Wahlberg's eagles and marsh harriers roamed in ceaseless quarry up and down the vlei. The ground was like a slaughter-house, while far above the Bateleurs, superior and grand, flew apparently uncaring into the thermals created by the hot earth. But they hunted too.

As we listened to the screams of the duiker and tried to ignore the sight of our gardener reaping into an old sack the rats that had fled into the garden (some tribes will eat rats, others won't), I felt the whole world was being given over to death. I alone was left a foolish penitent sentenced to sweep forever from the floors of the house the returning layers of charred grass.

A bush pig came into the garden and ate the tomatoes. "A bush pig never appears in the daylight," Martin said, until he saw it too. The carnivores were having a feast; this mainly vegetarian pig was starving. There was nothing much I could do about him. He weighed probably 90 kgs, was fearsome-looking with tusky, knobbly face and a back covered with long, coarse, wiry, brown bristles. Not to be trifled with and a known killer of dogs. We had to let him eat in peace. He was, after all, more my kin than were the predators.

And then the dust-devils started, twisting like supernatural beings across the black land. They seemed to embrace the filth in witches' arms, small tornadoes, taking up the earth to darken the sky and then depositing it on anything that still dared to live.

We didn't see the garden birds for a long time, and I dreaded for their safety. We knew them as individuals.

After a week a miracle happened. A green haze spread over the earth, and, without rains, spring came, and all the trees burst forth together. Beside the stone bird-bath a small yellow-wood tree became almost overnight such an intense lime green against the black bark it looked like a Japanese painting. In the vlei, stumps sprouted mauve and yellow flowers out of the rock-like ground.

Birds began to find their mates, and above the house a sunbird with scarlet chest wove a nest for his drab little mate, with a slender beak like a scimitar. The birdbath was full again, firefinches and waxbills chattering and splashing.

Across the dam three reedbuck played together. They were usually too busy attending to the business of staying alive to play, but now skipped like rocking horses – good to be alive!

It was spring and soon it would rain.

We've always lived in funny houses. Though they were generally pretty houses and in beautiful spots, but I sometimes felt I'd love to be a townie, just for a while, and live in a house with flat plastered walls, and doors that fit. Town friends said I was mad, but then I'd really enjoy going out into the countryside to "rough it", to observe the scenery and be part of the wind and rain for the weekend, knowing I could take my wet clothes and aching limbs back to civilisation. Such feelings weren't so fashionable then.

Now that children can experience the thrills of drugs and alcohol and sex and not just think about them, they will want more. The last thrill perhaps is the wilderness, as long as it remains.

At first in the house by the dam we had to cart all our water from the main farm, where there was a good borehole. Carting in galvanised iron tanks isn't the best method of acquiring water, believe me. Water is very heavy, and it slops and wrecks trailers and tyres on rutted roads. And when it arrives it is so earnestly needed it runs out again right away.

A neighbour came along and divined water for us with a forked stick: one that he had chosen and cut quite haphazardly from the bush. There was nothing to divining water once you knew how to do it, he said, and most people were capable of doing it.

And it did seem so. He took Martin and me into the garden, showed us how to hold the stick with thumbs down, and put his hands over our hands in turn. We walked over the ground where he had already divined water and sure enough I felt the weird, uncontrollable pull of the stick within a hundred metres of the house.

Then I tried on my own, and there was no trick - the stick could not be prevented from bending towards the earth in the two places, no matter how tightly it was held. Martin could feel the same. From that day I have never doubted the ancient skill of dowsing.

An old African was found who said he knew all about sinking wells. He worked for a long time and when a little water began to seep into the well he departed, leaving his tools and promising to return to deepen the well later. He left behind some of his surplus dynamite and Martin put it in the wardrobe, less than a metre from where we slept, as the only place we could lock up. The dynamite was weeping, but I didn't realise the significance of this until I read in the newspaper about someone who had his hands and part of his face blown off by similar sticks of explosive. Martin grudgingly consented to remove it from the bedside and bury it in the bush. He thought I was fussing again.

We could not use the water from the dam untreated because bilharzia was prevalent in most surface water in Rhodesia. Bilharzia (schistosomiasis) was a disease well known to the Egyptians and Chinese, and detected in 3000-year-old mummified bodies, but was not investigated till the middle of the nineteenth century in Cairo be Theodore Bilharz. There is even a hieroglyph for the disease, which was often mentioned in ancient records, but is not really suitable for quoting here (even out of hieroglyphics). It is carried by worms to host snails, which live on the edges of rivers and dams, and appears in two forms over the warmer regions of Africa – and many other sunnier parts of the world.

In the 1960s, while we were trying to stay out of the water, it was reckoned that 50% of Africans had urinary bilharzia and 25% intestinal bilharzia, while in the European population of Rhodesia it was less, 15% and 5%. Today it is calculated that 2000 million people are infected worldwide.

A person with bilharzia has adult worms like tapeworms; the female worm, 20mm long, lies snugly in the curve of the male worm, himself only 12mm long. The worms mate endlessly in the veins of the bladder or bowel and the eggs are released in the urine or faeces. If these eggs reach open surface water, they burst and become swimming organisms (miracidia). They now have 48 hours to look for one of two suitable species of snail living on the sides of watercourses. Find one and the miracidia will live for six weeks in the snail's liver, then change form to a cercaria, once more take a swim in the water and this time they're seeking an unsuspecting human taking a paddle, a swim or a drink on a hot afternoon. Bonanza! Into the bloodstream, into the bladder, causing bladder stones and septic bowel conditions and quite likely affecting the lungs, liver and appendix. Among the first noticeable symptoms are blood in the urine, a rash and itchy skin or a cough, then later, lack of energy and general lassitude. Treatment neglected, death could follow. Who's for a swim?

Bilharzia snails particularly love water-lilies to hide under, and whereas an English gardener will look at a pond of beautiful flowering water-lilies with admiration, Rhodesians would look with horror and clutch their children to them for fear they go near, screaming that even to touch the water can cause infection.

When we were in Rhodesia, bilharzia was incurable in severe cases. Those who were diagnosed and treated in time said the cure was worse than the disease.

Now that your toes have started to curl, the good news: treatments have improved beyond all belief and today a single oral course of praziquantel will effect a cure. You are even recommended to take it anyway if you've been near suspect water, without waiting for tests.

I don't know why we didn't all get bilharzia. Martin even built a small sailing dinghy we put on the dam the first year before the weeds grew. We warned the girls of dreadful illness if they touched the dam water. But it was only a hundred metres from the house and when Mom and Dad weren't looking there was always something in the water - water scorpions, clawed frogs and sticklebacks, and down the spillway after the dam had overflowed, exquisite quartz crystals, like dreams of diamonds.

We had a very complicated water supply to the house: in the bathroom we used well water, generally brown; we drank water carted from the main farm borehole, or, later, rain water collected from the corrugated iron roof into large storage tanks. This rainwater stayed clear and tasted sweet throughout the whole dry season, much to our surprise. We dared not flush the toilet too often, but the water was re-used from the septic tank outflow to water the peach and banana trees. The well water also watered the vegetable garden (we grew bountiful fresh peas and strawberries) and the orange and grapefruit trees.

But we did store dam water in tanks for forty-eight hours, trusting the bilharzia worm would die for lack of a host. This was the water we used in the kitchen, and we just hoped for the best.

When we dug a small swimming pool in the garden we used the dam water this time, allowed it to stand for two days and treated with chlorine.

The second year at the dam, we had bought a second-hand prefabricated cement asbestos house (yes, asbestos!), and now we had quite a mansion with five bedrooms. It was by far the largest house we've ever had. Painted and with new curtains and carpets, it didn't look like the old condemned house it was when it arrived on the back of a lorry. But we had to work at it all the time to stop termites and ants taking over.

When we first started farming, arrangements for acquiring milk - it could hardly be called milking - would have made the Health

Inspector, the RSPCA, Louis Pasteur and a time and motion expert collapse in horror.

Each night a few scraggy cows, ill tempered and of no definable breed, were penned at the back of the house while their calves were placed in a separate pen. In the morning an old reprobate who could be trusted with no other work on the farm, led the cows into a small enclosure, or sometimes just tied them to a fence with a piece of rawhide. Then, into a dirty bucket, he would somehow urge a few drops of liquid, while the half-wild cow kicked and leapt in the air. This was repeated many times with a dozen cows, and in the end a gallon or so of thin milk laced with cattle dung and earth would arrive at the kitchen door, and be tipped into the scrupulously clean pail kept for the purpose, then filtered through a cloth (whatever good that did it) and boiled.

The year we built the house, the dam filled up and covered eight acres and reached to the end of the cleared slope, some of it already lawn and garden.

The weeds had not grown round the edges and no water-lilies clogged the surface, so the water gleamed like an ornamental lake in the sun, and was populated by hundreds of wild geese and ducks, herons, egrets and storks. They were left in peace and their friends came. One day I counted 130 white-faced ducks and ducklings. These odd ducks don't quack as ducks surely should, but whistle, and they roost in trees.

Lots of happenings were odd, we found, in Rhodesia, a "down-under" country. The European cuckoo never says anything when he comes to Africa, while the African cuckoo says: "Oo-cuck, oo-cuck". And anyone who doesn't believe me can go and listen.

One little sandpiper would come for a walk with us in the evening round the dam - fluttering and chattering just ahead of us and bobbing his tail all the way. Fuji got so used to him she ignored him.

One season a pair of striped-chested swallows built their mud nest right inside the small verandah, up against the roof. We watched the laborious building fearfully, and when the nest was finished we had a tremendous rainstorm, the roof leaked, and part of the nest with its tunnel entrance was washed away. We were all so upset, and I patched up the nest with a piece of cloth like a sling underneath. Oddly enough, the birds did return to use the nest, though whether they raised their young successfully we weren't able to observe. So even if I can't milk a cow or raise chickens like a good farmer's wife, I can build a nest.

Susie grew up to love the bush of Rhodesia - the *bundu*. Paula was bored with it unless there was action involved, in which case it was no longer bush, but wide-open spaces made for activity.

But it was left to Paula, 28 years later, to visit the farm with her husband and children, and make a video. Our old house had been pulled down, the garden was completely overgrown and returned to bush, the well abandoned, and no sign of the fruit trees, but the dam was still there and I expect many of the birds or, rather, their descendants, watched the strangers (also descendants) from the trees and reeds.

Paula's visit was a couple of years before white-owned farms were invaded by the "war veterans" and youth gangs of Mugabe, when farmhouses were routinely destroyed. But that is another sorry tale and still unfolding in 2005.

Two

In the early years on the farm I never really doubted Rhodesia would last forever, any more than I doubted my children would always remain children, or the sun would shine in October.

But in November 1965 Rhodesia declared its independence from Britain, the storm clouds gathered (as was normal in November) and we wondered how long we could go after all, before we had to choose between emigrating or living in a country under laws of an inexperienced and understandably unfriendly black government.

Susie and Paula were still at junior school in Sinoia and it was always a tear-around at seven o'clock in the morning any weekday. On 11th November 1965 I hadn't much patience with them because I was planning to go to Salisbury (which is now called Harare) directly after dropping them off at school. I only just managed to hear on the radio news the announcement that the Prime Minister, Ian Smith, was going to make an important announcement to the nation at lunchtime. I wondered if I should still go, or if I might get caught up in riots. Even so early we had experienced our first taste of unrest.

I hauled them reluctantly through breakfast -- in those days we had a choice of imported goods: Kellogg's corn flakes, Heinz baked beans, white bread, eggs with yellow yolks and Robertson's Scotch marmalade. They had their packet of marmite sandwiches, a triangle of Swiss cheese and a bar of Cadbury's chocolate, with a peach grown in South Africa to follow. As it proved, two years later we had none of these, but they were whittled away so delicately that, like more important things in life, we no longer wondered at their absence.

Martin was working against time to plant a large land near the road as I drove out. Fields were often 50 acres or more and we called them "lands". Everyone was up to their ankles in mud after a good planting rain the evening before. A hundred Africans, men, women and children were working on and around the land: carting, carrying, distributing and hand-planting the leggy seedbed tobacco plants. He was trying to get as much of the land planted as he could before the sun became so hot the plants would straightway sag, lie down on the warm earth, and shrivel. If the majority of the plants survived he'd have a good start for the new season. The land was close to the seedbeds, and now was the ideal time.

I stopped in spite of the children's protests (I was always behind time and they hated being late), and managed to signal Martin - I didn't want to get my town shoes muddy so early in the day. (I was behaving like "the madam".)

The land extended up the hill and over the other side of the skyline. I'd brought his breakfast, which he would eat under a tree by the land to save time. He'd wash the egg sandwiches down with hot tea from a lemonade bottle wrapped in newspaper to keep warm. No niceties like thermos flasks for Martin!

I told him about the announcement: "Should I go to Salisbury, do you think? Will it be all right?" I always tried to get home before it got really dark. It was one-and-a-half hours' drive from the farm, these days on a good, tarred road, except for the six-mile dirt approach road to the farm. The main road had been improved from the "strips", like wide railway lines of tar, that we had known when we first arrived in Rhodesia.

Getting back before dark was a throwback from the days of the Afrikaner voortrekkers of a century before, when at sundown the ox wagons were drawn up in a circle, the laager, and everyone and everything was enclosed inside, protected from the terrors of the night.

"The announcement will probably be nothing - you're all ready now. It would be a shame not to go. If it looks as though there might be trouble you can always come home again right after lunch."

Martin was never excited about national threats. He only ever worried about personal crises he thought he could remedy -- the crops, or later, his job, or if we were on holiday the state of the tyres, or if we shouldn't find accommodation when we reached our destination. His main worry right then was that I might be making the children late for school.

To Martin, time was so important, to me it was an unacceptable impediment, and the only way of getting around it was to ignore it. Whenever I set my heart on doing anything it always seemed to be time that tried to get in the way.

So I hurried the children the twelve miles to school, then doubled back on my tracks along the main road, passing the farm turn-off and southwards to Salisbury. This was my freedom: the long open road and a day looking at shops and among people.

In the shops everyone was speculating about the announcement, but I didn't see anyone I knew to discuss it. For weeks the government had been protesting about the pressures Britain was trying to exert on Rhodesia, and many Rhodesians were screaming for independence.

There was utter silence in the store restaurant where I sat at lunchtime, as the speech that changed Rhodesia's future was relayed throughout the store.

Ian Smith's dry voice droned on around the cold meats and salads, and the imported salmon, and imported tea and coffee. It was surprisingly short:

"In the lives of most nations there comes a moment when a stand has to be made for principle, whatever the consequences. This moment has come to Rhodesia. I pray, and I hope other Rhodesians will pray today, that our government will be given the wisdom and strength to bring Rhodesia safely through.

I call upon all of you in this historic hour to support me and my government in the struggle in which we are engaged. I believe we are a courageous people and history has cast us in a heroic role. To us has been given the privilege of being the first Western nation in the last two decades to have the determination and fortitude to say 'so far and no further'.

We may be a small country, but we are a determined people who have been called upon to play a role of world-wide significance. We

Rhodesians have rejected the doctrinaire philosophy of appeasement and surrender. The decision which we have taken today is a refusal by Rhodesians to sell their birth-right, and even if we were to surrender, does anyone believe that Rhodesia would be the last target of the Communists and the Afro-Asian bloc?

We have struck a blow for the preservation of justice, civilization and Christianity, and in the spirit of this belief have this day assumed our sovereign independence.

God bless you all."

Some said these few minutes set back the clock or spelled out the country's ruin; some said it bought time, if it didn't save her.

So we cut ourselves off from Britain. Land of our fathers! We had talked about this possibility.

"It will be the finish of the tobacco industry," Martin had said many times. "It will have perhaps five years, the country ten."

I decided there was nothing I could do about the fate of the nation so I might as well have the afternoon at the pictures, the bioscope, as we called it.

"It will be the end of us," I said to the cashier at the cinema, when she asked if I had heard the news

She was amazed: "It's wonderful!" she said. "It's what we should have done years ago. Now we can really go ahead, stand on our own feet."

Our farm covered 3200 acres in the tobacco and maize-growing belt of Lomagundi, north-west of Salisbury. As well as a large farm we had a large bank account. Like the turn of the roulette wheel, it was just a matter of fortune it was in the red and not the black. Martin always promised we'd be rich one day, and we might have been fairly well off eventually except for that disastrous declaration and all that led up to it, and followed it, on that day, November 11th 1965. In Rhodesia, as in many parts of the world, it was also Remembrance Day, and a time to sell red poppies:

"That there's some corner of a foreign field
That is for ever England."

Well it was done, and at that time whether we loved England

better than we loved Rhodesia, or not, really didn't enter into it. We had a livelihood and property in Rhodesia, and two young daughters entering upon an important time in their education.

Martin and I came out to Rhodesia independently from England, and met soon after. He's fond of telling everyone how he picked me up from the roadside, which is absolutely true - I was trying to get a lift to the riding stables after missing the bus, as usual, from Mount Hampden camp into town. He came from Epsom and I came from near Derby, which made us a good racing certainty.

Martin had travelled quite a bit since he left school. His father had refurbished a motor yacht that had been extensively used by the navy in minesweeping operations during the war. They had worked for two years taking wealthy clients round the Mediterranean on charter cruises. Then, during his two-year British National Service he had served as a Second Lieutenant in the Royal Artillery in Korea, and had been stationed in Hong Kong and Japan.

His father and stepmother had already been in Rhodesia over two years when he arrived. Neither of us ever understood why Martin got involved in tobacco farming. He was so unsuited to it. I think in those days - the ten years after the end of the 39/45 War - it was the accepted thing for young immigrants to do, a left-over from the white man's burden, which we never hear a mention of these days. Everyone thought tobacco was truly gold leaf, and to many it was.

I had spent all my young life wanting to go on the stage. When I look back I seemed to have occupied all my evenings in dusty, bare rehearsal halls - church halls and school rooms - or shivering on even colder buses coming the ten miles back late at night from Nottingham or Derby. But I never got any further than an endless succession of amateur productions. I was nuts about Shakespeare and read Bernard Shaw avidly. When I won a scholarship to the Royal Academy of Dramatic Art in London I thought my way was clear.

Then one day, when I was twenty, I quite suddenly realised I was not interested in the stage any more. That heavy proscenium curtain had fallen on my own private stage, and finally. I wasn't doing well, and if I couldn't shine I didn't want to go on. I was utterly disillusioned, I think now, by the people, and the pettiness. I wanted to bring Shakespeare and all the beautiful English language and poetry to the people - to all the people who would stop and listen. This, I found, was not the aim of most of the stage world. And the world itself was not inclined to listen, not to me, not the way I was saying it.

Not able to do what I wanted, I thought I'd try and do some good in the world and be a nurse, but the ill-temperedness of the matron and senior staff, and the discipline, then, of hospital life was too much for me. I walked out. I did a stand-in job for the county youth service department for a few months, but when I saw an advertisement in the Daily Herald for young people to work in government offices in Rhodesia, all fares paid, it presented the opportunity to start my round-world travels that I'd always waited for.

I had worked in a bank before going to RADA and had sufficient commercial office experience to get a job.

My youngest brother, eight years my senior, had been one of the "Blue Perils" who had finished his wartime RAF pilot training in Rhodesia. In my teens after the war ended, I had been terribly excited and envious of his stories about Southern Rhodesia and Africa in general.

So I was destined to go to this "Land of Sunshine and Opportunity" or "Land of *Kusasa* and *Kabanga*" (tomorrow and maybe), as more commonly described by those who lived there.

I found Southern Rhodesia, as it was called in 1952, a great disappointment. Quite simply - no jungles. Just dry savannah, tall yellow grass and stunted trees as far as the eye could see. And dust.

There were a lot of us young new immigrants and we were all accommodated in an abandoned RAF camp of prefabricated corrugated iron and asbestos huts, some even in Nissan huts, at Mount Hampden, twelve miles from Salisbury.

Salisbury is on a plateau at 5000 feet, and at first I felt

excessively tired and often almost dropped off asleep in the afternoon in the warm offices. It wasn't helped by constant late nights.

The companionship of the camp was great. We were all in a strange land. It was funny, years afterwards, to see in the newspaper and on television so many of the old faces of Mount Hampden now bearing important government or commercial posts, when I remember them as young boys who didn't seem at the time to be over-bright. Girls weren't allowed in those days to progress in their careers. When women married they gave up work and became full-time wives and mothers.

All the girls were several years older than the boys - it was customary for girls to be attached to their momma's apron strings till they were well over twenty-one, whereas boys were expected to go out into the world and seek their fortunes pretty early.

Young people did not automatically progress from school into university or training colleges as they do now. Instead, they went out to build the Commonwealth. The Empire was out of date, but the sun still never set on the parts marked red on the map of the world.

But even though the girls were older, we were thin on the ground and in great demand, and we were rarely in any evening or weekend. But we were good girls and behaved ourselves according to the morals of 1952.

But in spite of friends, I was still desperately homesick.

Martin maintains we were taken out to Rhodesia to provide wives for lonely tobacco farmers. And it is true that of the four of us who found ourselves thrown together travelling out on the old Athlone Castle from Southampton to Cape Town, two of us did marry tobacco farmers and the other two also married and stayed in Rhodesia. Nearly all those who went to Rhodesia in that recruitment drive did stay for many years.

We organised a hockey team and used to run round the disused airstrip every evening for training. It was great fun. Sometimes we even persuaded the blokes to let us use their football pitch for practice, though it was so rough and full of termite holes we were just as well without their grudging licence. All our matches were "aways", and in spite of the surprise of finding ourselves playing real matches on rolled green lawn-like pitches we got into the first division after the first season.

People gradually moved from Mount Hampden into flats in Salisbury suburbs, and most of us finished up feeling a little on our own there. I followed the trend rather later. Unless a girl had a car she couldn't go out alone at night - it boiled down to that. Even in midsummer it was never light after seven. I borrowed a bicycle, took up fencing again at the Polytechnic (shades of RADA), and learnt "basic Bantu", a polite name for *chilapalapa* or kitchen kaffir, which was at least based on Zulu. But I was so nearly run down by slaphappy, partly inebriated colonial drivers, I was a little scared.

When Martin first started farming as an assistant on a large established farm, he earned £25 a month and lived in a lean-to shack by the side of the tobacco barns. He said we should get married right away. It was not acceptable to "live together" then. I was earning much more than he was and could hardly save on that, though I was earnestly trying to save my fare back to England. It's well we didn't marry then. The first house we lived in on the farm was basic enough, but we weren't awakened at all hours of the night during the curing season by the barn furnaces being stoked, with much noise and an accompaniment of whistling to keep the spirits away, as would have happened in his first house.

When we did decide to get married, Martin and his father were trying to buy the farm, and we lived a few yards from his father's and stepmother's house.

I couldn't cook, and any chance of my learning was stifled by the smoke that emitted from the old Dover wood-burning stove. The sticks stuck out of the front of the stove, never the right size, and had been gathered from the bush indiscriminately. We had electricity in the house but couldn't have an electric stove - something to do with the phases, I was told. Eventually we did buy a Calor gas stove, and at least I could get the pots to boil and the oven to heat up, but to this day I've never enjoyed cooking.

We had 18 tobacco-curing barns on Doondo and generally grew 100 acres of Virginia tobacco, 150 acres of maize, and ran a herd of about 100 rough-looking, crossbred cattle. Some maize was sold, some ground into mealie meal, popularly called *poop* from the Shona word *mpupu*. The farm workers were given rations of mealie meal from which the women made *sadza*, a porridge, which was the staple food. (It was also used to brew beer for the Saturday-night party.)

Each worker also received a ration of meat or sometimes dried fish, and dried beans or peanuts, which the family cooked with onion, cabbage or squash, often home-grown in the compound gardens, to make *ndiwo*, or relish.

On the farm we also had a small store that sold bread, dried and tinned fish, sugar, biscuits, sweets and rolls of cotton materials. A resident "tailor" would sit for many hours at an old treadle sewing machine making dresses to order.

When new sheds or barns were needed we had first to make the bricks. An itinerant brick-maker was hired, suitable ant-heap soil selected and dug, mixed with water and then poured into homemade wooden moulds. Kilns were built and the bricks baked. It took a long time, but how else?

When Susie was about to be born, we had a span of eight oxen standing by in the field behind the house, ready to pull us through the mud on the way to the maternity home in Sinoia. I have never seen rain like that year! As well as the vlei, the main river that was lapping over the low-level bridge near the town had to be crossed.

We went to look at the bridge every day. It was disappearing. A family conference decided I should cross the river while I could and go and stay in the hotel near the maternity home till the baby came. I didn't mind. I was bored with the farm and looked forward to walking to shops and drinking coffee in the cafe - even though there were only three or four of the first and one of the second. We couldn't really afford for me to stay in the hotel, but that could hardly be helped. The Sinoia Hotel was a real pioneer-style place with a wide red-polished verandah. Morning tea was brought to the room, at six sharp, heralded by loud knocking on the door.

By the time we decided to cross, the river had widened into a roaring, sucking torrent that swept on either side and sometimes lapped over the bridge that was so narrow there was only room for the wheels of a vehicle. A forty-centimetre high guardrail lined the edge of the bridge, and as the road surface itself was covered by the water we followed this guide. In the middle, the river roared and leapt, grey and evil-looking, taking whole trees along its course. The car was inches deep in the river waves, and the tyres slid alarmingly sideways. I was terrified and could see no way our lives could be spared, and particularly that of my unborn child.

But we reached the other side. A few days later it came over six metres above the bridge, but, amazingly, the bridge was still there when the river subsided.

I waited a week. Martin came to see me every day the river allowed and he could borrow his father's car.

He hadn't been able to come for a couple of days, and still my baby showed no signs of appearing either, though by now ten days overdue. Morale was low. I had no friends in Sinoia.

At the bridge a dozen or so cars were waiting for the river to subside so they could drive over. It would obviously be foolhardy to try and cross with the water over the guardrail. So Martin arrived on the tractor. The electrics were on the up-stream side, so he reversed across the bridge while the current caught at the light front wheels and tried to sweep him downstream. But he got across to the cheers of the crowd - loudly from the other side, from those who had been told of his urgency to get across.

At the end of the week the river went down, so I went back home. The bumpy ride must have set off the trigger and by dawn next morning I knew I had to return.

It was a beautiful dawn, with the narrow stratus cloud on the horizon fringed with gold and pink, while beneath awoke Africa to the calling of the doves and an oriole.

So Susie was born under Aquarius, the water carrier, and the next wettest time I ever knew was twenty years on, the day Susie was married.

When Paula was expected fourteen months later I felt I couldn't take all this again. We had £100 bonus from our tobacco sale, and with this I caught a train (three days), then a boat from Cape Town (15 days), and took my problem (and Susie) home to mum. So easily Paula became English born, with a National Health card and number, milk tokens, free orange juice, and the indisputable right to a British passport, and the automatic right to live and work in Britain.

It is difficult for anyone in Britain who is not a refugee to understand what an advantage, in troubled times, this can be. Our next-door neighbours on the farm had the greatest difficulty getting British citizenship for their children, as nationality was determined by the male line.

The father, who had been a kilted Argyll and Southern Highlander, and a Caucasian to the last drop of blood, was classed as Burmese because he happened to be born in Burma when his father was working there. So, as his daughter was born in Rhodesia, she was not allowed a British passport, though all her ancestors on both sides had never deviated from being born under the British flag, the British Raj, the British-to-the-core British. The mother's English nationality did not count apparently.

Whoever decide on nationality or race are an odd bunch.

Twenty years later this neighbour's daughter was not allowed to visit her grandmother in England, though after much form filling and appeals she was allowed in on a temporary permit as a student. The son, on the other hand, was permitted a British passport because his paternal grandfather was born in Britain. This was patently unfair, but the ruling has now been changed, I believe, as it has been in South Africa.

When Rhodesia declared her independence and was ostracised by the rest of the world, a British or South African or Irish or anything-but-Rhodesian passport (even Zambian later) became of paramount importance to anyone who wished to travel beyond South Africa, Switzerland, Spain, Portugal or Greece. Susie got her British passport because Martin is British. It seems I could have been Tibetan for all they cared.

There was a lot of ill feeling about to be or not to be British, understandably so, the way the British Government treated us during those eleven years. Many who owned British passports chucked them away in the early days, got Rhodesian passports and sat at home singing Rhodesia's praises to each other.

Martin came to Cape Town to meet his new daughter, who was by now three months old. We stayed aboard the Bloemfontein Castle round the Cape of Good Hope, by Port Elizabeth, East London, Durban and Lorenco Marques (now Maputo) to Beira.

Susie, eighteen months old, learnt to walk on the ship's rolling deck. In spite of my dad's best efforts in England, she had shown no interest in getting up on her feet, but could make rapid progress on her bottom, (she never crawled either, like most children). From Beira we went back to the farm by train, one night and one day to Salisbury, where my father-in-law met us.

Martin had spent the six months I was away in England learning to ride and play polo. It all started when he was looking for a horse for me to ride round the farm.

Rhodesian polo was much more a farmer's game - certainly without the snobbery of the upper class and wealthy polo playing and players in England. What he lacked in ability to hit the ball (it's a long way down there to the ground or to the flying ball from the top of a cantering pony), he made up for by his fearless "riding off" of his opponents from the ball. Over five years we collected around us six assorted horses, most of them not very suited to polo playing, though there was something for all of us. I started playing polo-crosse with a small club in Sinoia.

The prize pony, an ex-race horse we called Twinkletoes, was really too fiery for polo, and certainly with a man of Martin's excitable temperament on his back. Twinkletoes appeared to prefer women to men, so I tried to take him out every morning with a polo stick, calm him and show him the basics. I wasn't a skilled enough rider myself to do any good, but he was a gorgeous-looking horse, and I generally managed to stay on him.

Susie and Paula loved the horses and became much better riders than their parents ever were. Susie ran livery stables for many years, still trains horses, rides dressage and gives lessons.

She loves horses and does it very quietly and with kindness. Paula's three daughters are mad about horses, enjoy entering competitions and generally keep their parents occupied, if not amused, with driving horseboxes around Johannesburg suburbs to shows.

I feel it's mostly my fault – if I hadn't wanted to go riding horses, that morning or any morning, where would all this have been?

Three

Rhodesia's biggest export in the 1950s and 60s was tobacco. In spite of increasing health warnings in Britain, our main export market, everything in the garden looked rosy for the tobacco growers' future. Rhodesians did not believe the warnings - that included us. We were grossly undercapitalised on our farm, which meant that Martin spent a lot of his time repairing old tractors, and generally sticking equipment together with bits of wire. Even on our wedding day, he spent the morning underneath the old pick-up truck trying to get it going so he could drive to Salisbury to get married.

The day before, he had just escaped receiving a black eye for our wedding photos when the Heath-Robinson maize sheller threw its belt into his face. He escaped with a bruised face and nose, and scratches. My good friend Colleen and I patched him up for the wedding, while good friend Julie helped prepare the wedding reception and tried to keep everything on an even keel.

As it was a registry office wedding a bridesmaid wasn't called for, but Colleen was a good Catholic and appointed herself to the post. Her fiancé, in an up-market car he'd borrowed for the day and beribboned, acted as "father of the bride". The reception was at Julie's apartment. She'd let me share her flat for several months, and was now landed with my disorganised catering arrangements. Our best man, a Hollander neighbour, lent us his car for our honeymoon in the eastern mountains at Rhodes Hotel, Inyanga. (These old "new immigrant" friends are still our best friends).

The honeymoon over, it was back to the farm. In the planting season the day was turned back to front and put together again upside down. Everyone was up at 4.30. Before it was light the tractors were trundling the rough-woven baskets of young tobacco seedlings on trailers to the lands. The baskets had been made weeks before from stripped tree bark, by the women on the farm.

The lands were between fifteen and thirty acres, and each seedling had to be planted separately by hand. Unless planting started in mid-November there was no time for the plants to grow and the leaves to ripen by the time April brought cold nights, when the leaves would die rather than ripen, and be lost to frost. If the rains were late, each seedling was planted with a litre or so of water containing insecticide to ward off cut-worm. This meant the heavy watercart had to take water perhaps a mile or more over rough tracks to the lands, and only a few acres a day could be planted.

Now the spindly-looking, but hardened seedlings would start their battle for life pushing down their roots deep into the earth searching for moisture, until they lost their leaves and became merely a moist stump a few centimetres above the ground. If the rains came soon, the plants would still live and the land got a better start than if they had waited for late planting.

The days the big planting thunderstorms came were wonderful. Thirty acres could be planted in a day.

In those days everyone was quite off-hand about insecticides, and DDT was used liberally on the tobacco and in the vegetable garden. Friends of the Earth and others who told us we were ruining the earth and poisoning ourselves were told to mind their own business and let us get on with the job of ruining the earth if we so wished. Look around! There was lots more earth and lots more trees to cut down still.

The years before UDI was declared in 1965 were the peak years for tobacco in Rhodesia. In Britain three-quarters of the adult male population and two-fifths of the female smoked. High-grade tobacco leaf was fetching 70 Rhodesian cents per pound, which in those days amounted to a lot of money and showed considerable profit. The trouble was, some tobacco only got 10 cents.

Tobacco seed is minute, and from one level teaspoonful enough tobacco can be grown to make two and a half million cigarettes.

When we first started farming most of our neighbours were in the same situation as we were, and wherever we went there was only one subject of conversation - tobacco.

Will there be good planting rains, what to do about the cut-worm, will the growing rains come, should we top-dress, what to do about grasshoppers, when will it stop raining, what to do about eel-worm, should we top the flowers off now, what to do about the suckers, again when will it ever stop raining, how can we best drain the lands?

Just after we were married we went to visit our nearest neighbours three miles the other side of our small boundary stream, which in the rains was impossible to cross. We sat in the mosquito-gauzed and extremely hot verandah of their house at lunchtime, while the men and our hostess talked for four hours without change of subject about the trials of tobacco growing, while drinking two bottles of gin. I was good and pure in those days and didn't like gin. And there was no sign of the lunch we had been invited to. I have never been so insufferably bored. I should, after all, have joined in with the gin. I tried to make friends with the two mangy-looking dogs sleeping in the corner, but they were ill tempered and covered in ticks so I gave up.

When lunch was permitted to be brought in, it had been kept warm in the oven for three hours, after being prepared by the African cook. Not once during the whole proceedings had the mistress of the house left her chair to go and see how the lunch was progressing. It was no longer fit for consumption. *Kusasa* and *kabanga*!

I wondered how I was going to live through married life on the farm. I persuaded Martin to go off on tobacco discussions by himself when I could.

But over the years the new tobacco farmers grew up, and like their crops, some were weeded out, and conversation turned to politics instead. I am difficult to please and this was no more interesting to me than tobacco. I avoided visiting as much as I could. Consequently I suppose I was often lonely. But, when on my own any boredom I felt, I could contain and deal with. I think loneliness is like homesickness -- you know something is wrong but you don't quite realise what it is.

We watched the sky in agony for months. It never rained at the right time, it seemed, or in the right quantities.

Later on we made our own rain, by rocket. This was a tremendously exciting acquisition.

It was like a dozen super Guy Fawkes nights. The launcher was made of iron piping and stood about three metres high, and the rocket itself was like a bonfire-night rocket but over a metre in length. When the rains didn't come in November or at the beginning of December, we would look out for a good thundercloud, quickly load up the rockets and launcher, and away in the Land Rover to a spot half-mile or so on the windward side of a land we wanted the rain to fall on.

Light the touch-paper and retire... It is probably a very good way of getting your head blown off.

The awful pause while the fuse was finished, then, ZOOM! – a great swish like a hundred fireworks into the sky and, we hoped, the black nimbus cloud. And it did work. Sometimes we would get over a centimetre of rain and in the right place. It was often what saved a land from death.

Cloud seeding was also done from small planes, and we talked to the pilot. He loved it, and reckoned it was the most exhilarating type of flying he had ever done. The two-engine plane would set out deliberately looking for large thunderclouds - the sort of trouble a small-plane pilot usually avoids. Then he would be swept up in the thermals to 6000 metres and more. Oxygen masks had to be used. Here the air was cold enough for successful seeding with cartridges of silver iodide crystals, and an extra 100,000 tonnes of water could be expected to be released from the cloud. The debate still continues if rain can be made to fall, but we found it so.

A well-grown tobacco plant of Virginia type stands one-and-a-half metres high, and has leaves as large as tea trays, like soft chamois leather in texture, but covered with a gummy substance. The leaves ripen naturally on the plant, starting at the bottom, and each leaf had to be individually reaped by hand at the exact day of ripening. (Reaping nowadays does not rely on this.)

The leaves were then tied with string on long sticks, *matepes,* and hauled into high barns where they were cured by flue heating to temperatures of 32°C over several days. At this stage, wet sacks would be spread over the flue pipes to encourage the right moist conditions for colouring the tobacco yellow or gold. Then the sacks were removed and the heat raised to 75°C for three to four days.

The leaves were now cured, but dry and brittle, so they were left in the barns to absorb moisture from humidifiers, until they could be unloaded without shattering the leaves, and stored in large bulks in closed sheds.

When the entire crop had been reaped and cured, all the farm labour then moved on to grading and packing the leaf into bales before sending off to the sales floors in Salisbury.

This presented a very good excuse to go to town for the day, and do some shopping afterwards if the sales had gone well.

The tobacco sales floors in Salisbury were said to be the largest covered area in the southern hemisphere. The hessian-wrapped tobacco bales (roughly 75X60X50 centimetres and weighing 90 kilograms) were laid out in neat rows over the whole length and breadth of the floors. American auctioneers and buyers from all over the world with their retinues moved at a slow walking pace up and down the rows rapidly chanting "sixty-four, sixty-five, sixty-six, seven, eight, eight, nine, nine, nine..." As a visitor, it was impossible to tell what they said, even when, rarely, they stood still beside a bale singing in your direction.

When cigarettes are manufactured many flavours are added to American-type cigarettes, though English manufacturers concentrate on bringing out the taste of the natural tobacco by blending Virginian with Oriental and Burley tobaccos, which are air-cured types. Even the paper the cigarette is rolled in can change the taste so much it becomes a different brand. The size and shape, the amount of moisture in the tobacco, whether coarsely or finely cut, or tightly or loosely packed, and even the atmosphere and altitude of where it is smoked can seriously change the flavour of a cigarette.

35

In America a cigarette was more like a meal then a smoke: tobacco may be flavoured with menthol, cocoa, maple syrup, glycerine, spices, sugar, and then toasted. Much of this will have changed considerably since the 1960s when we knew it.

When filter-tipped cigarettes became more popular because of lung cancer warnings, coarser, darker tobacco began to fetch better prices than the lemon, unspotted varieties we had been striving for over the years. Unfortunately, it was later reported that the darker, stronger leaf makes the cigarette even more harmful.

Fashions change with tobacco like everything else and manufacturers were always having to bring out new brands to satisfy their customers' changing tastes.

Until recent decades, smoking wasn't thought injurious to health. The old apothecaries always had a stock of tobacco on their shelves, as it was thought to ward off many fevers. During the Great Plague of London in 1665 English schoolboys were compelled to smoke a pipe of tobacco each morning before school.

One terrible night we had a very large barn fire. Suddenly through sleep came the scaring sound of African labourers shouting, doors banging, metal clanging. The sweet, sweet smell of tobacco, which for months hung round the barns and homesteads, became a compulsive reality. Martin was on his way down to the barns before the man on barn duty arrived at the house.

Everything was alight in three barns and everything was ignitable - dry tobacco on wooden sticks, the gum-tree-wood barn tiers, and the barn rafters. It was too late to save anything in these barns, and of little use to close vents: the roof by this time was open to the air. All efforts had to be concentrated on saving the neighbouring barns by draping wet sacks over the doors to eliminate draught as much as possible.

We all watched as Martin started to climb up on to the roof and I was fearful one of the corrugated iron roofs would break under him. He dislikes heights so he was doubly troubled. With the help of his workers he closed the top vents and then hauled up buckets of water to stop the fire spreading into the adjacent barns along the purlins.

At last the fire exhausted itself. £600-worth of tobacco had gone up in smoke before its time.

Next day the scene was awful to view. Twisted, blackened corrugated iron, bricks, tortured metal flues, and, in the neighbouring barns, charred wood, spoilt tobacco.

But the reaping had to go on. The insurance assessor was no sooner through his business than the clearing and rebuilding was under way. In the middle of the reaping season every barn was essential to get the tobacco through. And, naturally, it always seemed to be the best barns of choice tobacco that caught fire. We could expect a minor fire in one barn every year. The dry leaves fell on to the flues, and at night the stoker was probably asleep and flames were away.

Throughout the world, tobacco was traditionally a peasant crop. It was even grown in Gloucestershire in the sixteenth century, but prohibited after a hundred years on the grounds the fruitful soil was being misemployed. Nowhere else, apart from Rhodesia at that time, were such large acreages grown by individual farmers.

I had a cousin who grew it in his back garden in Derbyshire, and he showed me round his four metres square of strange rank green plants. It seemed so utterly wrong to see tobacco where Michaelmas daisies should be. I was dumbfounded, and I think he got the impression I didn't like his pet tobacco plants, on which he lavished so much care. He told me proudly the tobacco kept him going in cigarettes the whole year through.

Our crop was enough to keep over 4500 people puffing away for a year at thirty cigarettes a day, with hardly a voice raised at the folly of such an action - thirty cigarettes was reckoned as normal. We, on our part, felt we were doing a good service to the population of the world by providing them with inexpensive enjoyment.

Many of the farm workers would make their own rough cigarettes quite casually as they worked. They picked up a few bits of scrap tobacco off the floor, tear a rough square of newspaper, roll, stick with spit and light up. Life can be simple.

Most of our farm labourers came from Mozambique and

Nyasaland (which was renamed Malawi on independence). They had no passports, but in those days passed freely between countries, generally travelling on foot through unmarked borders. They obtained a *situpa* from the District Commissioner, a sort of identity card, before they could be employed. They returned home every year after reaping season, when the annual bonuses were paid out, to their family *kraals* for a few weeks. They were paid pitifully low wages on the farm -- about £3.10s a month. But by having their wives and older children work also, they managed to save some of this and go visiting, smartly dressed and with a new suitcase bulging with presents for their parents and younger brothers and sisters. They must have a great feeling for their families to save the little they have in this way. Many of them also put their younger brothers through school on their wages.

Ours was a medium-sized farm, and we employed about fifty male Africans and their families. They lived in the compound, near the barns and sheds and the main farm homestead, building their own *kayas* - houses made from poles cut from indigenous trees on the farm and plastered with *daga*, which is mud from ant-hill soil that sets hard like plaster. The houses were thatched with dry tall grass cut in the vleis at the end of winter.

There was no running water in the *kayas* and no sanitation. The surrounding *bundu* was the toilet.

A small fire was kept alight in the house all the time and the smoke filtered through the thatch as best it could. To enter one had to crouch to get in through the doorway to the dark and windowless interior. But it was cool in summer and warmed by the fire in winter. Like the old kitchens of English farmhouses with large open grates, the fire was used economically for all purposes.

Birth control among Africans was almost unknown until 1970, so families were large. As the family grew, more round huts were built inside the grass fence which formed a garden and farmyard, where vegetables like marrow and pumpkin, and some irrigated maize were grown, while hens scratched around with their chicks. African people do not generally eat eggs, but prefer to let them hatch and eat chicken instead.

A black man might, by customary law, have more than one wife in Rhodesia, though many were Christians and would only remarry after divorce. By tribal custom, before a young man could marry, he must pay a bride price or *lobola* to the girl's father, in value according to her looks, education and upbringing. It might be ten or even sixty head of cattle, a dozen goats, and perhaps R$40. If she proved to be a poor wife and unfaithful or barren, he could return her to her father and reclaim some of the *lobola*, though this was often very difficult to achieve, as can be imagined. Because of this *lobola* system girls were assured a better welcome in the African world than in many societies. Sons, on the whole, agitated for a better education and with them there was always the urgency to pass exams so they could find better jobs in towns, away from the simple living on farms in both tribal and white areas.

We had a small school on the farm, which took children up to Standard 2, with a more-or-less trained teacher who was more-or-less literate. After this the children were obliged to go away and stay with relatives near larger schools, or become boarders, if they wished to continue their education. African education was not compulsory.

By custom, it was the African woman who did most of the household physical work. She fetched and cut wood from the bush, carried on her head the jars of water from the communal tap, or the river where the washing was generally done, gathered some foods from the bush, bore many children which she nursed at the breast till they were two years old, and carried them on her back till they could walk. She tilled the garden, cooked the food, brewed the beer, looked after the children through colds and chest complaints and measles, kept the home fire burning and often, on white farms, went out to work as well for a very low wage.

But African women generally knew very little about caring for the sick or injured among them, and it was left to the farmer's wife to play doctor, nurse and adviser on mothercare. We had large bottles of *muti* (medicine) in the store shed, in different colours

39

labelled "cough mixture", "diarrhoea mixture" and, unbelievably, "pneumonia mixture". Modern GPs could learn a lot about cheap cures.

When a black man is very sick his face goes grey and his eyes fold back. He would generally agree to be taken to hospital then, but not always - hospital was the place to die in.

And curses do work. We watched one of the Africans on our farm slowly being driven out of his mind by a curse. He was changed in a few weeks from what had appeared to be a normal working member of the community into a mental and physical wreck. He had been told he was going to die. He refused to sit down for fear he would never get up again, and walked around the farm all day and most of the night, waving his arms around and shouting: *Ndidzafa, ndidzafa!*" I am going to die, I am going to die! Everyone would stop what they were doing to stare when he worked himself up to a pitch of rowdiness. He was pitiful. In the end he had to be restrained and taken to hospital, and eventually he went back to his relatives in Nyasaland, and we heard no more of him. I often wonder if he did die of the curse.

But it was the *nganga*, the witchdoctor who specialised in medicine, who was the real influence in sickness and death in Rhodesia. Sophisticated, town-bred Africans were respectful to the point of servility to the *nganga*, as well as to the bone-throwing witchdoctor, who told the secrets of the present and predicted the future. Ngangas were generally good men, and their knowledge of herbs and roots is respected in modern medicine. Some *ngangas* are known to cure cancers, snake bite and cardiac diseases with their natural infusions. Laboratory analysis cannot always pinpoint the magic compound; the ingredient "Africa" is hard to define.

Faith healing was paramount, and surrounding all consultations and cures there was much ritual and noisy appreciation for the witchdoctor's power and wisdom.

We once visited the ruin of one major sixteenth-century settlement, Khami, near Bulawayo. The poor sufferer must have been about dead with fright by the time he reached the witchdoctor at the end of a long, low and narrow passage, which was originally heavily thatched and without light or ventilation. The passage climbed a steep hill, but before the supplicant started his horrifying climb (he was presumably sick in mind if not in body before he started) he gave offerings at the base of the hill.

It was said that one of the witchdoctor's acolytes then sprinted up the hillside, told the witchdoctor what he had been given in payment, and the witchdoctor still had a few minutes to decide whether to help the poor wretch or order him to be thrown down the cliff-side into the crocodile-infested stream below.

It could be life was even rougher in the sixteenth and seventeenth centuries for the superstitious Bantu than it is today.

Four

I was bringing the children back from school in Sinoia one day when we had our first experience of terrorists, even before the Unilateral Declaration of Independence by the white government in 1965, when Rhodesia broke away from the Commonwealth.

I shall call them terrorists because they were terrorists to us, not freedom fighters. Now in 2005, they are called war veterans (that is the few that were adults in the 60s, but not the teenagers of today who are adopting the title.)

Susie was eight, Paula seven. We'd just collected the weekly comics, and they were sitting in the car with heads down and concentrating hard.

Two helicopters were swooping low over the 150-acre maize land we drove through every day, and at the farm turn-off stood a military Land Rover with a mounted machine gun manned by a black soldier, and several others standing guard with rifles.

"Look at the helicopters!" I said to the girls (after all we didn't see many helicopters in Rhodesia). They took a swift glance to oblige, then sank deep again into the recognisable adventures of the picture world.

"Look, I think one of them is coming down," I tried again. But this time I was ignored.

Uniformed figures carrying rifles jumped out of the helicopter and rushed across the far end of the maize land. It must be an exercise, I thought, and after lingering for a while when nothing else happened, I drove on home.

When I got home the news was on the radio. A "battle" was being waged against terrorists near Sinoia, it said. In those days we got the news while it was still new, before the strangling clamp of censorship came down upon all news media.

A group of terrorists had crossed the Hunyani river on the next farm to ours, but they had been routed and many of them killed. The only previous incidents had been well to the north of us, nearer the Northern Rhodesian border, where terrorists destroyed cattle dips, stores and small, isolated African schools in the tribal areas. These were the symbols of European domination, presumably.

Some time later the parents of a little girl in Paula's class were shot on their farm in the first attack on whites in Rhodesia. The day before, they had brought their daughter the 40 miles into school from their farm near Hartley, due south in the Midlands of Rhodesia - the last place one would expect trouble to break out.

(As we lived only 12 miles from school, our daughters were day students, some students were weekly boarders and others full-term boarders).

In those days I can't say I slept very well. Our house was isolated, with the farm workers' compound over a mile away, and our nearest white neighbours, my parents-in-law, further still. Part of our house was constructed of creosoted wood, and the rest of two layers of prefabricated asbestos sheeting. It was plainly vulnerable to fire and bullets. I had a pistol by my side of the bed, Martin had a rifle beside his.

But Fuji, our Alsatian, slept well.

Even so early in the troubles many farmers were sandbagging and fortifying one room for the family to sleep in. Farmers on the edge of the tribal lands, particularly those who were suffering already from poaching and cattle thefts, began to look to their personal safety at home and while driving round the farm.

My parents and brothers in England read about the "battle" in the English newspapers and told us we must come "home". This was before every country got its terrorists and hijackers. It was amazing how, by the 70s, everyone's attitudes to terrorism changed.

By the time we had our real terrorist war in Rhodesia, Britain itself was prey to Irish and Arab terrorist attacks, and when people travelled on a plane they no longer wondered if the plane would crash, they now watched their fellow-passengers with suspicion and prayed they wouldn't be hijacked, or a bomb placed in the luggage compartment. Suicide bombers had yet to crawl out of the caves.

So when our real war began eleven years later, and terrorists were roaming the countryside ten miles away from us, it was no longer the cry "come home". By the time the new century began these early fears and attacks were but blips in comparison.

Sinoia (later renamed Chinoyi), where the children went to junior school and we did our grocery shopping, was the sort of town where donkeys and stray cattle walk down the main street unheeded. It is a hot town in a fold of low kopjes, and oranges grew well.

There was always dust in the air from the sides of the road and from the adjoining dirt roads, and nearly everything in this "cowboy town" was covered with a layer of orange-brown dust. Even the clean white sheets in the laundry. The water cart lumbered through town about nine every morning, spraying water on the verges of the road, but by eleven it would be dust again.

In the morning there would be dogs taking themselves for their morning walks after their owners had gone to work and the servants were making confusion of the house, sweeping the verandahs and shouting to their friends. One old boxer used to sit outside the butcher's shop and slobber every morning before eight. When I passed again to go home he had moved a little nearer, swaying dreamily. I never found out if he was living in a fool's paradise or if he got a reward for constancy.

The road that ran through the town was the main road north from Cape Town to Cairo, but you'd never guess. I often dreamed of driving on and on, right up through Africa to the great lakes of Nyasa and Victoria and on to the Nile, Egypt and Mediterranean Europe. But this road would never lead to Rome for us. By the time the children were grown and we were able to travel, the road led through "liberated" countries, not one of which would let a resident of Rhodesia enter. We heard so many tales of travellers languishing in African jails, it brought caution to us when older. In the 70s it became a popular route for young people who travelled in the backs of lorries or in old clapped-out cars. Australians, in

44

particular, all sunburnt and blond, took this route to Europe.

"Your hinterland is there", it says under Rhodes' statue in Cape Town, as he looks northwards to the interior. Rhodes' dream, my dream, will remain just that.

But in its own right Sinoia was a cosmopolitan town. The baker was Greek, and was heard several times to shout *Eureka!* to customers' delight; most of the shopkeepers were Pakistani or Indian and their wives were always elegantly dressed, with jewelled colours. The two grocers were Greek also and many of the farmers had immigrated from Holland or the Dutch East Indies after it became independent Indonesia. Many of the farmers in the district spoke Afrikaans as their home language. Most of the Africans were Shona - this was Mashonaland - but many came from neighbouring countries of Bechuanaland (Botswana), Mozambique, Zambia and Malawi, looking for work.

On sports day the school winners' list read like an Afrikaans roll of honour -- van der Westhuizen, Oosthuizen, Labuschagne, Cilliers, van Wyk, van As and on to van der Merwe. (Van der Merwe was a very common name and jokes were not about an Irishman, a Scotsman and a Welshman, but about van der Merwe.) Among South Africans with their reputation for worshipping sport, the Afrikaner is the worst of them, so it is not surprising they should start so young. We were always called Myers, the Afrikaans version of our name, especially if one of the girls managed to win a race.

Our children's school was a whites-only school, and it never occurred to us to question this.

Convicts seemed to do most of the maintenance work in the town. It never ceased to amaze me how groups of convicts, dressed in arrowed shirts in summer, or red and white striped jerseys in winter, were armed with iron grass-slashers, pick-axes and choppers and sent off to work in the morning around schools, hospitals and post offices. They were under the supervision of one African warder, armed with a shotgun. Would he shoot if he had to, I wondered. Or was it all show and he hadn't a cartridge?

In Rhodesia it was long ago discovered that the best way to keep down the grass, which every rainy season tries to take over all buildings and paths in town and country, is to use an instrument called a slasher. This is swung like a one-handed hockey stick at the seas of grass. A progressive plot-owner or school would buy a motor mower, but these were not designed for the tough grass of Rhodesia or the treatment they received from unskilled gardeners, so, after many repairs, out would come the slashers before the season was half through.

When Susie was six we'd had to decide whether to take her the twelve miles into Sinoia every morning at eight o'clock and fetch her back again at midday, or to let her have a correspondence course. This was run by the Rhodesian Education Department with parents supervising the lessons and sending them to be marked in Salisbury. We knew Paula would reach school age the next year.

Both the children were very shy, used to farm life and not happy in crowds. We felt they needed the company and competition of other children, so we decided on the daily trail.

The six miles of rough, rutted road varied between large holes and small lakes according to the season, before we reached the main tarred road. I knew every dip, stone and hump on that road after eight years. It would not have surprised me if the car had got up and driven itself. At lunchtime it was often very hot and we were pretty irritable and tired.

As they got further up in junior school, they took an interest in swimming, athletics and hockey, and a desultory interest in discussion groups. These kept them at school beyond the normal Rhodesian school day of eight to one. They could also do their homework at school. When they arrived home at half-past five they were pale and exhausted. This worried us, but I talked to other mothers and they assured me their children were the same, particularly in the summer.

European children in the tropics, as we were in, never had the rosy cheeks that made children look so well in Britain in those days. We just didn't have the weather for it. (Children now are pale in

Europe often enough, with computers claiming their interest.) They got tanned, but the tan wore off in winter and their faces became almost yellow. The sun seemed to dry them out. Children in Africa were, and still are, subject to a lot of respiratory ailments and virus diseases. Being a vegetarian, I think this is partly because people eat too much meat there, while the omnipresent dust in the air can't help.

When the time came for Susie to move on to senior school, we decided to send her to boarding school in Salisbury. I hated the idea, but we felt to keep her in the small, mainly farming community of Sinoia until she was eighteen was unfair. I couldn't wait to leave my home ground when I was young. The least we could do for them was to show them there was another world out there. Many of her school friends were going to boarding schools, and she seemed to be quite happy about it.

Because Martin had been to public school, he was anxious for her to go to a private school. He quite reasonably argued that as I had said what they should eat, he should say how they should be educated. I had vague hopes they might find more understanding of their vegetarian diet in a private school than in a larger school with hundreds of meaty mouths to feed, but I'm not sure this proved true, except in the few rare years when a competent and sympathetic caterer was employed at the school.

Private schools were the only multi-racial schools in the country. Because of the lack of good educational facilities in their own countries, many pupils were from neighbouring territories - President Seretse Khama's daughter from Botswana was in their house. Seretse Khama figured largely in our bit of Africa in those days -- now who has heard of him?

It cost as much as an expensive private school in England, but they both won bursaries, which helped. As Martin's parents were most anxious the girls should go to one particular school, the fees were paid out of farm funds. It was not a happy situation.

We rarely had any money to call our own beyond that needed to pay the grocery bill (to buy a new pair of sheets or similar articles was a major crisis), but we ran an expensive car (the farm's) and our children went to the poshest school. The farm in the end had to buy the uniforms, because we certainly couldn't afford them. It was hard work trying to keep up with the numerous leisure outfits they wanted to take. Fortunately they were the same size, which doubled their wardrobes. They were used to home-made clothes and soon started to make their own. Making your own clothes was usual then.

Paula, in particular, was quite a good swimmer (I know - proud parents are dead boring.) She wouldn't take private coaching because, she said, her shoulders would grow too big. She did take some diving lessons, but a year on, she wouldn't dive in case she lost her bikini. Who'd be a teenage girl?

This was before skin cancer warnings, and young Rhodesians spent long hours "catching a tan". It is alarming to think of it now.

Martin himself had basal skin cancer on his nose and underwent drastic radiotherapy, a treatment still in its early stages. But he survived relatively unscathed and it has been a talking point with any skin specialists he has encountered during his life. Later patches of skin cancer he has suffered have received much gentler treatment.

If I could have chosen, I would have risked bringing the girls home white-faced each evening. When your children go to boarding school they are lost to you. You no longer know who they are talking about, you can't follow their studies and small scholastic and sporting triumphs, and you can't put in your small offerings of advice and help, even though they'd take little notice.

Many parents sent their children to be boarders at incredibly early ages, without real need to do so. Others had no choice at all and their children went to boarding school when they were seven or eight, after two years of correspondence courses.

As it worked out, when we thought about leaving the farm, it made it much easier with the girls able to continue at their same boarding schools. The nearest senior school then would have been 250 miles down the road.

When the girls started school I decided if ever I was going to write I'd better start right away. Before I emigrated to Rhodesia I'd written odd bits of poetry and short stories, but I'd never had anything published. So I took a correspondence course in short story and article writing. I sent for all the prospectuses advertised in the "Argosy" and chose what appeared to be the most reputable. It was a tremendous help. Some people derive great pleasure in writing for themselves and their friends. My journalist brother scorned this idea, instilling in me the principle of never writing anything unless you are going to be paid for it. This can be difficult, but I felt to sell a story is to place a standard upon it which you cannot do for yourself. But it is not always the best of your work that is accepted.

I really benefited from my course and enjoyed it. A lot of what they teach about article lengths and studying your market is not obvious to the novice.

Sometimes I heard a story over the radio where even I could see the writer was really struggling in the shallows of his technique. The Rhodesia Broadcasting Corporation paid very little (three guineas for a story, half for a repeat), but as their standard wasn't high it was a real encouragement - you can't help getting a kick from hearing one of your stories on the air. When someone else reads it, too, many of the weaknesses that had escaped your notice stick out.

I read every book I could lay my hands on in Rhodesian libraries (some of the books were older than I was) about journalism, fiction writing, and about writers and their experiences in writing, and bought magazines for aspiring writers. We could still get overseas magazines in Rhodesia then, or send subscriptions overseas.

Like all would-be writers, I learnt to hate editors. They are not human.

There are few more oft-repeated and sickening experiences than the constant return of a treasured manuscript with those mortifying, faceless rejection slips attached to them. They can't even be likened to homing pigeons in their faithfulness, as, presumably the pigeon fancier wants his treasure to return. I truly never wanted to see some of mine again, in or out of print.

My tutor persuaded me to keep plugging away, altering and rewriting one of my stories till in the end he pronounced it was as good as it could be, and it was accepted by the only Rhodesian woman's magazine. I couldn't contain my joy. They paid me £5, and I thought I would explode with pride. When it was printed they had my name wrong on the top of the page.

I enjoy writing more than any other pastime, occupation or hobby. On holidays over the years I've always collected many pamphlets and guidebooks, and written something on my return. It helps pay for the holiday, but if I go on many more holidays I won't be able to get into the house for glossy paper brochures.

I wrote a novel - a novel is immense! Imagine 70,000 words on 280 pages, all connecting with each other. It was a poor novel. I got lost. It wasn't published.

One fact I've discovered about writing is that nothing you write is ever wasted like, they say, nothing you learn. Stuff you've written is better than a diary any day.

Some of the articles and stories I laboured over when I first started writing I took out, polished up and sold. One story that had been the rounds two years before, I cut down, gave a new title and sold twice - to a South African and to an English magazine. I even got two articles translated into Afrikaans. Odd! I hadn't the first idea what they said. But, at least, they got my name right this time.

The printer in Sinoia was trying to run a weekly newspaper. He was floundering, so I offered my invaluable (what else?) services for little pay. This was a great experience. I learnt by trial and error: my boss was so pleased to have someone to fill up the gaps between the advertising he never bothered to advise or direct. Now I had to write several thousand words a week, I had to go out and talk to people, I had to try and put down facts concisely, but to provoke interest. Reporter on the Lomagundi Echo - there's something to be proud of!

Most people said how much the paper had improved - what else could they tell me to my face? But unfortunately the circulation of 500 on good weeks wasn't economically viable, and we couldn't win over any more advertisers. The European population was only 2000, so there was little hope for much better. The Africans enjoyed their own news - a lot of football - and had little interest in the white man's world. My boss was not fit and was trying to care for a sick wife, so away went the paper and I hadn't a job.

When the children were older I tried to persuade the town council, who were supporting a sort of circularised diary, to withdraw this so I could start a newspaper instead. There wasn't enough advertising to go round for both, and I pointed out to them all my plans, how I could make this town really hum, how the advertisers would be falling over themselves to say their bit, but I've never been able to make town councils or any other august bodies listen to me. I wasn't willing to cast my pearls in duplicated sheets and for free, as offered by them, so I retired. I hadn't the money to take too great a risk: most of the major tradesmen were members of the council anyway.

We erected a 30-metre high television aerial behind the house as soon as television started in Rhodesia in 1960. There never was so much snow in Africa. The aerial was constructed of tubular steel pipes with supporting wire stays that reached way out over the ground. Every year the winds, which brought the first thunderstorms, used to blow it down, a twisted wreck. Martin no longer got "the man" out from Sinoia to fix it. His farm handymen got quite good at re-assembling it over the years.

The television reception deteriorated each time it blew down and was re-erected, but we had a lot of fun out of it - simple-minded bush yokels watching Z Cars in black and white. Programmes started at five in the evening and went off about ten. Before sanctions cut off the best serials and documentaries, we loved Danger Man, Bonanza and Roving Report.

Lots of people in Rhodesia, including my kids, couldn't understand what they said in Z Cars, and it was as well we didn't run to Coronation Street. At last, the world was being allowed to creep into our rural lives. Radio reception out in the country was very poor.

Dare I say how good TV winter sports were with the extra snowstorms thrown in? And how can a child grow up without knowing anything about cowboys and Indians?

The mistakes and amateurisms were hilarious at times, though the local shows made you want to cry rather, they were so bad. Sixteen years later when South Africans overcame religious prejudices (the Dutch Reformed Church in this case) and were allowed to have television at last, we watched while on holiday the same awful procedures taking place all over again in Natal. This time it was in colour, with no snow, and the mistakes glared out more gloriously: the pauses, funny make-up, men's odd ties, hands waved in front of cameras, announcers with oddities of speech so you couldn't quite catch the meaning. Wooden interviewers conducted interviews full of agreement with each other while sitting uneasily in easy chairs or in a flower-bewildering patio with spots of light which made the interviewer squint, and odd patches of white light on the beauty queen's pancake-makeup face.

What I liked most on our television were the loud crashes, and one Christmas time, the sounds of unmistakable cursing off-stage. Surely not Father Christmas. The lady announcer meanwhile smiled sweetly on.

In 1973 when Zambian television arrived in Livingstone just across the river from Victoria Falls, (we'd moved there by then, but more of this later), the Falls residents became quite hysterical at the antics of Zambian television. A record would be played, and the screen would show the record going round and round and round for the duration of the interlude. Then the announcer would have a news item about New York, while on the screen was a lovely picture of the Sydney harbour bridge.

Victoria Falls was too far from a Rhodesian transmitter to pick up a signal, so residents certainly had a different view of news from the rest of Rhodesia, with the two countries politically at loggerheads across the Zambezi river: President Kenneth Kaunda with his "One Nation, One Zambia" to the north, Prime Minister Ian Smith of Rhodesia to the south, still shouldering the white man's burden, running a country on apartheid principles, though he was not often accused of such.

FIVE

The year Rhodesia proclaimed the Unilateral Declaration of Independence (UDI) we came back from a three-week holiday in the eastern mountains and Beira to discover a leguaan over a metre long had set up house in the roof. If ever you were in any doubt, I can assure you it is possible to reside quite happily with a leguaan once you know it is not an oversized cobra or python, as we first thought.

Leguaans are Nile monitor lizards, so named by the early Cape settlers who mistakenly took them for iguanas.

We used to hear him dragging himself above the ceiling board in the sitting room (which had the only ceiling in the house), creating a loud slushing and sliding noise that resounded through the roof space. The first we saw of him was a very large clawed foot appear in the gap between rafters and wall just half a metre above our heads. Then came the hefty shoulder, followed slowly and laboriously by a soft yellow and black-spotted underbelly and a banded tail. He gave the impression he wasn't designed for this crawling around ceilings of houses.

He became quite a showpiece, but had to be approached in silence or he skitted back into the roof again. Visitors would not believe we had a leguaan living in the roof. So we would take them outside and creep to where he was often seen spread-eagled in the sun on the back wall of the house, where he could just squeeze under the breezeblocks. He did a fine job on the rats - much better than our misguided cat who concentrated on the bush rats rather than the ones in the house.

We would see him in the afternoons, when all was quiet, majestically swaggering his way down the garden to the dam for a break, and his dinner.

He lived with us for several weeks, even when we were in the first stages of erecting prefabricated bedrooms, with all the hammering accompaniment, but I think the noise did get on his nerves in the long run, and he departed down to the dam wall. One of the leguaans there was two-and-a-half metres long. I can't see that our ceiling would have held that one.

Leguaans look very like crocodiles as they flash into the water, and were often mistakenly shot by farmers keen to protect their workers' children and livestock. They make holes in the earth walls of dams, but as they eat crocodile eggs, snakes and rodents, many feel they do more good than harm, and they're interesting to watch.

Sometimes our little wooden house got a bit too much like a fairy story, and when a dormouse arrived we gave up struggling for reality. Dormice are the cutest of creatures, and I could see why Alice in Wonderland was so fascinated. They look more like miniature squirrels than mice, with bushy tails, furry grey bodies, big round eyes and big round ears.

One day he pinched a small ball of red knitting wool from the children's bedroom and took it to his ledge in the bathroom, where he slept all day. I don't know whether he was decorating the place or whether he caught his foot in the wool, but one morning we got up to find, right across the width of the bathroom, a festoon of red wool from the dormouse's ledge to a nail on the far side.

His feeding habits were a trouble: he preferred the fruit bowl, or pretty well any food left out in the kitchen, to his natural food in the bush. We also suspected we had rats, but weren't quite sure how to catch a rat without catching a dormouse. We hadn't acquired a cat then, which is as well for dormouse because he was careless and often fell from his heights. He was in the empty bath one morning, panic stricken, so Susie had to pounce on him with a towel and put him back on his wall ledge. As might have been expected, we didn't have one dormouse for long, we had three, and we knew them by name. After that there were a lot of dormice. They extended their territory to the wardrobe and our clothes began to smell. They urinated and worse on the shoulders of the clothes as they stood on their hangers. The home-made built-in wardrobes were made of rough wood, with large gaps between wall and cupboard.

In the end, sadly, we had to collect as many of the dormice as we could and take them for a ride into the bush in the Land Rover. We had already found what we thought would be a nice spot for them to live, by a rocky outcrop with trees. We left them some supper to start their new life, and returned to a strangely silent house. Paula was upset and sure they would die. Susie was very quiet about it.

Before Susie was born, and before we lived at the house by the dam, one of Martin's employees brought us a very young bush-baby (a lemur) that he said he'd found abandoned. He said I should care for it. It had probably not been abandoned permanently, but it was too late to do anything about returning it to its mother - it was rife with human smell. Experts told us, then, no wild animal will take back its young once the animal smells of humans, but we've proved this wrong several times, with birds at least.

So, without knowing anything about bush babies, we had to try and rear him. He was the most adorable little creature to look at. Bush babies have hands and toes with nails like monkeys. Including the bushy tail, they grow to sixty centimetres in length, but when we were given ours, he was perhaps twelve centimetres long. He was ash-grey with big rounded ears and the largest, most soulful eyes on earth. We kept him in a birdcage at first, out of the cat's reach, and let him out to play in the evening when the cat went out: he was by nature nocturnal.

We scoured through all the books we had to hand, but came up with little knowledge what to feed him on. We found he loved raisins, grapes and any fruits, and I gave him milk and water in a dropper, as he didn't show any inclination to lap. We then moved on to baby porridge and raw egg, and he was really a fit little chap and gave us no trouble with his diet right from the beginning.

He soon outgrew his birdcage, so we fitted up a box for him to sleep in with a wire-meshed front, and in the evening, when let free, he soon learnt to leap up on the bookcase, then up the electrical conduit to the rafters below the corrugated asbestos roof. He liked to catch insects by the table lamp, and loved grasshoppers. I can't say I enjoyed seeing my sweet, much-loved bush baby with a large half-eaten grasshopper in his hands, chomping happily.

After a while he would not bother to come down from the rafters to sleep, so we had to search and call around every day, though he came down for supper (his breakfast) every evening without fail. As a baby he was extremely cuddlesome and affectionate, though quick-tempered. We called him Tickey-widdles because of his habit of rushing up the conduit, peering down on us or the dog and cat, and swearing, "tic-tic" at us. He would then urinate on his hands and feet to improve his grip and streak off, up and away to the far end of the roof.

And he loved alcohol. In the evening if he found a glass unattended he would be there in a flash with his nose right in. Once or twice he got so drunk he wasn't able to climb, falling all over the place and dropping to sleep eventually, without any caution, in a chair.

He began going out into the garden, climbing to the top of the highest tree and letting out unnerving cries - sometimes a harsh bark, sometimes like a baby crying, then in turn swearing, laughing and growling as he swung about the branches.

As he became adult he also became very fierce, biting our hands till he drew blood. He was starting to appear only in the evening, announcing his arrival by thumping on the roof, and I'd put on a pair of leather gloves when he arrived.

I was very large and pregnant, and we were fearful for the expected baby's safety with Tickey-widdles snatching and biting anyone in sight.

He was living more and more in the bush, and for only a few months after Susie was born did he clomp back to the roof and down the conduit, though he took the opportunity to land on her in her cot once or twice, grabbing at her face with his clammy hands.

After he had finally left us, a bush baby would often come to the high tree in the garden and shout, and we were pretty sure it was Tickey, though he would never come down to us again no matter how we called. Twenty years after, bush babies still visited the high trees around the cottage and homestead at the main farm, yelling and crying at night. We hoped they were Tickey's offspring.

A smaller type of bush baby, usually called a night-ape, was a popular pet with schoolchildren. They were less fierce, but not so pretty.

One day we got back from a day in town to find a swarm of bees installed in the wardrobe, with a honeycomb already rich in honey. Such was our trust on farms in those days that we always left all our doors and windows fully open when we went out.

We slept that night on the mattress, which we dragged cautiously into the sitting room.

We hoped the bees would go of their own accord next day, but in the end, most regretfully, we had to close up the room and let off an insecticide bomb. We knew of no beekeepers nearby who might have helped remove them.

Wasps of all varieties would regularly set up house in our house. Most of them bore no resemblance to English wasps - more like extravagantly coloured daddy-long-legs. The mason wasps were the smartest with yellow-and-black football socks, which they trailed behind as they flew lazily through the doors and windows in spring, bringing each time a small lump of mud in their mouths to construct a dome-shaped nest on the ceiling, or behind the furniture or curtains. The plain-legged species preferred holes in the wall or even a folded newspaper to lay their eggs in. To feed the hatched grubs green caterpillars or large spiders (depending on the variety of the wasp), which had first been paralysed by the wasp's sting were stuffed in with the eggs. This wasp baby food stayed alive and fresh for days. Perhaps humans should stop trying to develop bigger and better deep-freezers and go in for stung foods instead.

Another sort for wasp, called a social wasp, made a paper nest. By painful experience I found I was violently allergic, and suffered anaphylactic shock, to the sting of the small variety of the social wasp, which is much smaller than a bee or English wasp. The second time I was stung by one, as I carelessly clutched it in my hand while picking a peach, I became almost temporarily blind, having difficulty breathing and with an alarmingly low blood pressure, before I managed to reach a doctor and receive an adrenaline injection.

When I go to Africa now I take a self-injection device with me, just in case. It's interesting, isn't it? How many other people are out there potentially allergic to the little social wasp? When Martin was stung by a scorpion, the doctor made the simple pronouncement that as he was still all right an hour later, he'd live. I have heard since that scorpion stings are generally not half as threatening as they are made out to be - no more than a wasp sting, but that doesn't do much for me. One thing I did find was that the wasp sting cleared away any twinges of rheumatism - like magic. We've noticed with many Alsatians that they will chase bees and wasps like crazy dogs, as if encouraging them to sting, and Alsatians suffer a lot from arthritis.

Over the years other wild creatures would adopt us and make use of our house temporarily. A field mouse would perform the same action every evening: peep round the door from the verandah, rush round the corner, skid on his bottom on the polished floor, then slide under the closed door into the kitchen. We found we waited for him.

Before I went to Africa I had heard strange stories about the praying mantis, but we found these delightful creatures, once you got over the horror of the way they cling to hair and skin. They appear to be very inquisitive and enjoy being part of a human household. They have a pronounced triangular head, which they move readily, and stare with five eyes. They vary between two and twenty centimetres long and come in a variety of shapes. And they pray, their two forelegs raised for hours in silent supplication. We had one that lived in the mosquito net over our bed, mopping up any stray mosquitoes that managed to get in.

The stick insect looks similar, but eats vegetable matter, and looks exactly like the grass, flower, leaf or tree bark he lives on. If a person is what he or she eats, then surely here is a prime example.

And there were, naturally, snakes: puff adders lying in pathways, pythons on rocky outcrops, boomslangs in the trees and spitting cobras in the wardrobe (a hockey stick comes in useful here). I was even bitten by a snake in the house once - it was all of twenty centimetres long and hadn't a hope of getting a grip on my sturdy leg.

We slept with a pair of puff adders for a week, when we holidayed at Lake Nyasa (now Lake Malawi), in a garden cottage of a hotel overlooking the lake. We had already moved from one room where termites kept dropping on us from the thatched roof - I think we were responsible for this, as we had sprayed the room with insecticide in the evening to ward off the mosquitoes.

Anyway, we found ourselves, next, sharing a room with bats. I am terrified of bats and insisted on sheltering under the mosquito net at bat-flying time - at dusk. Martin and the children didn't want to move again, and the bats showed no inclination to make a nest in my hair as I feared, so we stuck it out. The last morning, as we were packing up to go, one of the girl's shoes was lost. We moved the large, heavy, old Chesterfield armchair that stood between the children's beds and there, hibernating in the depths of the chair's undersides, were two large puff adders. Guess how long it takes to pack up when there are two puff adders watching...

One night at Christmas (which is a great time for insects, at the beginning of the rainy season), we were throwing a party and the biggest beetle I have ever seen joined in. He was over twenty centimetres long, in pale colours with large dark patches on his back. But, in spite of his enormous size and long weird feelers, he was not aggressive. He kept to the floor, and as it was at the end of a rather boozy party, we were going to extravagant lengths not to step on him. After our guests had left and we were clearing up and piling the worst mess into the kitchen, the beetle bustled to and fro as well.

To reach the bedroom, we had to walk outside and up a step to a different block of rooms. We had no desire to share our sleep with the beetle, so we carefully avoided putting on any lights. We were nearly safely in bed, when who should come triumphantly under the door but our old friend, the beetle. How he found his way to the bedroom, unless he smelt our tracks, I don't know. The dog looked embarrassed and retired to the far end of the room. (I find Alsatians always pretend not to see what they can't understand, or don't know how to deal with. I wish I had an equal facility.)

And the beetle? I persuaded Martin, by now almost asleep, to take beetle wrapped in a towel, for a long walk into the bush, and to try and walk back quicker than beetle.

One happening our poor Alsatians couldn't ignore was the tornado that swept through the house while we were out for the day in Salisbury. Fuji was nine years old, and when her heart began to fail we decided to get another Alsatian puppy, because not only could we not bear to be without a dog, we needed a watchdog in our isolated position. So we got Hayley whom Fuji immediately took as her own puppy, played with, loved and watched over jealously. Fuji took on a new lease of life, and after being thought to be at death's door, lived in good health for another four years. Thirteen was a good age for a large dog in a hot climate.

When Hayley was five months old we had taken the girls back to boarding school and had a quick supper in town. All the way back we saw terrific wind and thunderstorms, hail, rain, all that the heavens could dispense, and as we neared the farm, we saw a great swathe of destruction had been cut across the bush. Trees were down, telegraph wires dangled on leaning poles, and crops and tall grasses were flattened.

When we got to the house it was pouring with rain. The tornado had cut right through the house. The roofs of the dining room and kitchen were blown off and a stream was flowing through the back of the house and out the front. The dogs and Pixie the cat were nowhere to be seen. There were no lights in the house (by this time we had mains electricity) and, with the car lights on, we searched the bush with a torch for the animals. It was horrifying.

At last they came out of their hiding places, shivering, soaked, and in great shock. We could hardly approach Pixie for a week

61

afterwards. We towelled the animals down and captured and shut Pixie in the bedroom, where it was reasonably dry.

Then we tried to bring order to the house. We piled all the wet furniture and soaked carpets into the sitting room, Martin quickly dug a ditch to divert the water from the back door, and we swooshed out as much water as we could. In the middle of it all our silly young Hayley picked up a drawing pin in her pad and was hopping around the house on three paws crying. Without lights, we couldn't see the cause of the trouble for long enough.

We were lucky the bedroom block was fairly intact. We were up at dawn to try and retrieve what we could. In daylight the wreckage looked even worse. And now we were becoming very apprehensive about the amount of damage the storm had dealt the crops.

It looked like rain again, so Martin dashed away to Sinoia to get some sheets of corrugated iron and get a roof of sorts on the house before the next storm arrived.

Anyone who could be spared from reaping tobacco, (some of which had been beaten down and lay with leaves frayed), dug ditches, cleaned mud off the carpet and dabbed at the furniture now out on the lawn.

The dogs wouldn't let us out of their sight for weeks, and Hayley's ears never did stand up after that terrible night, in spite of her very good pedigree. She had hairy, heavy ears, but they had been showing signs of standing up like an Alsatian's should. After the storm they flopped forever. As she was also a very long-haired dog, she happily went through life looking remarkably unlike an Alsatian, and everyone asked what breed she was. But she was beautiful all the same.

SIX

In 1969 Rhodesia tried to count its people, and I got a job as a census enumerator. I hate to think how the African census-takers fared in the tribal areas on their bicycles (ten shillings a day bicycle allowance), because my only concerns were with the small village of Banket, with two hundred or so white people and their employees. I felt my count was inaccurate even though after my few days stint I knew every dog and dog-eyed daisy in the village.

In those days, certain urban areas were reserved for whites only, or blacks only, even though there was no official apartheid as in South Africa.

Banket was 15 miles from the farm, and blink while driving on the main road and you'd miss it, with its one store, one hotel, one school, police camp, sports' club, Roman Catholic Church, farmers' hall (which doubled as the Protestant Church), and acres and acres of eye-high grass dotted fragrantly with cosmos, Mexican marigolds and orange chrysanthemums.

Everyone I spoke to told me how disgraceful it was that "they" hadn't cut the grass: "And, lady, could you please tell your boss to come and cut the grass? You know, it is dangerous with all the snakes, and how do we know what else is lurking there?" How indeed? I sneezed agreement. All this had occurred to me.

Some told me they thought the television programmes had improved. It was really so notable an opinion that I felt there should be a space on the census form to record it - this was the time we were being told by Britain that "sanctions were biting", and we weren't getting good British programmes any more.

But no one cared to tell me how many people were sleeping on the property the night of the census, even though they had been warned *ad nauseam* through newspapers, TV and radio networks.

"Oh, man, how can I remember the name of that young chap Fanie brought home that night? No, man, I don't know where he came from - he met him in the bar. I think he said something about going down south. Hell, I can't remember. No, Fanie's working in Mangula now."

Seven years before, when the last census was taken, people had put "twice a week," and "yes, please" in the sex column, so the revised form was very carefully worded, and duller.

It is surprising how many households don't have a pen, and how many husbands don't know their children's ages or full names.

It is a sad reflection on the drunken state many people were in when they used to drive their cars that two householders were in hospital as the result of separate road accidents.

And an even sadder reflection on morals in 2001, when, in the South African census, at a time when HIV and AIDS were rampant, that census enumerators were issued with condoms along with their census forms.

I enjoyed my occasional jobs that took me off the farm sometimes. I tried market research interviewing also and found it great fun, but hard work. Unfortunately what few jobs there were in this line were generally confined to Salisbury. But this stood me in good stead eight years later, when we emigrated to England, and I was able to get jobs for 25 years or more because I could say I was an experienced interviewer.

But holidays were best! With the rest of the white population of Rhodesia, we used to rock our way down to Beira, on the Indian Ocean, in Mozambique, which was still a Portuguese colony (Portuguese East Africa on the map then). It was 400 miles from the farm and the road was really awful the other side of the border.

The Portuguese had an odd way of making up the roads. They sent out an African labourer with a wheelbarrow and a spade: *"Hamba longisa lo mugwaga."* (Go and mend the road.) It was only 200 miles long.

At some forgotten time the road had been tarred to a roughly two-metre width, but as it broke up the wheelbarrow man filled it up with grit, and we never saw any real construction work being done, all the years and times we went up and down the road in search of Portuguese wines and the miles of sloping sands, and beautiful clean surf.

Kids loved Beira, and the man who dreamed up moving Rhodesia to the Estoril at Beira regularly every school holidays made millions. He built, right on the edge of the sea, a rather nasty complex of huts served by the most unreliable lavatories and grubby showers that no self-respecting Rhodesian would have let his child go near normally, if they had been nearer home.

As the people rolled in, bringing their Rhodesian pounds (or, later, metricated Rhodesian dollars), which were the common currency of Estoril, the entrepreneurs built self-contained flats, which were cleaner, but the lavatories still didn't work.

We started our camping holiday life with a motor caravan. They were uncommon in Africa then. Ours was a factory-converted Commer van with lifting roof. Like children, we were thrilled with the wardrobes, table, built-in stove, drawers and cupboards and seats that converted to beds. Attached we had a self-standing tent. It was a fun-wagon always. Even before we left the farm we felt we were on holiday, sitting high up, and it was ideal for game watching.

No searching for an orange, all things right to hand - fruit, drinks, and lunch – we could stuff ourselves silly. Susie and Paula would do their drawing, read puzzle books or play cards at the table as we went, or just lie back and read or go to sleep on the wide seats. No seat belts in those days! It was slower than a car, but we found we got to a place as fast as anyone else, because we hardly needed to stop. (Martin wouldn't stop.)

When going to Beira, we used to take what we considered the essentials of living - bread, butter, cheese, fruit - we even took growing lettuces in a seed tray - because foodstuffs there were so expensive, and the bread dry and inedible.

Most people revelled in the large prawns. Some said we missed a lot by not eating them, but we managed to avoid the digestive upsets at the same time, as a bonus. The Portuguese wine was good and cheap and helped the greasy chips at the pavilion wash down well. Lots of people had to return home early with dysentery, malaria, sunstroke and sunburn, but they were natural hazards and they travelled down again the following year.

The little boy from the caravan next to us had to undergo a series of fourteen daily anti-rabies injections in his belly while tests were being made on the brain of a stray dog that had been roaming around the beach and petted by many children. The dog had died from unknown causes.

To Rhodesians the town had a magical Continental atmosphere, and restaurants serving "foreign" foods. The nightclubs were seedy, and prostitutes came in all colours - it was a big port. Aids was apparently unknown then.

One day there was no water at all on the chalet and camping site, and a great many people had been out the night before to celebrations of garlic, seafood, oil and exotic drinks. All morning chalet cleaners and gardeners ran up and down the beach, to and fro from the loos to the sea, fighting a losing battle – these employees bore little resemblance to Swiss chalet maids or Butlin's blue coats, which was perhaps as well.

It was exceptionally hot and the smell lay on the torpid air.

We left before noon, a day earlier than planned, and stayed a couple of days in the mountains, on the Rhodesian side of the border, enjoying the sweet, pine-scented air. It was marvellous to go to Beira; it was such a relief to get home again.

Our last year on the farm was also the last time we went to Beira - and at night! It was just before Easter and we drove the caravan down through the pampas and the swamps, and the endless lantana and scrub bush by the light of an odd-shaped moon that lay before us all the way.

It was a beautiful journey. We had supper in the border town of Umtali and the girls went to sleep on the big bed in the back. We stopped once only over the border for unrationed petrol on the 200-mile drive. The whole countryside was lit by the strange white and wondrous light of that unforgettable moon. We saw only two or three cars on the road and nothing else but nightjars, owls and a few scared-eyed bucks. It was our world and the Pungwe River, silver, winding and serene, our river.

Beira was Beira when we got there, and we enjoyed it.

On the way home again we stopped at the Gorongoza game reserve, just off the main road in Mozambique, on a great wide plain, which is surely the nearest approach to the old and famed great plains of Africa, teaming with game, that the hunter Courtney Selous wrote about at the end of the nineteenth century. Now that poaching is rife in Africa, and the Frelimo terrorists have roamed the area, it may be the last time anyone will see the spectacle. All across the wide grassland were zebra, wildebeest, giraffe, buffalo, sable and buck of every variety, while in attendance were jackals, cheetah, hyena and vultures.

The lions lived in houses. They had taken over a deserted rest camp, and we went to see them in the heat of the day as they lay stretched out on the concrete floors, leaning against the flaking white-washed walls. There were several full-grown lions, six or seven lionesses, and many half-grown offspring. They were too lazy to look up. Flitting in and out of the houses above the lions' heads were endless successions of small swallows, tweeting in high bat-like squeaks. When dusk came the bats themselves joined in.

It was hard to believe they were real wild lions, and to resist the temptation to get out of the car and pat one of them on the head, all at one with St. Francis.

Within five years, Beira, that bare-foot paradise of white Rhodesians, had been returned to Africa. Frelimo soldiers camped in the huts and flats and it was their turn to taste the delights of *vino*, lager and the prostitutes - at least so they thought. But there was no money to import the wine, the breweries ceased, and prostitution was banned by the Marxist government, which only goes to show what much higher-minded rulers were the Frelimo than were the Portuguese. But I bet the lavatories still didn't work.

The harbour silted up after a few months, and few ships came and went in a port which had once carried Rhodesia's best luxuries and, perhaps, her lifeblood. Rhodesian residents were not allowed through the borders, neither had they any desire to go.

It was no longer possible for anyone to drive along that road to the sea in safety, even in full daylight - it was unthinkable to undertake the journey at night or, indeed, any night-journey through central Africa north of the Limpopo.

A couple of times we had been to Victoria Falls for our holidays, and into northern Botswana by the Chobe and Zambezi rivers. At the time there wasn't a proper border post there. We went through the formalities of immigration and customs in Victoria Falls, travelled the forty miles of rutted dirt road to the game fence, which marked the border, and then went to look for the policeman who kept the key to the gate. It was all very friendly.

Ten years after, this became the only road open between the black north and the white south of Africa. Great trucks and pantechnicon vans wound their way round the bush roads, which were still mainly unpaved, from South African ports to Zaire, Malawi and the Zambian copperbelt. At the border, they sat for hours in the hot sun in the simmering, sandy roadsides, waiting while customs officials went over their vast cargoes and trucks with a toothcomb, searching for guns and drugs.

On one side were the black officials, slow, deliberate and stolidly officious, finely avoiding being rude to the whites; on the other side, white officials, overheated, impatiently officious, rude to the blacks. It was no longer at all friendly.

As the children outgrew the bunks in the motor caravan, we bought a trailer caravan, but it wasn't half so much fun. It was too smart and civilised and we weren't "with" all our holiday stuff. The children fretted, too close together in the back of the car, and they wanted to stop for cool drinks, ice cream, apples, oh, just stop! We could never really account for why the extra space and comfort of the trailer caravan didn't suit us better.

It was much more convenient once you arrived and set up camp to have the car free for touring, we told ourselves. But as with a room, a house, a town: it's a feeling, and no amount of factual argument can make you like or dislike it once the first feelings have established themselves.

If we'd had a good season with the tobacco, we went to South Africa. We loved the mountains of the Cape and the rugged shore, and yet it took four or five days, our speed, to get there. Durban was nearer, with its sandy north- and south-coast golden beaches that seemed to stretch for ever. We have pictures of the children from babes in white sunhats to bikinied teens, snapped (unwillingly) in front of the lighthouse at Umhlanga, north of Durban. They didn't seem to change much, in our eyes anyway.

Young Rhodesians loved the water. In their own country it was so precious and jealously stored. To live in a land-locked country is to see, through winter and spring months, the rivers become dry sand-beds, and in summer fast-flowing rivers that are suicidal to swim in. Everywhere are dams, to be sure: most farms have their own, some like sizeable lakes, and all full of bilharzia snails.

When I first arrived in Salisbury, I was surprised Rhodesians did not flush the lavatories after use. I was told there was a grave shortage of water following a drought year. Bricks in water cisterns became common practice

But when dams were built near the towns, the gardens and parks bloomed gloriously. Salisbury, particularly, had beautiful private gardens (and some still have, judging by the television pictures in 2005). In Bulawayo, where reticulated water was used in the municipal parks and on roundabouts and roadsides, the greenness of the lawns was unbelievable to visitors after the miles of faded grasslands and mean scrub they had driven through to reach there. And, lining the streets of all towns and *dorps,* were flowering trees and shrubs: jacaranda, flamboyant, bauhinia, spathodea, franzipani and poinsettia, while golden shower and jasmine covered white walls vigorously.

On Rhodesia's northern border, where the Zambezi has been dammed, Lake Kariba is more like a sea - 180 miles long and the far side lost in haze.

But it is the light over Kariba that makes it so fascinating: on the hot dry days when the air seems to sing, a soft, light grey-blue haze suffuses the lake, so that there is no end to the lake, no beginning to the sky. In a boat you are utterly alone on a horizonless sea of doldrums. Except that here and there, even way out in the lake, stand thin dead trunks of forgotten trees, which do not rot under the surface of the water.

And the sunsets are unforgettable, when the haze becomes orange and the sun a mist of light.

But there are some unheralded and severe storms on the lake. One morning we were going to the other side of the lake to Bumi, a sort of paradise 36 miles from Kariba, when one of the engines of our boat broke down and, instead of planing the two-metre-high waves we had to slide and rise into the troughs and crests of each wave. Nobody felt well, and the owner of the boat was sick, trying to fix the motors.

As soon as we got there we were told we would have to go straight back to be in before dark, in case of further trouble. I said I was going to cool off in the hotel swimming pool come what may, and Martin said he was going to have a beer, so help him.

As he was obliged to wait, the boat-owner managed to fix the engine now that the boat was still, so he had a swim and a beer as well and we shared a large plateful of sandwiches.

We sat at peace and looked out over the endless blue water with white caps on the waves, and at an elephant and a fish eagle by the shore. Bumi is a world on its own, remote from the other side of the lake, and there is no road to it.

We were all at peace now, restored and ready to go back over the waters into a normal time-cycle, with the permission of the river god, *Nyaminyami,* without whose permission the Zambezi was dammed.

Many Africans really believe that this god lives now far beneath the waters of Kariba, where before there was a treacherous stretch of rapids. While the dam wall was being constructed, the river came down in the highest flood ever recorded, causing a catastrophe which it was estimated might occur only once in a thousand years.

How else could this have happened if not by *Nyaminyami* taking his revenge?

SEVEN

There's nowhere quite like Victoria Falls to live and work. The village sits poised as if on the edge of the world. Except for a long, long and lonely road and a tenuous railway line, the area lies cut off from most of Africa. Yet the rest of the world comes to experience the grandeur. The falls, no matter when or how you see them, are instantly and bewilderingly dramatic. Whether in sunlight, moonlight, mist, rain, at dawn, sunset or in black night, their intenseness is irresistible. See them in full flood in April, when the throb and roar deafen, or in October when the waters fall like lace among black rocks, and you will be aware that here you stand as nothing, while the great Zambezi river puts on a show of power, beauty, terror and delicacy which is decked in the most luminescent colours in earth or heaven – *Mosi oa Tunya!*

Anyone who doesn't believe in a God, or in other worlds, or in himself, must go to Victoria Falls, because there he will begin to believe in beauty, or splendour, or power or glory - something that may pass for divinity.

Martin had been applying for all manner of jobs for years: harbour master on Lake Malawi (we opted out of this as we had young children to educate and we weren't sure we wanted to live in a newly-independent country), coffee growing in the eastern mountains, tobacco growing in Nigeria, tobacco grading in Northern Rhodesia, selling cars on Fiji. This was in addition to all the jobs he'd applied for while in England in 1961. At the end of every growing season he would say: "I can't face another season on the farm." So we updated last year's applications, got out the best typing paper:

"Dear Sir..."

This was the way things were done then.

Anyone who has indulged in the soul-destroying occupation of looking for work without having any qualifications will know how it feels. It starts with pins and needles in the legs and rises to ulcers in the stomach, tightness of the chest and blinding headaches. Symptoms horribly like those of several fatal illnesses. No-one wanted to employ an independent, self-employed tobacco farmer.

We had a good manager on the main farm section, and my father-in-law on the farm also. With tobacco cutbacks it was easy enough for us to leave without too much upset. In fact it was obvious from our economic difficulties someone had to leave. We volunteered.

And Martin got two jobs simultaneously, and we had to choose. He decided to take the post of assistant manager at a motel, with a job for me in the office, and it was the best decision he ever made. So we went to Victoria Falls, at the other end of the country, and not really quite in the same country, we were to find out. Victoria Waterfalls, how we all grew to love it! But it beat us in the end, I think, as it did everyone else, including David Livingstone.

We got to the Falls a little more comfortably than Livingstone 115 years before, but even then it was quite an expedition.

We had five days to clear up sixteen years of living on the farm, and three of those Martin spent at the Falls on a look-see at his prospective job - after all these years of job applications we didn't trust anyone, and we were wise not to.

Immediately Martin left to catch the plane, dear old Fuji came on heat. I was trying desperately to pack up, throw out, sell, give away - anything, anything, oh, heavens above, let me get rid of all the clobber of a hoarding life!

We were going to live in furnished rooms in the hotel and, as most of our furniture was pretty tatty anyway, we decided it was not worth the expense of hiring a furniture van over the 600-plus miles. We would pack all we held most dear into the caravan and store things like the gas stove, beds, wardrobes, carpets, books and crockery - the items grew - on the farm.

When he saw how badly I was doing with the preparations to move, my darling husband went through the house like a flash, chucking out or, rarely, stowing in boxes. Our employees did very well out of it.

I just felt so sick. As usual I got bogged down with small jobs while Martin got on with the real job in hand.

We set off in convoy - me in the mini pick-up, with Pixie, the cat, on the passenger seat in an apple box. I was to set the pace and Martin following, with the dogs in the car, and towing the caravan. The caravan was terribly heavily laden, and took some keeping in trim. We dared not overload the ten-year-old mini too much.

Susie and Paula had always driven the mini around the farm during their school holidays, even before they were old enough to own a licence. With it they could go and visit their grandparents and friends on the next farm, keeping to farm tracks.

After a while we saw the mini was doing so well on the journey, we started to off-load a few heavy items like boxes of books and garden chairs on to the back of it from the poor overloaded caravan.

We took two days over the journey, camping at Bulawayo, just over half way. The vet had given me tranquillisers for Pixie. They did anything but make her tranquil, and she howled and scratched to get out of the box all the way. When we got to Bulawayo she had to stay in the car with a sand tray, but at least she stopped howling, now out of her box. Some large male dog got wind of Fuji and she had to be kept on a lead, and Fuji on a lead was just something else - she had always had a free run of the farm before.

I can't remember if we got anything to eat that night, but I do remember we managed to get baths in the surprisingly luxurious bathrooms of the camping site, and crept thankfully, still a full complement of five souls, into the caravan - and bed, after removing half our belongings off it. It was a good thing the children were at school. Paula would have been disgusted with the whole proceedings, and rightly so. We felt like disorganised gipsies.

The 260-mile road from Bulawayo to Victoria Falls is the original road that has no turning. It was an excellent road, like all the main roads were by this time in Rhodesia's history, but there was nothing on it. It is even without hills for the first part of the journey. Outside Bulawayo were signs, in kilometres, "Lupane

160", and as you drive along the road and the numbers lessen on each sign, there is terrific excitement when at last you approach Lupane, no matter how many times you have travelled the road and should know better. At last you're in Lupane, past it - where was it? What was it?

There is a mission and a church on the hill and a bridge.

But 36 miles further on, thank heavens, was Halfway House. Rest and a drink, and let the dogs out.

It was extremely hot when we dropped into the lowveld, and the heavily-taxed car began to flounder. When we set out we thought the mini might not make it, but I had gone ahead in the mini and had to double back, to find Martin labouring up the hills, moving fifty metres or so at a time, then having to stop.

I went on ahead again and managed to find a mechanic at last, and we both returned to the stricken car. This garage near the hills must make its living out of the relentless sun and the long road. Even at the beginning of winter the heat was defeating.

Because of the temperature and the general stress and worry, poor Fuji looked as though she was about to have one of her angina attacks. I quickly gave her one of her tablets and tried to cool her down and calm her by sponging her head and neck with water. By the time the engine was fixed she seemed to have recovered a little.

After the delays it was dark by the time we reached the motel, which was half a mile up the road from the town and a mile from the falls.

Since we had last seen Vic Falls while on holiday, there had been few developments: the old Victoria Falls Hotel, the Casino, a restaurant and still little else. Peter's Motel was a year old and first impressions were of brightness, with modern buildings full of colour and set among green lawns round a swimming pool; a pleasant spot.

I suppose when you do something so dramatic in your life as we had, you expect the town band to turn out. There was no-one around to even say "Hello". We found a rather disinterested receptionist (we discovered as we became acquainted with the tourist industry that most hotel receptionists are disinterested.) Martin had given the place and the people such a build-up after his three days there; it was something of an anticlimax.

We had been allocated a two-roomed place with a bathroom - one of the motel family rooms, which would normally be let out to visitors, and, we discovered later, would still be. It was very pleasantly furnished (once we'd got our bits around), and we proceeded to mess the place up with all our pets and junk.

My job was to relieve in reception and do some of the accounts. It was the first time I had worked full-time for sixteen years, and I was really keen to make something of it. The accounts had not been done efficiently, or kept up to date, since the motel started up, and the confusion was indescribable, with all those hundreds of little pieces of paper largely missing, and accounts added up wrong and months behind.

Martin liked his job. We stayed two months.

If Martin had been wiser or less conscientious, smarter or lazier, or a drunkard, we might have been there for many years (and perhaps got ourselves shot, as it turned out.) The manager and his wife retired to their flat, and many bottles from the bar retired with them. Martin, with three days experience in the hotel trade, had full control of the hotel, and it was busy. He was up at 5.30 in the morning to open the kitchens, and the bar closed at 10.30pm. Except for two young girl receptionists, there were no other white or trained staff members, and everything had to be locked up in the kitchen, bar and reception, such was the reputation of African staff at that time.

He was so steeped in the fine public-school and army-officer traditions, he wouldn't even let me hold the keys to the kitchen for two hours in the afternoon, while he had a rest. The world does not forget to go round if he relaxes for ten minutes, but to this day he will not believe it.

Susie and Paula flew to the Falls from Salisbury at half-term. This was really a big step for them, after being farm children all their lives. They enjoyed the chance to meet young people at the hotel, and being able to order cokes and ice cream round the pool. Susie was fifteen, Paula fourteen.

Because of some quirk of our hotel manager's, we had to keep changing rooms. There were only four family rooms like the one we occupied, so it was just hard luck for us if our room happened to be booked for a weekend or so. The motel's system was that whenever anyone booked, they were immediately allocated a certain room in the reservations book. We managed to wangle it so that we had to move as little as possible, but after four or five moves we had practically all our stuff back in the caravan and a suitcase to live with. The dogs were always going to the wrong "house", and Pixie wisely stayed up on the roof and found us where she could, after much rattling of dishes for her supper. I stayed up for hours at night trying to re-arrange the bookings. Martin complained I would miss someone out and they'd arrive to find no room for them. It was all right for him (as long as he remembered his room number at 11.30 at night) - he was never "at home" anyway, but I had to do the moving each time.

The manager was naturally irritated by Fuji being on heat, as his little Maltese terrier was always wandering off in her direction (his dog was better at finding our place than we were). He refused to restrain his dog in any way, even to call him back. We kept Fuji shut up, but the hotel servants would let her out by mistake. There was little I could do with her unless I took two days off and took her the 260 miles back to Bulawayo to the nearest kennels, then fetch her back a few days later. We had hoped there would be kennels at the Falls, but at that time there were none. She was already so distressed with her funny heart by the move, the unaccustomed heat, and her heat, I didn't want to upset her further.

Relations worsened as the second month progressed, and it was obvious it couldn't go on.

When we made our fated departure from Peter's Motel, we both decided we loved the area, and having come so far, we were going to stay. We'd get work somewhere else at the Falls. Whatever else happened we would never, but never, admit defeat and return.

But first we had to find somewhere to live. The Victoria Falls Management Board was, as always, behind the times. Tourism, which was the dominant industry and employment source at the Falls, was expanding rapidly, but there was nowhere for new arrivals to live. I have never known such a tight situation in Rhodesia where one could usually find something, no matter how unsuitable.

The girls were back at school, fortunately, so we lived in the caravan. We were fairly happy, except that no pets were permitted in the caravan park, which was inside the game reserve near the river. Ours were hardly the sort of dogs you could hide, but as there were no kennels, we persuaded the warden, whom we knew by now, to let us stay with the dogs and cat while we looked for somewhere to live. He was very reasonable, but the caretaker who looked after the place was characteristically officious. He was afraid of the dogs and did his utmost to oust us and make life as miserable for us as he could.

I got a job in the offices of the touring company. It was interesting work doing the vehicle control and there was a lot to learn. But it was also much hotter than we were used to, and the pay wasn't all that good.

We were living with all our belongings crammed in on top of us in the caravan and tent. We wondered why on earth we hadn't left more things behind, like a couple of bookcases, pictures, ornaments (the survivors of the farm storm again), curtains, bedding, table lamps and my writing appendages - cuttings, files, unpublished manuscripts, and even copies of manuscripts that had made their mark, and innumerable magazines for "market research", letters and the portable Olivetti typewriter.

We worried about Pixie, too, because of the dozens of times she had moved house with us during the last two months, but she was very good about it, and stayed most of the time inside the caravan or underneath it where the cool breeze blew. She hated the monkeys - the little black-faced vervet monkeys that came into the site regularly and slid down the tent roofs, steal anything left out, and really enjoy themselves. Fuji and Hayley went wild chasing them, and we went wild chasing Fuji and Hayley.

One day Martin came to the office with a radiant face - he had found somewhere to live. The rent was only R$20 a month. My boss's face fell when he heard where it was. He didn't actually say: "You can't live there!"

Some said the cottages, glorified by the name "The Chalets", had been condemned for 25 years, but there was nowhere for the tenants to move to, and no buyer for the ground anyway. If the town had a centre, they were in the centre of town, and used to house the District Commissioner and his staff back in the early 1900s.

With our background it took more than crumbling walls to faze us. One side of the living room was protected from the dust only by mosquito gauze, and the access road to the chalets further up the "crescent" ran right outside. The kitchen was practically non-existent, and could be ignored (as it was ignored mainly, except the sink came in useful when the drain wasn't clogged up), the bathroom was odd, and when it rained the water came up the plughole. But it had two bedrooms, and we were expecting the girls home for school holidays in a few days.

It was nice now to have our bookcases, table lamps, pictures, bedding, curtains, mats, mosquito nets and ornaments. While I was at work, Martin fixed up the house with the camping table and chairs and camp beds, in the way he was good at, and the first day when I returned from work the place was home. In the kitchen space he rigged up the caravan two-plate-and-grill gas stove.

As part of the deal we had agreed to buy two beds, an old armchair, curtains and an ugly and ornate self-standing metal ashtray, which haunted us for years afterwards.

We knocked our landlord down to R$30. for these, (the amount the former tenant had owed him for rent before he disappeared,) and they were really a terrific bargain - everything was worth twice as much by the time it got to the Falls - but we were desperately hard-up by now and it was becoming a case of beds or food.

The touring company was always short of couriers at short

notice. (Our tour guides were always known as couriers in Rhodesia.) One day I suggested Martin could fill the bill. This was something of an innovation, a man courier, but we weren't proud. From then on I tried to wangle the tours so he could get a few jobs every week. The rate was R$3 for an afternoon's or morning's work, taking people round the falls and sights, or up the river with a commentary on the launch.

He fell into the job as though he had been born to it, in spite of a certain over-anxiety for the well being of his passengers (this concern was a new light on couriers, we learnt). He has a naturally pleasant, strong voice, and an easy way of expressing himself (though I shouldn't be saying this). As he progressed we discovered he is no mean raconteur. People never knew whether to believe his stories or not: "Martin's Myths" people called them later.

Susie and Paula were really good about that awful house. They tried not to ask for money, they didn't grumble about the camp beds they had to sleep on, or the rail that served as a wardrobe, or the odd meals they were dished up with. By this time Martin was working most days, so they looked after the animals, did the shopping and got a salad lunch for us all with fresh French bread or rolls. We had no fridge for a long time and with temperatures hovering around 30°C, daily shopping was essential. They even managed to get themselves holiday jobs in curio shops and the hairdressers, so they could be independent financially.

As teenagers they must have been sensitive to the situation, but, and in spite of the house (they never admitted to anyone where they lived), they seemed to enjoy themselves that first holiday there. They could walk to a selection of posh and free hotel swimming pools, or down to the falls or the river. They sewed themselves dresses on a rickety table with my old hand sewing machine, (the materials and patterns we'd brought with us along with everything else), caught beautiful tans, and were more than pleased not to have Mom and Dad around all the time, and grandparents too, as they always had on the farm.

The tiny record player would sing out all day with Neil Diamond and the New Seekers and a dozen others I can't recall now, though if I hear them on the radio in an "oldies" programme, I'm immediately transported back to that funny house.

It was while at that house they grew, those little girls, and had their first love affairs and learnt about a different world.

It's strange, isn't it? Martin and I actually liked that little house. We were happy together there, everything we did was together. The bedroom was pleasant, with small windows - I love small windows in bedrooms - with wooden frames and looking away from the rising sun, and with flowers on the curtains. It's daft what unexpected, unlikely things you learn to value, and remember best.

I often used to go down to the river with Fuji and Hayley, and there is no more beautiful place on earth, and of more infinite variety. It was National Park land all along the river, and officially dogs were not allowed, though a blind eye was turned for residents as everywhere was in the park, and we had to take them somewhere. I took them down to the river in the car to save the hot walk through the bush, and to ensure they didn't chase the wild game and get us into bad books with the Park's staff.

The river was well over a mile wide above the falls, flowing rapidly, while clean, fresh, wild water that swirled round palm-bordered islands. Along the riverside leaned huge water berry trees with roots like mangroves, and yet more date palms. And birds: herons, kingfishers, hornbills and African robins; it was always beautiful and exciting.

I was somewhat scared for my dogs always, and for me. There was real danger of meeting a hippo, elephant and baboon on the pathways. We often saw them, but luckily never too close when we were walking, though one man we worked with suddenly came upon lions as he was walking near the main road, a hundred metres or so from the river. He lived to tell the tale.

Once I had to beg a tourist to give me (plus dogs) a lift in his car back to my own car, because I dared not pass a troop of baboons, which had spread out from river to road, some of them as large as ten-year-old children. Baboons are reputed to attack dogs, though I have never tried out this theory.

The dogs always wanted to swim in the river as they had in the dam on the farm. At intervals along the river were signs: "Beware of Crocodiles". All the years I was at the Falls I carried a picture in my mind of one of my dogs being carried along in the current towards the falls. It nearly happened after we had been there several years, after Fuji had succumbed to old age and died.

Hayley chased a leguaan, a monitor lizard, into the river beyond the pools of quiet water and into the full stream. Too late she realised where she was and started to swim back, against the current all the time. By the time she was a few metres from the bank she was exhausted. She was gradually being swept under a great mound of Kariba weed floating on the surface, and once under that there was no hope for her - she would suffocate. I went in after her, grabbing on to the roots of the water berry trees till I could almost reach her. When I let go the current took me too, amazingly fast. I grabbed her collar in passing, and between the two of us we managed to struggle away from the horror of the weed, towards the reaching tree roots further downstream.

Hayley shook herself, had the grace to look a little perplexed, and bounded back in the direction of the car. My hair was full of weed, my watch full of water and my sandals on their way to the Devil's Cataract. I stank of river shallows. I felt a little foolish in case I met anyone, and a little afraid in case I didn't, wondering if anyone would have known where I was if I hadn't managed to get back with my dog. I met no-one.

The Chinese say that if you pull a man out of the water from drowning, that man's life is yours, and you must then look after him for the rest of your life, or his. The dog's life was mine now, and I surely never loved an animal as I did Hayley. She was my child. I do not care if people say it is wrong to love an animal so much. It can only hurt eventually the one who loves, but the hurt will never overtake the amount of the love.

I did not love my husband, my children, my parents and brothers and friends any less for loving that dog. For each of these I would have swum into the river - and for you, the stranger on the bank, too.

I was in trouble when I got back and told my story.

Years later when we had left the Falls, Paula, while visiting friends one weekend, fell or jumped off the boat on the Sundowner Cruise (the booze cruise) into the river. By the time the boat had turned, she had disappeared in the fading light. The stretch of river was about five miles above the falls, but the current was strong. The police boat was called out, and everyone was looking for her - the army and the National Parks staff - even to the point of keeping a watch on the Devil's Cataract to see if she was swept over the falls.

But they did not know about Paula's swimming trophies (big shoulders and all). So she reached the bank easily, in her heavy jeans and denim jacket, and then set off on bare feet along the river path a couple of miles or so to the hotel. All the wild animals were out at this time of the evening, and she must have been petrified and very cold.

We did not hear the story till a year or two later, and then not from Paula, or Susie. Everyone at the Falls apparently knew, and everyone in the touring company, except us. How the secret was kept, I don't know.

EIGHT

That Christmas holiday Paula had a singles record "Ode to Joy" recorded by a male singer to a popular version of Beethoven's Ninth Symphony. At all times of the night and day it pervaded the little house.

Rhodesia had been undergoing competitions for several years for the words and music for a National Anthem. It was fast becoming the national joke, as one unsuccessful competition after another failed to resolve the somewhat embarrassing problem of what to do with the silence preceding public occasions, now that we had thrown out "God Save the Queen". I was amazed when I woke up one morning to read in the paper that "our" tune had been adopted with suitable patriotic words:

"Rise, O voices of Rhodesia, God may we
Thy bounty share;
Give us strength to face all danger and where
challenge is, to dare.
Guide us, Lord, to wise decisions, ever of Thy
Grace aware;
Oh, let our hearts beat bravely always, for
this land within Thy care."

Many people recalled it was also the tune to the "Clockwork Orange", which, even in the backwoods of Rhodesia, we knew as a controversial and violent film. An English newspaper suggested if Beethoven's Ninth was heard being whistled down a dark alley, it did not necessarily mean a mugger was nearby, but rather a homesick Rhodesian.

Its performance taxed the skill of the national police and regimental bands to the full.

But I naturally loved it. No matter what happens, it will always be the song of Rhodesia and of joy for me. To adopt Beethoven's Ninth was one of the nobler actions the Rhodesian government brought off during those twelve years of isolation called independence, the UDI type of independence.

Many years after we hear it as the anthem of the European Union. What are they singing now in Zimbabwe in 2005? Do many Zimbabweans have anything to sing about?

The house leaked disastrously at the first and worst thunderstorm of the year. I was on my own in the house when suddenly the tin roof was a sieve. The girls' bedroom was hopeless, and I moved everything on to one side of the living room away from the open gauze side. I ran out of buckets, bowls and saucepans placed to catch the worst. The water was over an inch deep in the small bedroom. When the family arrived back after sheltering from the storm, the water was mostly mopped up. I couldn't impress upon them how the roof leaked as it never leaked so badly again, with such a driving wind.

Paula found her record player from the shambles and we had a Song of Joy again.

By this time Martin had been taken on as a full-time, temporary courier, if there is such a thing, but with a low salary.

We were so utterly broke we even thought of asking Martin's father for a loan on the farm account. This would have been an ignominious admission of defeat. Now when I think of it, I don't know why. It was our farm, after all, and Martin had "spent the best years of his life" developing it and paying off loans on it. I think we just wanted to make our escape complete.

Then at the beginning of December I received a cheque for the equivalent of £60 from the Fair Lady magazine in South Africa for a story I had written while still on the farm. Any wonder this magazine had my undying affection! (It is a mark of the times it no longer publishes fiction stories. Or the standard of my stories?)

Then the blow fell after Christmas: Martin was told he could not be kept on. We thought we had no choice but to turn our backs on the Falls. Martin went off in search of a job. We couldn't even afford the train fare to Bulawayo and Salisbury (the children's fares were generally paid by the farm as part of their education packet), which were the only likely places to have employment vacancies, but he managed to get there by driving touring company vehicles back to other branches.

He couldn't find anything, and we tried to keep calm. He was offered two jobs managing small shabby-looking cafe/shop combinations at the Falls; hardly a brave new world. He had really enjoyed his job as a courier, and he knew he was good at it. The decision not to keep him on seemed inexplicable.

Then the company bosses changed their minds. Would he like to be head courier with additional charge of the river boats for a much more reasonable salary, and get a house thrown in?

It was a palace, that house, with firm white walls, real floors, huge waterproof and tiled roof, drains that drained, and a beautiful, equipped kitchen. The girls' bedroom was very small, which meant they were still thrown together too much, but they liked the house, and covered the walls with posters and their own paintings, and even told people where they lived, and invited their friends.

We had to start from scratch with the garden - the man living there for a year before us had removed every plant when he moved, and even some of the lawn.

The soil was deep, red Kalahari sand, which needed only the introduction of compost to make the plants go wild. We found an African labourer who was good at digging holes. This was the extent of his gardening prowess, but he dug some mighty big holes while he was with us. Our idea, as we were not good gardeners, was to plant what grew best in all the neighbours' gardens. We planted bougainvilleas, poinsettias and bleeding hearts, and they grew all night and all day, winter and summer, because of the heat.

The bougainvilleas we planted against the fence as a protection against the dust from the access road to the flats next door soon began to take over the street as well as the garden. We reckoned after a year the trees and creepers we planted round the house lowered the inside temperature by at least 6°C.

At lunchtime we would put the garden sprinkler on the open front verandah, and if there was a wind, it acted as an air-conditioner.

The touring company uniforms for women were crimplene (all the rage at the time), and much too hot and sweaty for the Falls. As soon as I got home at lunchtime I'd pour the garden hose over myself, dress and all, and Hayley would play with the hose also and soak herself. By 2 o'clock I'd be dry again and refreshed (underclothes were wet all the time anyway from perspiration), and Hayley would retire to her favourite place under the bed, where it was cool, to sleep away the afternoon. No one dreamed of locking or even shutting up their houses.

Most overseas visitors came to the Falls by plane and were predominantly American or German. The Victoria Falls was the highlight of most tours of Africa, some of which took only three weeks to cover the continent from Cape to Nairobi before going on to Rome, round the world and beyond.

We got groups also from France, Italy and Japan, but after UDI the only Britishers who came were as individuals, probably with relatives in Rhodesia or South Africa. They came against the advice of their travel agents, and gave the impression they thought they were rather intrepid, and would look with surprise round the foyers of the big hotels at all the other nations also gathered there. We would sometimes get 15,000 visitors a month during the peak year of 1972, though the local tourist board would never publish official local figures in case of overseas sanctions repercussions.

After six months in the main office I moved down to the tours sales counter at the Victoria Falls Hotel, where most of the overseas visitors stayed.

I could not forgive anyone (of any nationality) for failing to appreciate the falls. The water from the Zambezi river falls over a sheer precipice of black volcanic rock 108 metres deep and 1700 metres wide (over a mile), into a gorge which takes the water rushing directly in front of the falls before turning off over three-quarters of the way along in front of the falls. This means it is possible to look at the falls level with the river and at times only 100 metres away. This promontory where you walk in front of the falls is the Rain Forest.

No matter how many times I walked round the falls, I was surprised each time by their beauty. In the afternoon on a sunny day they are perhaps at thcir most awe-inspiring. Rainbows leap from the gorge as the sun begins to lean over in the sky. Rainbows and double rainbows, and outside of these another, and all this combined with the spectacle of white spray and luminescent green water.

And the noise! At the end of the rains it is impossible to hear anything above the roar, and sometimes it is impossible to see anything either, for mist and spray.

When taking a tour party around, we would arrive down at the falls entrance in the bus among the dry yellow grass and bleached trees, and people would just not believe it would be wet, and that those wretched plastic raincoats we had urged them to hire would be necessary. I doubted it myself some days, and yet, after walking 200 metres along the path, we would be drenched, and some huddled under umbrellas, with cameras tucked in plastic bags. Sometimes people would bring their own nylon showerproof raincoats or heavy gabardines (the English were guilty here), scorning plastic. Within seconds of being in the Rain Forest they were drenched to the skin.

The rain runs down your neck, between the buttons of your raincoat, streaming into shoes and out the other end. Standard wear for female couriers was beach flip-flops with their uniform, sometimes a plastic raincoat and an umbrella, which she generally lent out to a tourist. No attempt at the white gloves and high heels worn by the air hostess who had shown round the 1952 group, when I had first seen the falls.

I once found a Scotsman sheltering under a tree in the wettest part of the forest. "I'm waiting for the rain to stop," he said. He would have been waiting there still, poor chap, if he'd not been persuaded to walk 50 metres further on out of his Scotch mist to where the path was dusty still. It is one of the few places you'll find where the rain comes from below.

We'd get back to the car park, sit in the sun for five minutes, and we'd be pretty dry and ready to carry on the rest of the tour.

Travellers had paid thousands of dollars, yen, and pounds to get to this place. Even if it is raining (from the sky), they must be made to see it in a good light. When a tourist says: "We never did get to see the bridge", "We weren't shown the Big Tree", "That courier said we didn't have time to see the Craft Village", "They should have things better organised"; then that was a bad courier had taken them round. How many times have we all been round ruins or castles and been overwhelmed and bored with streams of facts that we have not wanted to know, and which would have been forgotten five minutes later anyway? Martin was determined this should not be the style of tour guiding at the falls. He said the couriers should know the facts, if asked, but should never be told what to say, so that a tour could be varied according to the people on it. How many times on long, hot tours of Greek or Italian ruins have I wished the local guides had been told this.

It seems obvious really, but, if it is, why don't these presumably intelligent people take notice?

In exasperation, Americans would sometimes say: "When are we gonna see the falls?"

They had been tripped up the river and trailed round the curio shops and heaven knows where, and this was not the courier's fault, but the travel agent's who made up some very odd itineraries way back in Illinois.

In October temperatures were often 35° plus for days or even weeks on end, and even residents said it was hot: "but hot, man." Visitors wanted cool drinks every half-hour. This could present a real problem when conservationists in the area were striving to avoid any development like the environs of Niagara Falls. When they were hot and tired, city Americans must be reminded (gently, of course), they have come because it is "wild Africa". The custom of carrying around bottles of spring water has solved this problem to some extent now.

Something I found with many visitors, and Americans in particular then (perhaps it has changed now), is that though they are longing to be in the bush, "no ways" will they accept the discomforts of the bush. This is particularly true for those who flew in at tremendous expense for three-week hunting and photographic safaris. They must have cold Martinis, Scotch, lots of ice, hot showers and epicurean food served on a table with a clean tablecloth and napkins, and regular beds. And if they were in an hotel, air-conditioning.

One American director old enough to know better brought his latest young starlet out to the middle of Botswana on a hunting safari. So he had to have a double bed flown out by private aircraft from Vic Falls, 240 miles away, for their two-weeks' stay.

Did he tell stories to his pals back home about how he had roughed it in the middle of darkest Africa, I wonder? Certainly it provided us at the Falls with a giggle.

I don't know how the Rain Forest, where it "rains" all the time and is warm all the year round, knows when to declare spring. But in September, suddenly, the bright red fireballs, *haemanthus multiflorus*, thrust up the soggy leaf-mould ground, which serves as soil, and in every sheltered patch these great balls of fire, often twenty centimetres across, rose from the weeds.

One National Parks warden decided to make a hand-laid stone path along the whole length of the falls. Everyone looked sceptical, but he and his workmen finished it in a year or so, before he was posted to another location. It was a labour of love. I imagine it is still there, beautifully laid and has prevented many thousands of visitors from sliding on the muddy path, yet not noticed, just one man's achievement, with colonial-style help.

The path became lined with blue lobelia, tiny maidenhair ferns and other "greenhouse" ferns, while further on were pale yellow wild gladioli. Twining among the tall ebony and fig trees were lianas, nightshade, honeysuckle and convolvulus. And standing with roots always in water are the red-fruited water berries.

On the fallen trees - they often fell because their roots were waterlogged - grew mosses and orchids. Sometimes from a horizontal tree trunk would grow up several other trees, where before, branches only had been.

The monkeys and birds loved the golden dates and Cape figs, which thrust straight out from the trunks.

High in the trees, in spring and summer, could be heard the raucous, unearthly cry of the trumpeter hornbill - like a child's trumpet, or an animal in pain, or like a spirit called back to this narrow stretch of forest.

It was said that there were as many different species of plants in the Rain Forest as in the whole of Ireland. Some were still waiting to be discovered, and three at least have not been found anywhere else in the world.

David Livingstone, when he went to the falls in 1855, built a garden on one of the islands on the edge of the falls. The river, he said, would look after it. He loved the Zambezi River and had followed its course from where it rose on the borders of what are now Angola, Zambia and Zaire, on its 1800-mile course eastwards across the middle of Africa. In his island garden he planted peach and apricot pips and coffee beans which he brought from Luanda on the west coast.

Instead, the river destroyed the garden through its agents, the hippopotamus. The only time he was ever moved to carve his name on a tree was on this island. As ever restrained in his descriptions, he wrote in his journals: "Scenes so lovely they must have been gazed upon by angels in their flight."

One of the biggest thrills when we were there, and the most accessible way to see the falls was in one of the two-engine Cessna aircraft, which took five passengers on the "Flight of Angels " every half-hour. The rainbows seen from above are fantastic, moving in the afternoon like gloriously coloured curtains in the high spray. Only from a plane can the whole mile-wide spectacle be seen, and the pilot would fly up-river and find hippo, like shadows in the clear water and crocodiles basking on the sandbanks, then down the gorges, low as a hunting hawk.

It was part of my job to sell this "flip round the falls", though when I first arrived at the Falls, I was very nervous of flying, particularly in small aircraft. I overcame this one day in an odd way: I had to go to Salisbury, but could not get on the normal direct flight by Viscount - we were given rebated fares if the planes were not full. So I had to fly on the Dakota, which made stops at Wankie Game Reserve and Kariba. I was full of apprehension and tried to avoid looking out of the window, when suddenly I looked at the ground. We were flying fairly low with wings flapping when I discovered I was not afraid, and I was even enjoying the experience. Since then I have never been scared of flying, and can recommend the cure.

People said at the Falls that anyone who went to live there had to have their watches repaired after a few weeks (as the nearest watchmaker was in Bulawayo, you remember these things). No digital or new-fangled watches in those ways: they ticked and had to be wound up every day. They said this was not through walking in the Rain Forest and water seeping into the watch, but the vibration from the falls. This vibration could be felt miles away, and any door left off the catch would rattle in ghostly fashion.

In the village, we were always aware of the falls, the roar, and the spray above the trees down the main street. On a cloudy day the falls would make their own cloud and at early morning in spring the village was mysteriously veiled in fine, warm, white mist.

Dawns at the falls were mystic, brilliant red and awe-inspiring. Sun, sky, river, and spray - all are crimson.

In the moonlight, too, the white time. White light on the leaves of the trees, white reflected from the raindrops, a pall of white smoke above and below, gushing and rising. And across it all a filigree bridge like finest steel: the lunar rainbow.

There were more misconceptions about the lunar rainbows than there are rainbows themselves. All a rainbow requires is a light (sun or moon) fairly low in the sky, rising or setting with the spray in front and your head in a line roughly between the two. The lunar rainbow doesn't need an absolutely full moon. Sometimes one may be seen down in the gorge, but if your luck is in, you may arrive in time to see it across the top of the gorge, bridging forest and falls.

At full moon the silver bridge may show edges of the seven colours, faint and elusive in the rising and falling mists.

One night we were walking in the forest. The water was as bright as the shade was dark, and there, standing still, right on the lip of the falls, looking out, staring at the falls was a beautiful waterbuck, its curved horns silhouetted against the silver water. Sometimes elephants would walk on the river side of the falls from island to island during the dry season right on the edge of the precipice where the water fell. What did they think as they strolled along, I wonder. And in October when the river was very low, local fishermen from Zambia waded along in the pools, metres from the drop, and appeared to care no more for the current and the danger than they did for borders and politics.

South of the falls is the Wankie Game Park (now called Hwange), which is about 90 miles long and 70 wide. It was run on much the same lines as the Kruger Park in South Africa, but much less developed. Most of the roads were dirt. When we lived there, people generally stayed in three main rest camps in the park. Later a luxury hotel was built to the south of the park, mainly to accommodate overseas tourists.

Towards the end of 1971, Martin went to relieve the manager at one of these rest camps for a month. Since he had been working full-time, he hadn't had one day off, and being in the tourist industry, that meant he worked a seven-day week. He was naturally afraid of losing this job he loved so much, and which had been so hard to come by, but I felt there was a limit to a man's endurance. Often he would work from seven in the morning till seven at night, and in that time he would include two tours of the falls, getting soaked to the skin both times. He'd forget to have a drink, let alone lunch.

The manager of our branch came to work every day. He never took a day off himself (he even worked on Christmas Day) unless he had to go to Salisbury for a meeting, and it grew up in the office that all the rest of the staff were hesitant to take their allocated seven days a month off also. It resulted in a fall-off of work standards, general lassitude, nervous breakdowns, and a very quick turnover of staff. Other branches, we learnt later, looked on in amazement.

I insisted on my days off (my father was a great fighter for workers' rights in the early days of trade unions at the beginning of the last century). I was unpopular for it, which was one good reason why I was glad to get out of the main office and among the couriers, who, like me, enjoyed having a life in their free time. If we had to work on our days off because of rush of work, we expected to be paid for it, like dad said.

So in the end my nagged-at husband agreed to go away for a couple of weeks in the school holidays, but first he had to go to Sinamatella Camp at Wankie for three weeks, relieving the manager there, who was, oddly enough, taking a holiday. He would be paid extra, giving us some money to go down to South Africa. We had decided to sell the caravan, fingers crossed we'd not need to live in it again, and by some stroke of luck, we were able to buy a new car, a Peugeot, in Bulawayo, and trade in our Austin 1800. New cars were very scarce in Rhodesia, and only French or Japanese cars were available for many years. Don't ask me why these two. No one asked.

Martin had been at the Wankie camp for three weeks when the children broke up from school and flew back to the Falls. We loaded up the caravan, and set off on the 80-mile journey to join him. I was not altogether happy about being entirely responsible for this entourage. Pixie, the cat, was ill and I didn't want to leave her at the new Victoria Falls cattery, where the nearest vet was at Wankie, so I packed her off to Bulawayo in a box by plane, to be collected at the other end by a woman from the cattery.

When it came to dropping off the dogs at the newly established kennels, which were on a nearby farm, we nearly came to grief early in the expedition on the long, Kalahari-sand track, with the car swinging from side to side, scraping the bottom on the ridge in the middle of the road, the day already crazy hot, and Susie and Paula refusing to sit in the back with the dogs, or in the front together.

After such an auspicious start, we all needed a bath and change of clothes, but we carried on.

We hitched up the caravan and were away, already late. As we were about to sell the car and caravan we hadn't bought new tyres. The car had a cracked cylinder head and was liable to boil. The caravan brakes were faulty. So the tyre blowout was not altogether unexpected, when it happened halfway to Wankie. But the crazy careering down the hill till I could find a place to pull off the road was. We perched near the edge of a steep embankment. We all piled out. I had never changed a wheel before, much less on a car attached to a caravan on the edge of a precipice.

"We must unhook the caravan," I said, not knowing where I'd learnt this startling piece of advice.

We couldn't. So we found the jack and decided to jack up the lot, if we could. It was a nice empty - one could almost say deserted - stretch of road, and I was not feeling up to this emergency. I took to wringing my hands and looking around for help. Susie was sick of me. She was sixteen and mother was being a bore. Paula looked helpful, if rather pale.

We managed to raise the whole contraption, and while I fussed around trying to thrust rocks in all the wrong places around the wheels, in case everything started rolling down the hill, Susie and Paula took command, changed the wheel, let down the jack, and we were ready for away. And I had thought they were still children.

They had to trust me in the driver's seat. The tyre was showing canvas.

Three miles on and water started to spurt all over the windscreen. We stopped, we had to stop, because I couldn't see, and the engine boiled merrily.

We opened the bonnet and surveyed the enigma mechanics call an engine. Water and steam were shooting out of the top radiator hose.

With nail scissors we cut off strips from an old plastic raincoat we had wrapped round tools in the boot, and bandaged the damaged pipe. We finished off the job with a layer of wide elastoplast, filled up with water (which we always carried with us for such an occasion) and away once more.

We were boiling again after a few miles and the bandages dangling.

This time we discovered an old bicycle tube, which had been shoved (you never know when you might need something like this) ages ago into the toolbox. We cut this now into strips laboriously with the nail scissors, bound the pipe, and Susie finished it off with a neat knot with her small fingers. We filled up with water again, and just as we were ready to go, the first car we'd seen, with three men in it, stopped. They had come from the rest camp, and Martin had asked them to look out for us. It was as well we had fixed ourselves up by this time: they looked far too clean and smart for our sort of enterprise.

This time our repair lasted the twelve miles to the outskirts of Wankie, and it wasn't yet five o'clock and the garage would still be open in the camp. We were really in luck. We filled up our water cans from the municipal parks' tap at the entrance gate, filled up the radiator again and cruised into the garage. We presented a sorry sight. We were all three covered in dust, grease, dog hairs and general filth, and well streaked with dirty water rivulets. Between us we scraped up enough money to buy a tyre and have a new radiator hose fitted. It was a good job the girls had some of their holiday spending money at hand. No credit cards then! And no mobile phones.

I rang Martin from the garage to prevent his sending out a search party - dusk was setting in rapidly, and we had 15 miles of stony road to go to Sinamatella. We made it!

Sinamatella Camp was a beautiful place. Set right in the middle of the game reserve on a sixty-metre high ridge overlooking a great plain, with views as far as the eye could see to the distant pale hills.

The vegetation was sparse and yellow, and in the heat-haze of the next day, groups of elephant, giraffe, zebra, and many kinds of buck could be picked out walking casually through the trees. We sat and watched a family of lions with several lionesses and older cubs walking, running, cavorting, even hunting just below us. Being directly below, with the sheer drop in between, they were not aware of man's presence - or didn't care, in the way lions are.

One of the best thrills of any game reserve is to spend the night in it, even in a civilised manner in a cottage. No matter how high or how apparently secure the fence around you appears in daylight, at night you are sure the lions' roars sound from just outside your window, and the hyena shrieks from inside the camp. The hyena sounds like a maniac at night, so small wonder most Bantu tribes have many stories and superstitions about *Mfisi*, the hyena.

Once on holiday, when the children were very small, we slept in a tent in Kruger Game Park in South Africa. It was a large tent permanently erected in a camp and hired from the park. In the small hours of the morning the baboons came and played slides down the canvas side, my side.

"Martin, Martin, can you hear? What is it?"

Long pause. "It's only baboons. Shake the tent wall." With that he went to sleep again. The baboons were on my side.

"Shake the tent wall" is now an established reply in the family to any sounds in the night.

At Sinamatella, a hyena used to climb the almost vertical hillside every night to raid the dustbins, and in the morning visitors had the thrill of picking out his footprints in the sand. (The camp staff had the thrill of picking up the rubbish again and putting it back in the bins.) We saw honey badgers for the first time when they arrived in the evenings before the lights were put out on the verandahs of the dining room and bar.

We often drove to a small dam about nine miles from the camp, and one late afternoon, in particular, I shall never forget. The dam was full and clear, even at the end of the dry season, and from the lookout shelf we watched a kaleidoscope of events. It was so leisurely and orderly with the slow pace we had become used to over the last few days that it was more like a tapestry than a view.

Lions had killed a young elephant beside the dam the day before, and the tragedy and the victory unfolded itself in the almost

97

still figures by the dam.

A small group of elephants, cows and calves, stood motionless on the left, and behind, what was surely the dead calf's mother moved slowly backwards and forwards, her trunk waving aimlessly. Three giraffes stood halfway up the slope, watching and waiting to drink. Down the well-worn game path another group of elephants slowly lumbered to the edge of the dam. A herd of impala stood, delicate and drifting to the right, their eyes staring in one direction. And to the far right, walking slowly from the water towards a patch of short green grass were several lionesses and young lions. They settled slowly, yawning, on the grass.

On the fringe of the dam stood vultures and maribou storks -- bloated and comatose. And on the trees, watching the spectacle, a grey heron, a fish eagle and several great white egrets. A darter dried its wings and crowned plovers stalked in and out of the great footprints in the mud.

The second group of elephants finished their drink and ablutions and marched single-file away. The giraffe moved down. As they moved away another group of elephants appeared and came down the path to drink.

The mother elephant continued to grieve; the evening breeze blew cool across the dam, and an unseen hippo bellowed his disdain of the world.

We returned to camp.

But in spite of these wonderful sights, there was no swimming pool, no young company, it was extremely hot, the days long, so the girls were becoming bored, and Paula more so. They were pleased when we all four set off for Bulawayo on the next lap of the journey, Martin's relief job finished. This time we drove at night in the rain. It was much cooler and the engine didn't boil once.

NINE

Anyone who knew thought we were crazy to spend our holiday in Johannesburg.

We found a high-rise flat so new the lime was still on the windows on the floor above us. We had an introductory offer, and less 20% because we were in the travel business.

Very cheap, and all around us were shops and cinemas and traffic, and scurrying people with plastic carrier bags from the supermarket. They looked like so many termites rushing to their nests with pieces of dry grass stalks in their mouths. We didn't have to be nice to them, they wouldn't ask us questions or even talk to us, even if we talked to them. We had a great time and the girls saw what a big city was like and loved the "mod" shops.

We had to go to the films at ten in the morning, as the prices doubled and trebled as the day went on. A couple of times we hauled Susie, always a late sleeper then (when permitted), out of bed, fortified her with orange juice and then straight off to the pictures.

We discovered a wonderful delicatessen supermarket that stayed open twenty-four hours - we could not believe it, a shop open all day and all night! We spent hours wandering around the shelves. The world of retail business had moved on since we'd been shut away in darkest Africa, with an ill-stocked, sanctions-bedevilled, end-of-the-railway-line store at Victoria Falls.

Fresh bread all shapes and sizes and nationalities, enormous sausages hanging from the roof, frozen food, canned raspberries from Switzerland, salads with olives, cheeses from everywhere. We carried so much back to the flat we were hardly justified in going out for a meal ever.

Our activities weren't entirely prosaic and utilitarian - honest! - we did go the rounds of the museums and art galleries.

No one today would dream of spending any time in central

Johannesburg unless they wanted to experience what it feels like to be hijacked, mugged, robbed, pick-pocketed, or just have their car stolen. All life now for "respectable" people, black, brown or white, is in the suburban shopping centres. Many go to the shopping centres regularly on Sunday in the same way people used to go to worship in the churches, once upon a time.

After a week we went back to the farm for Christmas, and stayed with Martin's father and stepmother. We hadn't seen most of our old friends for eighteen months, we all had a lot to discuss and it was great fun. Without exception, everyone was amazed we had no desire or intention of returning to the farm. My father-in-law wished we would. The girls, more than us, were appalled at the idea of living on the farm again.

They need not have worried. Paula is the only one who has ever been back, even for a visit, since then.

Apparently many of our neighbours who had left farming were finding it impossible to settle down in town - even though many of them had their own big houses and swimming pools and all the rest of it. Only one of our neighbours who had made the break was happy - he, like Martin, had never been a farmer at heart. At the time, when he was young, it was the accepted thing to do and he couldn't think of anything else he could do. He made a poor farmer and his young family had gone to bed hungry often enough. Like us, he left farming after many years suffering from lack of capital. After a year he had regained his natural cheerfulness and self-confidence and was making a name for himself as a great public relations man.

And we wondered why we hadn't made just that bit more effort to get away before. The dream of becoming wealthy tobacco farmers was just that for many, and could become a nightmare.

Thirty years before, author Doris Lessing's father had followed the dream in much the same district as we had farmed, and ended as poor as he had when he had started, at least financially. In other ways it was a rich life, a memorable time in undeveloped bush. A life that will probably never be available again.

Just by the way, because she was a communist, Doris Lessing's books were not available in Rhodesia during those sanctioned years, and she herself was banned from returning home to her beloved country and the farm of her childhood for many years. By then the grass was no longer singing the same simple tunes of the virgin bush.

We got back to the Falls ready for the boom year in Rhodesian tourism, and at the Victoria Falls in particular - 1972.

Twenty years before when I had first visited the Victoria Falls on a day trip, all the development had been on the north side of the river at Livingstone, in what was Northern Rhodesia. They were building a new international airport there, while on the Southern Rhodesian side there was nothing but one old hotel, which was built ahead of the railway in 1904, a cafe, two curio shops and an airstrip. An old boat plied up the river to Kandahar Island where a large white man dressed in a leopard skin jumped out of the boat to welcome the tourists to the "desert island" of waving palms, monkeys and hippos.

The story went that one visitor was chopped in half by one of these hippos on Kandahar Island when he found himself between a female hippo and the river while taking big-game-photographer-take-home snaps. People in the village tried to keep the gruesome story quiet.

Like all booms, no one expected it. Plans were put forward for new hotels when the people had already arrived and were demanding beds. Extensions were being built all around and under the feet of the tourists. The Victoria Falls Hotel was now undergoing vast transformations - new wings, bathrooms knocked in, air-conditioning in all rooms, dust everywhere, hammering and plaster and paint.

Ours was a real complaints counter - the host of things that had gone wrong with the touring company passengers from Rio de Janeiro through Nairobi to Cape Town and back was retold to us. In the midst of it I'd peep out of the door and see a seven-seater bus arrive for 30 passengers.

The tours departed at last; then it was time to reassure a mother whose little girl had been scratched by a monkey, dry the new courier's tears and tell her that's the way nasty Americans/Germans/Frenchmen always spoke to people doing their best for them, tell twenty people a day the way to walk to the falls, twenty the way to the loo, and point out the hotel reception desk (they were practised in hiding) when visitors found no towels in their rooms.

We accepted payment for tickets in South African rand, American dollars, marks, pounds and francs - even in Rhodesian dollars - without batting an eyelid, unlike cashiers in Europe when Euros were introduced. And no calculators at hand.

I was knocked out at the end of the day and no-one could understand why. "What a gem of a job you've got," they'd say when all the buses had left. True! But my coffee was cold again.

The very worst person I ever came in contact with was an Irish doctor. He carried a blackthorn walking stick and was always late. His plane was late (could it have been his fault?) and he was too late to catch the afternoon cruise if he had lunch. He told the entire large foyer he intended to do both. He refused to take the evening cruise or go without lunch, and if the bus started without him he intended to go out there into the hotel car park and lie down in front of it. This was a bit of Irish if ever there was any.

When he left the dining room after an hour and a quarter I can imagine the relief he left behind, till dinnertime. Then he proceeded to my corner, thumped so hard on the counter with the blackthorn stick I feared for the plate-glass top. I dodged out of reach and announced as bravely as I could the bus for the cruise had left an hour before.

He threw such a tantrum as I have never seen before and, if this was the way he lived, how he hadn't suffered several heart attacks by now was amazing. It was almost comical except he wouldn't stop. By this time we had the undivided attention of the whole foyer - hotel staff and visitors. He would not listen. Every now and then he stalked outside to rage at the non-existent bus. I phoned Martin at the office up the road to come down for support, but he couldn't calm the man either.

In the end our Irish doctor blasted his way into the hotel gardens to walk down to the falls, full of threats that he would report the whole branch to head office. I felt sure he would, but I felt the other twenty-nine people in the bus would have protested with more justification while waiting for him in the full two-o'clock sun.

And he wasn't late for the evening cruise. I had made up my mind beforehand the bus would go on time when everyone else was seated, whether he was there or not. No one chucked him into the river, either. Perhaps he'd taken a couple of tranquillisers.

Young English doctors were about the worst. I must quickly say that since returning to England in1977, my job has meant meeting many doctors, all ages, and I have found them, with few exceptions, very likeable people, but during their escape to Africa something changed their behaviour patterns. They could be picked out not only by their accents and clothes (we must remember this was thirty years ago when doctors talked "posh" and wore safari suits in Africa), but also because they were travelling with their wives and young children. They were too young to have the money that had brought them there. It seemed that, having broken away from the discipline of their long training, they were now determined to throw their weight around and have their own back on some of the wretched population who normally demanded too much. So hotel and touring staff met the brunt of it. They would have their children's meals when they wanted, they would go on their tours what time they wanted (and to hell with the other thirty five on the tour), they would hire cars even though they hadn't brought their driving licences with them - of course they held driving licences in Britain, you silly apes (this would always happen immediately after we'd had yet another directive from head office that on no account must we hire out cars without seeing licences.)

In the meantime, while they were waiting for us poor fools to sort out their perfectly straight-forward requirements, they would order large glasses of iced water in the foyer, at the wrong end of the hotel from the kitchen, drink an inch of each, leave them, and let their really badly-behaved children spill the rest on the chairs.

They were generally booked with some out-of-the-way travel agent who didn't have an idea what they were booking them on, and when their arrangements were obviously wrong, blamed us. In all fairness to the travel agent, he probably hadn't had the doctor's requirements explained properly in the first place.

But there was hope for the doctors. Elderly doctors, when they arrived, were charming, knowledgeable and interested. In the intervening years they were presumably so busy, and spending all their money educating their children in the right manner, we did not see them. Perhaps French Provence was more lucky.

All nationalities are difficult in their own particular and peculiar ways, and it's no good trying to belong to the whole of mankind on earth, saying all men are the same, because they aren't. And not only are there peculiarities belonging to a particular country, but when you get used to spotting them, there are traits belonging to a certain part of that particular country too.

It is as pronounced as regional accents; you can cut it down to part of a state, part of a country, shaving it finer and finer if you're observant enough, till you can almost find the suburb or village the person comes from. You would think that with so much world travel and television regional characteristics would melt into a smudge, but they certainly hadn't then in the globe-trotting community of the middle-aged and elderly, or even in the twenty- and thirty-year-olds.

We all have a picture in our minds of an Englishman or a German, and get a group of them together in a strange place and they are so, ten-fold. They behave exactly as everyone says they do.

Germans were always right on time everywhere. Tell them to do something and they would do it. Once a courier realised this, life was much easier. In return they require first-class service, strings of facts, facts, facts about the sights they are seeing and the country in general. Most German tour leaders who travelled with their parties could string out the facts themselves, because they did not trust the local courier to know it all (very wise!)

Most of what he knows is not entirely true, but what does it matter when there is so much of it? Who really cares how wide this particular stretch of water is? Such facts are immediately forgotten. But all the same, a German will ask, and have to be told. And eat! If a German or French group was expected we had to warn the hotel of their nationalities, even if they were having merely a casual meal. And in the small Japanese-manufactured buses that we used, Germans must be allocated a seat-and-a-half.

If they were French the hotel was warned for a different reason from giving out larger portions. No matter how hot the day, how strenuous the touring programme, how tight the schedule they were expected to keep, a Frenchman would take two hours over his lunch, and he must draw it out with the best wines, French, of course. Even then, drink French, speak French was their motto. Where the fallacy that many French people speak English arose, I can't guess. Those who came to Africa couldn't - and in my experience, those who stay in France can't - or won't.

It is more than not being able to speak other languages; it is the wanting to understand. If you're a reasonable person, and a fairly intelligent foreigner is earnestly trying to speak your language, no matter how poorly, or even just speaking his own language simply, with lots of sign language, you can generally get the drift of what he's saying, or at least you can pretend to. Not with the Frenchman. As far as he is concerned lingua franca means French, properly pronounced, in France or out of France, or so we found.

But we did find their manners superb. Courtesy is natural to them, appears in the most surprising moments, and always pleases. Being a courier you would start to close a window, or pick up a dropped paper, but suddenly one of your tour was doing it for you. Looking up in surprise, suddenly it dawns - here is a Frenchman. Maybe it is no longer true of the majority of Frenchmen, but I see why the word *gentile* cannot easily be translated. With most nationalities, including the English, a lifetime is spent not requiring the word.

And Italians were noisy in their love of the falls, and describe them in such beautiful words: *"fantastica", "bellissima", "meravigliosa"*, that I can forgive them anything. It would appear that they are surrounded by so much beauty and art in their own country they had been bred to beauty like a racehorse. But get a group of them in a confined place and all the silken drapes of all the palaces of Italy could not absorb the sound. But I can quite see why English and American heiresses loved their Italian Counts in those days: few can excel Italians at making a woman feel as beautiful as she dreams of being.

We got quite a few of the Spanish aristocracy, or at least the upper class, mainly from the Argentine. They spoke beautiful, measured and impeccable English and dressed carelessly in the most elegant clothes (they always appeared to be dressed in silk but this couldn't be true). They were extremely grateful and even touched by any small service that we, feeling like peasants in our awkwardness, were able to offer. Such people make me want to cry at the futility of my presumptuousness. The opposite happens with any contact with members of the English upper classes, whose presence makes me want to shout socialist slogans.

The bulk of our passengers were Americans who generally came in groups of twenty or so. Some of them made a whistle stop at the falls their only visit to Rhodesia. Before the bridge to Livingstone and Zambia was closed, one particular touring company group would fly in every Monday afternoon from Johannesburg, take a run round the falls in three-quarters of an hour (some members of the group were so tired by this time they wouldn't even get out of the bus so they might catch a quick sight of the falls), then on to Livingstone for the night before flying to Nairobi, to become, no doubt, as expert on affairs Kenyan as they were now on those of Rhodesia, and all in twenty-four hours flat.

Nearly all Americans who found their way to Africa on tours were elderly and unfit. Colleen, my old friend from Eire, once told me she hated the English as a nation, as individuals she loved them. This was very much how most people at the Falls felt about the Americans. At the sight of twenty or more haggard, mistakenly-dressed, noisy tourists sitting in the foyer writing postcards, a courier would take a deep breath and put on a big, brave smile before approaching. But if they stayed long enough to make their acquaintance, they were amiable, interesting, and interested in you, like the best of any country. I think American people, and women in particular, from some parts of the States, should really make a big effort to get rid of that terrible whine they have in their voices. The sound pervades the ruins of Europe, the streets of Paris and the "sights" of Africa to such an extent it closes great barriers between the outgoing Americans and their jealous observers from the rest of the world.

Then there are the beautiful blonde girls who holiday with bare midriffs and beautiful brown legs and buttocks below their cut-off denim shorts. They bring joy to fellow travellers. I wish they could be told that, although they are absolutely fascinated by the "difference" of the polite black bus driver, it is not the custom of the country, and particularly among the African peoples, for young girls to approach and engage in long conversation with men of any race, particularly while their T-shirted breasts brush sweetly against his shoulder.

The driver is obviously flattered to the core and utterly overwhelmed: his wife after seven children and thirty-odd years of manual work really can't compete. Little Miss Sweden is not promoting good relations, or helping the downtrodden blacks by behaving like this. Tomorrow she will be gone into the sky in a big steel bird, while he is left to readjust himself to driving a bus full of tourists he has to be respectful, polite and even deferential to, and these will include racists. He's "cheeky" if he smiles too much, surly if he doesn't smile at all. After all, would she try and "get off" with the Manchester father-of-seven bus driver because she found his way of life so exhilaratingly different, and was sorry he had to spend his life in such a dreary, wet climate? Perhaps she would.

The Japanese who came, fitted into their buses so nicely it was like an organised dream. I loved to watch them taking up a small space. Conversing was so difficult one could only watch and smile and bow.

They were the direct opposite of the Americans when they sat in the foyer of the hotel. They would take up only the exact width of their hips on the bench seat. They drew their elbows into their sides to allow someone to sit right next to them if necessary, and carefully placed their small bags on the floor between their feet. They kept their knees tightly pressed together, and everything was done not to offend that very close person next to them. Communication was very, very difficult, because although many learnt English (or rather American) in school and post-school business training, they learnt written English and many of them had no idea how the words were pronounced. With the difference in alphabets it was impossible for them to guess.

One day when I was on the counter a dear elderly Japanese couple arrived on their own, heaven knows how, and with not a word of English between them. The man had an amazingly comprehensive phrase book, which covered six languages. He would point to the relevant phrase in Japanese, and I followed the line along, through Spanish and the rest, to English. Then came the search for the English reply to point out. It was a lengthy affair, but I wasn't busy. We must have made significant progress because he got to his room, and returned at 2.30 to join the tour of the falls. The falls at least were self-explanatory, and going on a tour ensured he saw what there was to see at least.

To take a Japanese tour around was an experience. At the end of the morning we were all, occidental or oriental, bowing to each other, and our manners had taken a leap forward. "T'ankyou, t'ankyou" all the way.

We expected the great months of tourism in early 1972 to last. In the first four months of 1972 Rhodesia earned six million Rhodesian dollars (£6M then) from tourism - a fortune then and an increase of over 17% on the year before. It was mainly South

Africans that made up the 100,000 visitors, and even the Director of Tourism went down to the great grey-green greasy Limpopo River to count the cars coming through in June, and imagine the happy clink of cash tills they would cause throughout the country.

And as usual when people began to enjoy themselves and spread a little money around, someone else started to mutter.

The Minister of Tourism, that glorious personification of a public schoolboy, P.K. van der Byl, said: "The government intends to prevent the Falls township expanding to the point where it becomes a city." Victoria Falls then sported about 500 whites and 2,000 blacks, so it showed what big ideas Rhodesia was getting. It was a bit of a laugh.

Then on came the conservationists. The Rain Forest beside the falls was becoming smaller and trampled. I'm sure they were right: they spent enough on expert investigation. "We must close the Rain Forest!" they declared. "Only a certain number must be allowed in each day," and they proposed to charge entrance.

We felt the Victoria Falls belonged to everyone. There were great outcries from the Falls residents, nearly all of them reliant directly upon tourism for their livelihoods.

(It was not until after Rhodesia became Zimbabwe in 1980 that a charge for admission was levied, and then a preferential scale of charges was introduced: a high rate for foreigners, somewhat less for South Africans and very little for Zimbabweans. When we returned on a visit several years after a black government had been installed, Susie told them at the entrance she was a Zimbabwean (as Rhodesia was Zimbabwe she was so), but the sellers at the gate laughed and would not believe her. She settled for being South African, which was the only thing she wasn't, though she lived there, but still held a British passport.

But back to 1972, a Yorkshireman was put in charge of the Rain Forest, and he promptly put up a dry-stone wall, so he'd feel more at home. (This Yorkshireman was later transferred to the Zimbabwe Ruins where the whole place was a mass of dry-stone walls.) And a high wire fence was erected which distracted greatly from the looks of the place and destroyed the "natural" look everyone was striving for. But the vegetation inside certainly improved, though whether this followed naturally on a series of better rainy seasons or not is hard to say.

Politics intervened, the boom never materialised, and today there is no need to limit numbers, as insecurity is doing that. Anyone who arrives at Victoria Falls these days should be given a bonus, not the special charge for foreigners.

Then South Africa devalued the rand for the second time in a few months. Instead of receiving a Rhodesian dollar for a rand, South Africans only got 83 Rhodesian cents.

Rhodesia suddenly switched from being a cheap holiday centre to what they described as a "swizz". Hotels and restaurants were still cheaper than their South African equivalents, but it was the psychological effect of not getting their full dollar for rand that they hated.

Several schemes were started as time went on to persuade South Africans to come to Rhodesia. In tourist centres rands were accepted on dollar value, and visitors were now happy they were getting something for nothing and how we all love that feeling. Except when there was a terrorist scare on, business did improve. But on the whole it was fear, even in those early days, which kept South Africans away.

The young women who stayed as couriers for more than a couple of months lived on their nerves. They ate rarely, drank a lot, smoked a lot, and got involved in glorious, all-in love affairs which ended in babies, abortions, or for the lucky just weeks of tears, transfers and emigration. Some of them had their nervous breakdowns on the job, some managed to slip exhausted away, to have them in peace among normal surroundings, or at home if they had one.

They all had their own ways of charming their passengers and of running their tours, and altered their talks to fit what they hoped were their listeners. They'd needed to be travel-wise even to arrive at the Falls. They, too, had been round museums, French chateaux and Greek ruins and been bored silly by the set spiel that local tour guides inflict on us all. (Oh, the joy of being given the complete history of Greece according to ancient myths over three hours at 35°C!) A Falls courier grew tough while avoiding the brickbats that flew around, as she couldn't spend her life in tears, and had to be reminded about the 99% who had enjoyed their tours with her.

Generally at the Falls there were fifteen or twenty full-time couriers, all white while we were there, though that was about to change, and only three of them men, who on the whole had to work harder to win their passengers over, and had to know a little more because (so long ago this belief), people expected men to know more about politics, history and economics. "From where I sit now", I can't think why.

The couriers came from many parts: Switzerland, Germany, New Zealand (Kiwis perhaps the best), Britain, Holland, Kenya, Denmark and Ireland. Very few Rhodesian girls ever applied for a job, or South Africans. The three who did were good because they had real background knowledge of Rhodesia, its history, the social set-up and customs, the African tribal customs - things that no amount of learning could ever make an impression upon foreign guides. I wonder if the critics were right and the children of Rhodesia were brought up so soft with servants, sun and swim, none of them would take on such an arduous, demanding, and in many ways servile occupation.

At any one time three or four of the girls would be employed primarily because they were German- or French-speaking, but languages were not as important as one would think.

Hard to believe now, but Martin trained fifty-three of these couriers while we were at the Falls. Most stayed only six months or a year. When he'd taken over the job, a courier generally would stay only three or four months. He managed to draw this out to one or two years for many, but if a courier stayed for more than eighteen months, she was often so mentally and physically exhausted, she opted for a job on the sales counter of one of the hotels.

The worst qualification for a girl as a courier was if she declared: "I like people". Let her love horses, stray dogs or hamsters, but if she thought she liked people she was finished. She must pretend to like people: each and every one of those awkward, demanding people on her tour. She must be selfish, concerned with self-preservation, dying to get home and go to bed with her flu, but appear to be ready to give her day, her wealth of knowledge, her charm, her smile, just for each one of these delightful people she is lucky to be showing these glorious sights (which she has been around six times this week already). She is an actress playing the part of a well-informed and charming hostess, showing off something she loves. She knows in her heart she is not at all charming and by now is bored with the place.

But if she is a good courier, and doing her job properly, one great thing to spur her on is the sense of giving pleasure to others, and the feeling of *entente*, which she gets from her audience, the passengers.

Just about the whole of Victoria Falls went to see the film "If it's Tuesday this must be Belgium", and we laughed ourselves silly. We watched it outdoors on the wide lawns of the Casino Hotel with the falls roaring away as always in the background. There was a grand feeling of comradeship; this Tuesday Belgium was our way of life - the life of the whiz-round tourist - and we were filled with a great sense of completeness with this film and the cocky and excellent courier. And we recognised each one of the passengers.

Art Buchwald, the American humourist, wrote a prayer for tourists:

"Heavenly Father, look down on us Your humble obedient tourist servants who are doomed to travel this earth, taking photographs, mailing post cards, buying souvenirs and walking around in drip-dry underwear.

We beseech You, oh Lord, to see that our plane is not hijacked, our luggage is not lost and our overweight baggage goes unnoticed."

He goes on to plead his hotel reservations are honoured and hot

112

water in the taps, that waiters will be friendly and that the natives will love them for what they are, not for their money.

"Grant us the strength to visit the museums, the cathedrals, the palaces and castles listed as 'musts' in the guidebook. And if perchance we skip an historical monument and take a nap after lunch, have mercy on us, for our flesh is weak."

The husbands pray the women will not spend all their money in the shops, the wives pray the men will not make fools of themselves in the nightclubs and look at foreign women.

"And when the voyage is over, and we return to our loved ones, grant us the favour of finding someone who will look at our home movies and listen to our stories so our lives as tourists will not have been in vain."

Some of the couriers at the Falls were working their way round the world. They'd pitch up one day, and the next they'd have a guide book shoved in their hands, then, after a few days, a pep talk, a few trips up the river and round the falls with Martin and a good courier or two, and they'd be ready to be thrust, petrified, on to a bus to face thirty expectant faces. In that environment, the only way to learn to be a courier was to be one. An intelligent and sensitive person would learn and read as much as she could on her own in self-defence against the questions she was repeatedly asked by her passengers. No one likes to look stupid, and there's a limit to how much you can talk your way out of.

Martin maintains that people became couriers because they desperately needed to be loved. (He didn't say where this put us.) On the face of it this was a contradiction, because generally the girls who became couriers were charming, well spoken, intelligent, had good figures and were never short of men. One was an ex-beauty queen, French and fabulous, but she was one of the worst of those who needed to be reassured, and loved.

One was a high-society, debutante type. She always had to go to the loo and comb her hair at the last minute, so someone else had to put her people on the bus, because she wanted to leave to the very last moment having to face them. She had a rather weak voice, but spoke faultless French, and appealed to many with her rather little girl lost look. But on the whole those working with her, or for her, were not sorry when she decided to return home and marry her, presumably, very suitable boy friend.

But at least there was all credit due to her: she had tried to break away and experience a different life.

Then there was Val, who spoke many languages badly, including Welsh. When she spoke German everyone could understand her. It was a sort of converted kitchen Swahili. (She was in Kenya before.) Her few words of Welsh came in very useful, oddly enough. She won the everlasting goodwill of the Welsh rugby supporters' clubs. These gallant Welshmen would sail along the Zambezi on the evening cruises (which had a free bar on board) and with a couple of drinks under their belts and Val as courier to lead them, they would pour out the songs of the Welsh valleys till everyone, singing or not, had tears in their eyes to: "There'll be a welcome in the valleys." The voices sounded unearthly and beautiful in the still air of the river, with the sun setting red behind the palm trees and the hadedas bawling their homeward song as they flew level along the river. I wonder what the terrorists watching from the other side of the river thought of it all. "Wales, Wales..."

One girl was a self-confessed nymphomaniac. "Let's scare the pants off this lot!" she'd say as she took a deep breath into her big breast and called "Tour of the Falls" across the foyer. Martin generally gave her the cricket tours and the football groups and they were happy, which goes to prove that everyone had their own way of doing a tour.

Another of the girls would often get invitations out to dinner after her tour. And often she would return to her flat early. "Some men! He expected me to go to bed with him for the price of a dinner." This was about thirty years or so ago, before this became the norm, or so we are told, though I don't believe it.

One of the German couriers professed she hated Germans, her own countrymen, and sometimes would almost refuse to take any

114

more German groups. She would list all the faults of the German people, and she was exactly describing herself.

German groups treated Swiss German-speaking couriers like servants, till they were unwilling to take any more Germans. It must be something to do with some part of European history, which escaped us Rhodesianised Englanders. Sometimes it would be preferable to give a German tour with a known ill-tempered tour leader a courier who spoke no German. He would then translate as he wished, the German passengers would treat the English or New Zealand, or other nationality girl politely - for what reason we failed to understand - and all would be happiness.

And everything being contrary in this game, having said all this about the make-up of a good courier, perhaps the best courier was one who betrayed most of the faults. She approached the job in an amateurish fashion, she worked only part-time, she was far from young, and she "loved people". But she knew the falls and Rhodesia inside out, though she never paraded her knowledge as most middle-aged and half-professionals were apt to. She got to know her passengers by name after a few minutes, and she made them love her, and the country, as much as she loved them. She was truly exceptional, and I wouldn't advise anyone to try and emulate her. She loved people so much she insisted on working (while over-caring for her family) when she should have been at home quietly resting a faulty heart, and at last, loving people too much killed her.

She had, after all, that fiery spark that all the best couriers had.

TEN

We were not without reservations that this "end of the rainbow" was an ideal place to bring up two young girls. Without doubt they loved it, particularly Paula. This was where it was at, if ever there was an "at" in Rhodesia. During the school holidays we wondered if the "Sprayview", where young folk (and some older) danced outside in a space between the tables to a loud African band, really was the best environment for two teenage girls. I think we were too free with them, but they so hated the confines of their school in term-time that we tried to let them have considerable freedom in the holidays.

We contented ourselves with the thought that the boy friends they found themselves always seemed to be decent young boys or men, and they promised us they didn't drink or smoke. There were drugs around, "pot" they called it then. If they indulged we didn't know, and it doesn't matter any more. Now they are anxious to prevent their own children from drinking, smoking or taking drugs.

Paula, oddly enough, was more constant than Susie with her boy friends. Her second boy friend she kept, in her heart at least, for years, and contented herself with breaking her heart several times over this young man. We loved, rejoiced, wept, rejected and were rejected, with her from the time she was fourteen. He was not so constant and the competition was overwhelming.

She would be the last to tell me anything then, or now even. Sometimes I could get the odd sentence out of Susie about her, and the rest was painted around it for a bizarre picture. In those days it was not the custom for a girl to sleep with her boy friend, and young girls were definitely never given the pill.

For my little blonde vegetarian's love was a white hunter. He made his living taking rich clients into Botswana on big-game shooting safaris. Presumably without a second thought she condoned the bagging of lion, zebra, buffalo and as many varieties

116

of buck as they could muster for American hunting "trophies".

He invited both the girls to go and stay at the main camp once, when he wasn't busy. The four American clients there at the time were seemingly as entertained by the idea that their hunter had a vegetarian girl friend as by the wonders of the hunt. The young man laid in stores of baked beans and sweetcorn for them while the rest ate buffalo steaks. (At least that's what we were told. Paula stopped being a vegetarian later.)

During the trip they travelled the length of Botswana in a Land Rover with a dead buffalo in the back (a present for Sir Seretse Khama, the President of Botswana). It must have been getting a little high by the time they got there, and I would have retched, but my darling daughters were apparently unmoved.

We saw a lot of South African Police at the Falls when we were there. There was some agreement with the Rhodesian security forces that they protect parts of the borders, though it was never admitted to. They weren't too popular with the residents of Vic Falls as they behaved like all young men in a group away from home. While stationed in a camp by the airstrip a mile from town, they found it difficult to get passes into the town, and increasingly so as more and more complaints were raised against them. But Susie's friend was a rugby player, and worshipping sport as South Africans do, he was allowed to make his evening training runs down to the river, and that naturally took him past our chalet house.

He was a nice lad. His friend was Paula's friend too, but he couldn't seem to get it into his head that we were not willing to let Susie, then fifteen, become serious about any young man. He was Afrikaans (South African Dutch) and spoke very little English, though he was an intelligent boy and intended to go to university after his police service. But Susie soon knew a lot of Afrikaans. He asked permission to marry her when she would be sixteen, and we were horrified.

Perhaps we shouldn't have interfered: he later became a Springbok rugby forward, touring France and playing the All Blacks and was a national hero.

On the same lines as Paula's white hunter, Susie next found a snake-man. He worked as a taxidermist and in the snake park in the village, and was crazy about animals, dead or alive. He told us he used to work in the lion cages at the London Zoo.

Whenever they got a chance, preferably on a moonless night, the girls would go out with him in the mini pick-up, armed with torch, forked sticks and sack. The girls were a little reticent to their old mother about the part they played in the capture of poisonous snakes: "Oh, no, Mom, Jules does all the catching. We don't do anything, or go near them."

Paula had always been afraid of snakes, but I heard by roundabout means some months later what a whiz she was at catching boomslangs (tree snakes), said by many to be one of the most deadly of African snakes, though back-fanged, and certainly without any antidote in the country. When they weren't catching snakes, they were looking for scorpions in the holes under the cattle grids on the main road, or catching toads and frogs to feed the snakes; another pleasant occupation for my two young vegetarian daughters. Jules later went to Hollywood and was described on the internet as "Hollywood's top animal trainer", starring in a film "Jules Most Dangerous: Wild West". It looks at actors performing with animals, and catches on film the ten most dangerous animals in the western United States.

Susie's next boy friend was blown up in a booby trap following a mine explosion near the Zambezi River. This time he was a Rhodesian policeman attached to the Support Unit, which was sent around wherever there was trouble. They rode about in "rhinos", the first of the ungainly, weird-looking mineproof vehicles. Unfortunately he was not in his rhino at the time.

The day before, two South African policemen had been killed in a landmine explosion in one of the first incidents near Victoria Falls. All day the Rhodesian Support Unit had been searching the area. In the late afternoon they returned to the Falls. As far as he knew, Susie's young friend was free for the rest of the day so he asked her out to dinner with him. It was quite an occasion, as Sue had never been formally invited out to dinner at a restaurant before.

In the middle of the dinner he was called out. For reasons unknown to man, he was ordered to patrol the area again in pitch darkness. According to Susie he was really afraid.

"I don't want to go," he said. "I feel it is wrong to go. Something terrible is going to happen."

And a few hours later he was struggling back to a farmhouse near the river, his eye full of shrapnel, and more than thirty slivers of shrapnel in his chest, face, hands and legs. At the time he thought he had been blinded in one eye. (We learnt later he recovered most of his vision after treatment.) He was half-way to becoming a commercial pilot, and his reason for working for the police was to pay for his training. He could never become a pilot after that.

Several weeks later, after lengthy operations in Johannesburg, he returned to the Falls for a day, to say "thank you" to the many people who had helped him. I never saw such a changed man. He could not keep still, his face was strange and bruised-looking, his eye all colours. His hand trembled as he sat. We wondered at the futility of this Rhodesian war.

Susie and Paula left Arundel School in Salisbury; Susie with her A-levels, Paula with her O-levels and a flat refusal to go back to take her A-levels. We persuaded her to go for at least one year more to a government (non-private) school in Bulawayo, to study for her M-levels, the normal leaving exams in Southern Africa. This entailed one night's journey by train, and with many other schoolchildren on the train. When they were at school in Salisbury they had a train journey of two nights with a whole day to pass in Bulawayo in between. We were never happy about these night journeys; all sorts of odd people found their way on to the trains, and there was even a murder on the train near Wankie one night. But the airfare was very expensive for the two of them and our friend, Julie, with children their age, took them to her home for the day in Bulawayo. Susie had always said she wanted to join the police, but we had taken it as a bit of a joke. Now it was time to do something. We couldn't persuade her to go to university. She said no professions her science subjects might have opened to her interested her.

If we had still been on the farm she might have looked at the world with different eyes.   I think we were wrong to let her leave off her formal education as we did; she would have tried for a scholarship with a little persuasion. But Martin felt there was no sense in prolonging the agony if she didn't know what she wanted to do. So she started her police training the day she was eighteen.

A new uniform had been designed for policewomen, and those on Susie's intake were the first to wear it. The police were starting a big recruitment drive, and were anxious to give the girls a new image, and the uniform was very attractive in a bright blue with smart hat.

We were excessively proud of her at her passing-out parade.

After a while she was stationed at Wankie (from which the game reserve took its name), the coal-mining town sixty miles from the Falls. One day, on the way to Bulawayo, we called in to say "hi!" and met her coming back from attending a road accident in a police Land Rover by herself.

"Did you have to see to everything by yourself?" we asked in amazement.

"Well, no, fortunately the ambulance arrived just about the same time. I only had to take the details."

"Why you?"

"There was no-one else."

As we got to know the police ways better, we discovered there was always "no-one else". They were perpetually understaffed and trying to do a dozen jobs in different places at the same time, and generally with no transport to take them there.

Whenever a policewoman went out she was supposed to take a black constable with her, to defend and translate, but as far as we could see Susie invariably by-passed this little rule when she could.

Another time we were waiting for her at the police station when she arrived by herself in charge of a Land Rover full of African prisoners. Once again, why you? And the reply as before.

"Do you think it's safe, Susie?"

"Oh yes, Mom, don't worry, they've got their guard with them." To be sure they did have an African in uniform with them, but he didn't look very alert, or capable of defending my little eighteen-year-old girl from fourteen convicts.

I wondered how many murderers, rapists or robberies-with-violence she had in that crowd. But surely they wouldn't let that sort loose, like that, would they? Well, would they?

She'd wanted to see life and she was seeing it. She was sometimes on night duty and had to go and help clear the township beer halls. They were a pretty rough lot in Wankie, being a coal-mining town. This time she did have one or two African constables with her.

"They never touch anyone in uniform," she assured us. What faith! (Now tell that to the Metropolitan Police Force, and others...)

The Minister of Tourism forecast that by 1990, tourism would double at the Falls to seven hundred visitors a day. He did not add "God willing", "African nationalism willing", but he should have.

The government decided on a brave plan to buy up all the privately owned land south of the Zambezi to the borders of the Wankie Game Reserve, which took a great sweep of country including safari and hunting concessions. These would be joined to the Wankie and Victoria Falls game parks to create the largest game reserve in Africa.

A civil case brought against the government haggled over the price in court for forty-nine days and became the longest court case in Rhodesian history - how times have changed! The government offered a farmer R$227,500 for his Paradise Ranch by a most beautiful stretch of the Zambezi. He was determined to continue cattle farming and growing tomatoes, in spite of large predators and hippo, and demanded two-and-a-half million dollars. The case dragged on for years, by which time the government was spending its money fighting terrorists and didn't want the farm after all. All such major developments were being quietly forgotten.

But for now in 1972, people were forgetting their fears, and one Sunday over a hundred people flew in on the day excursion alone. They took us by surprise and we were falling over each other in the Rain Forest, and the river began to look like the Thames (we thought!) with a hundred people and more munching away at picnic lunches as they steamed along. No self-respecting elephant would have dreamed of approaching the river, but the monkeys thrived on the titbits they got on Kandahar Island. It was a terribly hot day, and they might as well have gone to Margate on a bank holiday for all the feeling of "Africa" they managed to find.

When February skies opened and the falls looked at their worst, the cruise ships began to arrive at South African ports, full of rich, middle-aged Americans and Frenchmen. The Victoria Falls was one of their inland trips. They had a great itinerary through Africa: the Murchison Falls, Kilimanjaro, Marrakech and Timbuktu. They were just romantic names to me, but to some Africa was only part of a round-the-world cruise, in style.

One of the most memorable experiences of my life was taking a tour of 130 French people, in groups over four days, round the falls in the pouring rain, proper rain from the skies, and then up the river on a cool windy evening with only the aid of cokes and fizzy lemon.

The day before the first of the French group arrived off a cruise ship, the young Swiss girl who was to direct and translate, turned her boy friend's car over. She wasn't hurt, beyond bruises, but she was too shocked to work. Before, Martin and I had been appointed to assist. We had neither of us had much to do with the French language for twenty years.

Together we went in there and it was excruciating. I would gladly have sung the Marseillaise - at least I knew the words for that. I did not know the words for: "The Zambezi river is three thousand kilometres long and rises... the fruits of the palm trees attract the elephants to the river, where they shake the trees with their trunks... the Sunderland flying boats used to land on this stretch of the river until 1951... no, this is called Kandahar Island, but they do not make carpets here... look at the hippos, you can just see their eyes and ears, yes, that is what hippos look like in the water, I don't know if he is standing on the bottom right now."

It occurred to me you're taught the wrong words at school, and the French literature evening classes I had attended fitfully hadn't helped much. Never once had I occasion to mention the pen of my aunt or, thank goodness, that the lightning had struck the postilion.

One of the Swiss girls stationed in Salisbury had very quickly translated a formalised commentary, so I trotted that out, and naturally all the French people picked holes in it. Some of the words, they said, were Swiss. It was all beyond me and by that time I didn't care. I had delivered the commentary three times and I was utterly exhausted after trotting round the falls and up the river trying to think in French for four days.

When I went to the airport to greet the last group, I approached a likely-looking man with a smile: "Bonjour, monsieur!"

"Oh, bonn-joor to you, ma'am," he said with a broad Middle-west accent. "I can't speak one word o' that, but it's very nice of you to say so."

It reminded me of the nervous Australian woman who shuffled apprehensively up to the counter one day. "Excuse me," she said to me, "do you speak English?" She had a terrible accent. No, and I wasn't rude and didn't reply: "Yes, do you?"

My second most arduous task, when I really had to pull out all the stops, was taking an ordinary mixed group of eighty people, including children, up the river on the launch one holiday afternoon and getting caught in a tropical thunderstorm. We all had to sit/stand/ perch on the enclosed bottom deck, while the rain trickled through in numerous places from the top deck. The windows were entirely misted up, because every time anyone tried to open one an inch or so, the rain beat in.

The whole damp lot of us were wondering what in the name of tourism were we doing on the river on a day like this, but they had paid their R$2.50, and it was my job to try and alleviate their misery, or try to.

123

So I talked. I talked for the full forty-five minutes it took to get up the river. I can't sing or tell jokes, or I would have tried that. I was afraid to ask for volunteer entertainers among the passengers in case I got some club comedian who told dirty jokes (and then watch out for the complaints from the mums). So I told them, bored them stiff, those that listened, with all I knew about the river, David Livingstone, Cecil Rhodes, the history of Victoria Falls and Rhodesia in general, all I knew about wild life on the river and in the game park and Wankie game park, about the flow of water over the falls, the plants in the Rain Forest and along the river, the birds on the river (out of sight), the rainfall (obviously a lot), the seasons, population and tribal customs, and after a bit I ceased to worry that what I said might not be quite true - my myths this time. They didn't complain directly. I had become a counter-irritant. Better to have them muttering to themselves: "Why doesn't she shut up?" than to sit morosely in the drips.

And then the sun came out. We landed on Kandahar, we walked round the island, saw hippos on the other side, had tea and biscuits, fed the monkeys, and sailed down the river in beautiful wondrous silence. Waterbuck came to the water's edge to drink, and an elephant shook the palm trees to get the mulala nuts, just as I had told them they did on the way up, though no-one had cared enough to believe me.

After two years with the touring company I left and went back to Peter's Motel as receptionist. The complaints and harassment on the Victoria Falls Hotel counter were beginning to defeat me and I wanted a change. I was also working for Martin, as he was in charge of sales staff as well as couriers, and I've always been noticeably deaf to anything Martin "tells" me to do.

The new manager at the motel was a very pleasant young chap and I couldn't believe my luck when I found myself among visitors who were happy with their accommodation, happy with their food, happy indeed to be on holiday. They bought postcards and chatted and said how lovely the falls were, and told me about the crocodiles at the farm, and the monkeys on Kandahar Island. They asked if I ever went down to the falls, and had I been on the launch?

I heard the Rhodesia Broadcasting Corporation was looking for someone to act, when required, as Victoria Falls correspondent. The local tourist board director recommended me and I was delighted and amazed when I got the job. They required three sorts of news: news of national interest; short local items for their district news bulletins twice a week; and "voice reports" for newsreel programmes broadcast in the evenings.

The voice reports had to be about two minutes long, and if anything happened in the area that was worthy of a two-minute talk I phoned it through for recording on the afternoon of the programme. It was a real thrill to hear my own voice - and my own reporting - coming through on the scratchy radio together with national items. And to hear all the faults in my presentation, which were "something else", as we used to say in Rhodesia.

The temperature was 37°C and it looked as though it would never rain again. My first voice report was for a programme near to my heart: no rain. I had served a long apprenticeship in watching for rain on the farm. Most of the reports from other districts were about the grave situation for the farmers, but I went to see the witch doctor, and followed the rain-forecasting movements of the elephants, which came across from Botswana in drought times. As the rain stayed away, the newsreel on rain or no-rain became a regular feature.

Another time a trainload of steam-engine enthusiasts arrived at the Falls by steam train (how else?) and I thought it was worth reporting that they didn't like the bits of soot that flew into the windows. The son of a Falls pioneer still living in the village had his book reprinted, and a memorial service to David Livingstone was held round his statue by the side of the Devil's Cataract. The falls were such a romantic setting you could make a story out of anything, except, perhaps, the endless conferences. I always missed the salient points of these, if there were any. (Twenty-five years or so later the "war vets" found it fun to stone the statue of David Livingstone. They should have read his writings first.)

This, though, was before the shooting started and the news reports could become serious.

An evening of tribal dancing at an African village ten miles from the falls was the brainchild of the local photographer and newsman, Dave. He asked Martin to present it and, never willing to refuse a challenge, husband then had an evening job as well.

People were really enthusiastic about it, not only visitors from overseas, but South Africans and Rhodesians who had seen lots of tribal dancing before. And even locals who were not taken in by any showmanship at the "native village", but knew some of the dancers as part-time waiters and gardeners, used to love to go to it.

We drove out in the short dusk-to-dark over a long, sandy road, through scrub and woodlands, and the people who lived in towns or had never been to Africa really believed we were driving right into the middle of darkest Africa. The road was rutted and deserted, and only served to make it all the more mysterious and frightening. There was always a real risk we might get bogged down after a thunderstorm.

Often on the way we met wild animals like waterbuck, kudu, zebra, jackal, serval cat. The road led alongside the game reserve, but we didn't tell visitors that.

And when we arrived out of the darkness, we were greeted by a procession of all-male Shangaan dancers carrying flaming torches and wearing only skins round their middles, with anklets and armbands of impala skin and feather headdresses. The Shangaans stamped and shouted greetings, but many of the visitors were truly afraid to get out of their minibuses. Reassured these were entertainment warriors, they huddled along the dark path between the thatched huts of the village, guided by the dancing Shangaans, and the dancing shadows on the walls. The braver ones stopped and admired the babies and young children sitting by the fires or plucking at their mothers' breasts. They progressed towards the cleared arena where the dancing started noisily with drums and the welcoming dance.

All around great bonfires sent sparks high into the black sky to join the stars, and beyond there was nothing but the silent bush.

Martin gave a short explanatory introduction to the dancing. He kept it short and it carried the interest along to combine each dance into the story of African village life. He said something about the tribes and how they came to be in Rhodesia now, and the differences each tribe carried forth in their attitudes and ways of life.

He tried to make his part unobtrusive, yet at the same time stopped the dancers running on too long or becoming too monotonous, as African dances are inclined to do. By all reports he managed a way of doing this that satisfied most people.

Drums are hollowed-out tree trunks of different sizes for achieving different tones, with skins stretched over one end. The skins must be warmed at an open fire to sound a true note.

Shangaan dancing is all kicking feet and jerking arms and tossing legs, dances of the hunt and war. It was very dramatic and a good introduction to the evening.

As the pace quickened the shouting became more guttural, the stamping more vigorous, and the dust rose from the sandy arena, "Sa,sa,sa. Sa,sa,sa," as the gleaming black male dancers waved backwards and forwards in lines. At the end of the line the little warrior, all of six years, danced with his father and uncles, watching them all the time, to learn the dances which had been passed on in this way since long before the white man came to Africa.

Sometimes a frenzied dancer would break away on his own with a scream and perform cartwheels and head-over-heels and handstands, carried away by the hypnotic chant and rhythm.

Beyond the dancers the sparks and flames jumped, and the whole atmosphere was alive and awake. It was impossible not to be moved by the performance.

On and on they went, pulling faces in the agony, till they dropped exhausted in the dust. Then quiet.

The next dancers were from the Makishi tribe, and their costumes and style of dancing were completely different, so that you wondered if they could be all the same Bantu people. They wore a sort of cat suit of natural palm fibre "knitted" and coloured with vegetable dyes in a horizontal striped effect. Each performer played the same part all his life: an owl, hyena, martial eagle, goat or spirit. He wore an ornate mask and headdress depicting his part grotesquely. His identity was supposed to be kept secret even from his family.

Once again only the men danced, though the women were allowed to play the chorus at the side of the arena, chanting and clapping wooden blocks. They dressed in bright lengths of cotton cloth wrapped tightly around their bodies and legs, which permitted a traditional shuffle dance only.

Some carried their babies in a cloth on their backs, with only a small black cherub face showing as the child slept peacefully throughout the cacophony and jogging, and was part of the dance before he or she was even aware of life.

Sometimes visitors were not entirely happy, particularly some Americans. They said this was a show being put on, and they had come to Africa to see a genuine village dancing. They didn't realise that as soon as a foreign person (which means not only from another country or race, but also another tribe) enters a village, then the village ceases to be genuine. When Dr Livingstone or Selous walked through the country in the nineteenth century, they no doubt found the genuine dancers, and were witness to them.

But they still would not be half as interesting or entertaining as these at the village, unless he happened to be an anthropologist.

Today if he travelled long and far over appalling roads that soon disappeared altogether, through riverbeds and rocks, he might find a village about to have a real dance in the dust and the firelight. But the dance would be part of a beer-drink, the dancers not good performers, and the costumes would sport scraps of plastic and bottle tops among the traditional leaves, while they banged baked-beans tins together to give rhythm. And if it were a real initiation or circumcision ceremony, they would not be allowed to watch. There's no way to step backwards now in Africa.

In this village near the falls, all the best performers - drummers, acrobats, dancers and singers - had been encouraged to come and live there. It was a show, to be sure, but it made other stage shows featuring African dancing, which toured the world earning great acclaim and great fortunes, look false.

Many of the Makishi dances were derived from circumcision rituals. At that time young boys were often sent away into seclusion in the bush for three months to learn tribal behaviour and customs, and how to hunt and fight. At the end of the period the witchdoctor circumcised them, without anaesthetic. Afterwards, to prove their manhood, they performed arduous tasks of endurance, bravery and physical strength. When the tests were over the youngsters returned to their village amid loud welcomes from their families, and several days and nights of festivities followed.

At Shangaan Musha these rituals and celebrations were all represented in dances with fanciful, exaggerated costumes, (a man played the part of the mother with a "child" on his back, as women were not allowed to take part). The climax was attained when one of the initiates shinned up one of two twenty-foot poles and performed a hanging dance on a rope suspended between the poles. Dressed in feathers, he was said to take on the strength of *kanjanjenje*, the martial eagle, largest of all the eagles known to his tribe.

Another dance featured terrible cries from the dark bush, which gradually got nearer until spirits dressed in white with tall white hats, and walking on stilts, appeared suddenly from the trees carrying lighted tapers. They stomped about the arena frightening away the other performers, their path across the uneven ground made more dangerous by their stilts being actually tied to their legs. The villagers were genuinely afraid of *Toyi-toyi*, the spirits.

The evening came to a close when a Shangaan picked up a ninety-kilogram length of railway line in his teeth. Before he could perform the feat he had to work himself into a hypnotic trance, helped by the dancers and drums, even by the audience, with clapping, stamping and singing. There was no trickery, and at the end it was as much as a strong-looking man from the spectators could do to carry the iron out of the arena in his hands.

A group of American dentists went to see the show and were vastly impressed, after the show keenly examining the Shangaan's teeth and mouth.

One evening we came across a tiny sable antelope and its mother in the headlights of the minibus. It had just been born and the cord still hung from it. It was a memorable experience.

The show was greatly in demand and after a few months an additional condensed version was put on in the gardens of the Victoria Falls Hotel, in an enclosure with a mock-up of African huts as a backdrop. Many more people saw this show, as it was cheaper and shorter.

If there was no performance at the village, Martin would sometimes fill in by compering the show at the hotel, but he didn't enjoy it much there. It lacked the atmosphere of the village with no dark journey through the bush as a build-up.

One night at the hotel performance, the Makishi dancer fell to his death from the top of the twenty-foot pole while performing his initiation dance. Investigation revealed he also had taken to town ways and instead of weaving the rope of palm fibres according to the tradition, he had hit on the idea of making it of plastic-covered electrical wire. The constant turning and twisting of the wire had broken it, but the broken threads were hidden beneath the plastic covering. By ancient custom, the man who performs the pole dancing is also responsible for making his own rope. Most people watching did not know that Willie Carson, the jockey, had joined in the dancing a few weeks before, and had himself climbed the pole and swung like a Makishi on the rope between the poles.

Some years later, a South African illustrated magazine came out with a dramatic story in colour about the terrible ceremonial circumcision rites that were still practised in an "isolated village" near the Zambezi. The village was Shangaan Musha, the village where the dancing took place, and the pictures presumably taken during a performance. It was a good try.

A German-American film company made a fiction film at the falls after we had left. We went to a Bulawayo cinema when it was released, and there were the dancers, the railway-line strong-toothed man, the leader of the dancers, and the drummers all playing the parts of warriors running through the Rain Forest (which played the part of the jungle), defending Ursula Andress, to the death, from ivory racketeers. All good fun and we had a good laugh picking out all the folk and performers we knew, playing bit parts and crowds, now heroes and villains.

Years later when we were living "safe" in England, Martin let on that he had been very scared when he used to drive out to the village each evening on his own to be there before the visitors arrived. He went at the same time most evenings of the week, the first vehicle along the road, so any terrorist wanting to place a mine on the dirt road knew exactly when and where to put it down, to cause maximum confusion. He had never given me any inkling of how he felt then.

ELEVEN

The bridge across the gorge at Victoria Falls was part of Cecil Rhodes' dream of a railway from the Cape of Good Hope to Cairo. This dream was never realised and never will be now. It was constructed as near the falls as possible because Rhodes was an incurable romantic (millionaires can afford to be) and wished the passengers to feel the spray from the falls, which they did on many days.

The bridge itself could be a lot more beautiful, and the view itself more beautiful without it, but it was started in 1903 and now the gorges are stuck with it.

Building this bridge in the middle of Africa, spanning the Zambezi, was quite an enterprise, and it was completed before the railway reached the river. It was constructed from either side simultaneously, and all the heaviest material had to be ferried across the drift, a narrow, treacherous and swift-running channel five miles up river. One of the first over the bridge was a leopard, which must have been surprised to find itself living out the rest of its days on the wrong side of the water.

And a word for woman's lib: the first locomotive over was driven by a woman, the sister of the contractor. Then seventy years later another train was parked in the middle of the bridge for a conference to promote peace between the black and white leaders of Rhodesia, and thereby agreement between the northern black governments of Zambia and Malawi, and those of Rhodesia and South Africa, then still white-controlled.

The Victoria Falls bridge is only two hundred metres long, but is arched in a single span a hundred metres above the Zambezi across a dramatic gorge, with swallows and swifts and eagles sweeping below it, and aloes clinging precariously to the black basalt cliffs.

In January 1973, Rhodesia, without warning, closed the bridge to all road and rail traffic except for through traffic to Zaire (formerly the Congo). It was a direct protest to Zambia for the obvious harbouring of terrorists who came over the river, laid mines, and returned to Zambia.

Four weeks later, presumably because Rhodesia received assurances this would be stopped, the Rhodesian government opened the border again, but the Zambian government immediately closed it. And that was the way it was to remain for a long time.

I was working at Peter's Motel when it happened, and many people staying there from the Copperbelt were stranded by the jolly movements of the politicians. After thinking they were nearly home, they were suddenly a long way off. The crossings to the east were also closed at Kariba Dam wall and at Chirundu, on the direct road from Salisbury to Zambia. For the first, and most likely the last time in history, the new border hotel at Chirundu was full to overflowing.

"Chirundu has the attractions - hunting, game viewing, fishing - to become a tourist resort in its own right," the owner said. "We can make a go of things here without the passing border traffic."

This was typical of the head-in-sand attitude that overcame most Rhodesians for fifteen years from the Unilateral Declaration of Independence till a black government took control in 1980. In fact this attitude prevailed and was even more pronounced in some white Rhodesians, who had now become Zimbabweans. They stubbornly refused to acknowledge that things were going to get much worse, which, we know now, they undoubtedly did.

So the only way stranded travellers from Zambia could get home then was to drive back to Salisbury, leave their cars and fly from Salisbury via Blantyre to the Copperbelt, a round trip of nearly 600 miles driving and 600 flying. This many did, hoping the trouble would not last long.

The only route by road was not immediately obvious, rarely having been used before. This was along the poor dirt road into Botswana and across a dilapidated ferry, then on another bad road to Livingstone. This made the round trip to Livingstone over a hundred miles instead of eight. From the riverside the sun could be seen shining on the buildings of Livingstone in the evening, as it could be seen shining on a perfectly good bridge that would allow them to reach the town in ten minutes.

The United Nations sent a delegation to the middle of the bridge (the Zambian side) to assess the help they must give to Zambia because they had done the "right" thing and closed it. The Rhodesian policemen on the bridge waved cheerily to the delegation, and the Zambian representatives pursed their lips.

But the Zambians got their money, as usual. In spite of great efforts to bring in goods by road from Dar es Salaam and other east-coast ports, and Lobito in Angola and the swift building of a railway to Dar es Salaam by the Chinese, the border closure cost Zambia about ninety million pounds in the first sixteen months.

Many families working on contracts in the Zambian copper mines felt obliged to return to Britain and South Africa when high school children could not easily attend Rhodesian schools. New arrivals had younger children who went to special mine schools, but they in turn chafed at the shortages of European-type staple foods and the non-existence of fresh vegetables and fruit, butter, bread and flour in the shops. Before the border closure they would come over to Vic Falls to stock up every month. White South Africans still occupied most of the senior positions on the mines while black employees were being trained to assume control.

Two or three trainloads of trucks went through each day with goods said to be destined for Zaire, though we knew many were for the Zambian Copperbelt. The trucks were backed on to the bridge as far as the painted white line in the middle, then picked up by a Zambian locomotive and drawn over.

Walking to the borderline on the bridge became a tourist attraction. From the bridge there was a beautiful view of the falls and, at times, an almost 360° rainbow. The extra excitement of the sight of the Zambian paramilitary policemen standing by the line or by their shelter over the other side, with rifles at the ready, was an added thrill and cameras clicked smartly. By the time a visitor had got this far in Rhodesia their sympathies were always on our side. South Africans loved to have photos taken by the sign "You are now entering Zambia".

But after a while it became obvious that the Zambians were becoming trigger-happy, the game of bridge walking might become like Russian roulette, and people were advised strongly by border officials on our side of the bridge, not to go on. We no longer took our tours there, but the baboons continued to play on the rails, thumping along on the trucks that were waiting to be picked up.

Then a Rhodesian train driver stepped over the white line on the bridge to check the brake coupling of the trucks waiting to be pulled over. He was arrested and chucked into a Zambian jail for "fiddling in a very suspicious manner with the locomotive trucks". So the Wankie rail men refused to handle any more rail traffic to or from Zambia, and after eight days the driver was released unharmed, and reported he had not been too badly treated, except for having to sleep on a concrete floor with the cockroaches.

Over the next few months, several tourists inadvertently crossed the border and were clapped into jail for their pains - an elderly German couple who had no knowledge of English, and two young German students who drove over for reasons best known to themselves. They were dubbed "the suicide kids" by the Zambians and kept in jail for eight days.

And at Kariba, our third border post with Zambia, a Power Corporation official who was inspecting the dam wall was snatched, carted off and suffered ill-treatment. In the end a charter plane flew into Lusaka to get him back and into hospital.

In May 1973, a party of eight young people from overseas arrived at the Victoria Falls on their way north through Africa. They stayed at the rest camp in tents and Land Rovers.

Four of them decided to go for a walk down into the gorges below the falls, within sight of the Victoria Falls Hotel. There were two Canadian girls, Marjan and Christine, aged nineteen and twenty, and a young American couple, John and Carol. Marjan remarked to her friend Christine how pretty it was down the path to the gorges, and suggested they try and get right down to the water's edge. Marjan led the way. They had on their bright shirts and holiday shorts, and Marjan even had her orange swimsuit on still, from sunbathing by the pool.

It is beautiful, lonely and wild country down there. The roar of the rapids in the gorge dominates everything. It is dry and hot, and a steep climb down to the re-entrant. Few people walk in this desolate spot, and the waterbuck, reedbuck, eagles and guinea fowl are unafraid.

They set off about lunchtime. They had been sitting by the pool with the rest of their friends, as they had been doing most days since they arrived. It was school holidays and Paula knew them quite well.

It was extremely steep in places and they had to use foot and hand holds. When they got down to the river they walked upstream to the bend. Here the Zambezi narrows from over a mile wide at the falls to 150 metres. It is tremendously fast-flowing, deep, treacherous and fearful.

They had been walking and scrambling for about an hour-and-a-half. They followed the water's edge for 800 metres, although the country was so rough there was no direct path towards the tip of the spur where the river zig-zags back into the third gorge.

They stopped about 500 metres from the Zambian power station, which was on the other side of the torrent, and discussed turning back, but Christine said she had been told of a path which led round and back to the hotel.

There were eight men walking around the power station, and the girls, thinking they were workmen, waved in friendly fashion.

Christine led the way to the point, John behind her, then Marjan, and further back, Carol. When they were in full view of the men on the opposite bank the Zambians opened fire. At first John could not believe they were firing, but thought it was fireworks.

Christine ducked and said: "What's going on?" She was crouched over a rock.

"Don't shoot," John shouted across, and tried to get Marjan away from the exposed rock, where she was standing rigid.

The second burst of fire left John in no doubt about fireworks, as blood covered his face where he had been hit in the eye, and pain stabbed at his groin. Marjan was hit: "What are those idiots doing?" she shouted, then she fell, or jumped into the river. She was swept down and around the point where she sat clinging for dear life on a jagged rock.

Christine was lying quite still. She had been shot in the head.

John turned to his wife to see if she was hurt. Carol was standing petrified, and John tried to hurry back to help her to safety. Dizzy and confused from his wounds, he fell into the edge of the river, but managed to scramble out. He reached his wife at last and shouted to her to get behind the rock. They were now partly in cover from the opposite bank.

John could hardly move with the pain in his hip and leg, or see from the shrapnel in his eye. He could not see the girls.

On the far side of the river people were trying to stop the Zambian soldiers from firing. Fifty people were in the vicinity and saw everything, it was reported later. The five men responsible for the firing with automatic rifles and machine guns would not stop. They had been drinking and were full of confidence.

When questioned later they said the four people on the other side were aiming to blow up the power station - that three were girls, as could plainly be seen at the water's edge and through binoculars further up the cliff, meant nothing because the Black September movement, they said, had used women to blow up Israeli airliners. The soldiers were sweating profusely and obviously longing to get back to their drinking.

They could see John's feet sticking out from behind the rock and were trying to hit him again. Marjan could not be reached because she was behind the promontory. She did not appear to be badly hurt and was clinging to the rock

So the Zambian soldiers set up a new vantage point three metres above the river, mounted a machine gun like a Bren on a tripod, and after some delay and discussion (while one man pointed out that it was obvious from her long blonde hair streaming in the water, that she was a girl) they opened fire on her once more. The watchers on the Zambian bank heard a high-pitched scream, and she disappeared into the river.

Altogether the firing continued for about three hours.

Even when the sun went down it never really got dark because of the illumination from the power station. There was too much light for Carol, the only one alive and uninjured, to risk going back for help. The two survivors crouched, curled up behind the rock, and waited.

At nine o'clock they decided it was now quiet enough to risk struggling back a little to the cover of a larger boulder.

In town the alarm was raised by the four other members of the party when their friends did not return, and the gorge rescue team set off, made up of ten volunteers, mainly from the police and National Parks staff.

Shots had been heard during the afternoon from the hotel swimming pool, but little had been thought of it. As the Member in Charge of the police station (who was a member of the rescue team) said: "They're always letting off pot-shots down there on the other side to relieve the boredom."

The team had only vague clues which direction to take. They had to go with painful caution because to use lights would have invited trouble from the other side, where they could pick out silhouettes and shadows of the Zambian troops. They were obviously being watched. They tried to keep in the shadow of the gorge.

At 10.30pm they came upon the American couple. Carol would not budge from the rock. She was so badly shocked she thought the rescue team were Zambian soldiers.

The rescuers rounded the corner to look for the girls and were then fully exposed to the opposite side. They found Christine's body, but there was no sign of Marjan. Because of the rugged territory, it was impossible for them to haul Christine's body across the rocks. Eventually they were obliged to tie her up in a parcel of blankets and float her a hundred metres down the river to a more accessible spot. There they had to leave her for the time being.

The party of rescuers and survivors struggled back up the gorge faces, keeping cover where they could. It was now bright moonlight, or they could not have contemplated the hazardous climb. At 4.30am the rescuers left John and Carol in a sheltered spot with the South African police doctor and a small escort.

The rest of the team scrambled up the gorge to be out of sight by daylight. They must at all costs avoid a major confrontation, they had been told.

That morning a stretcher party brought up the Americans, after twenty hours in the gorge. They were flown to Wankie Hospital by helicopter.

The news did not break until next morning. It was amazing how the secret was kept so well in such a small community.

I was on duty in the reception of Peter's Motel when Martin rang - he generally heard any news pretty soon from his office in the Falls Hotel foyer, Vic Falls' own Piccadilly Circus.

I had to make sure it was substantially true before I phoned the RBC newsroom, and simultaneously, on the verandah of the hotel, a man arrived who had just come through the Kazangula ferry in Botswana, from Livingstone. He said he had seen the shooting, but he wouldn't say anything else. He was obviously very scared and disappeared while I was making my call, so I didn't get to interview him.

The head of the news service arrived from Salisbury in a Rhodesian Air Force plane with a camera crew that afternoon, but they were premature, and nothing at all could be seen, neither Rhodesian nor Zambian, as we walked (my day's shift over) around the tops of the gorges. There wasn't time to get into the gorges that day, even if we'd dared.

This RBC newsman was afterwards berated by the television critics in the newspapers (who were not in political agreement with the RBC and RTV), for presenting the programme as a propaganda item on the lines: "Everything is beautiful here at the falls, and tourism is going on as usual." He had even said that everything would be all right as long as the Press didn't play things up. The Publicity Association and the hotels were, of course, right behind him. Just how they imagined they could prevent the Press from many countries of the world, who were already there, or on their way, from spreading this news he didn't state. If it were to the detriment of Rhodesia's already shaky tourist industry, then that was in line with sanctions' policy and to be exploited by the rest of the world.

That, so suddenly, was the end of the tourist boom in Rhodesia.

Although in the end it was all blamed on five trigger-happy, drunken soldiers, I wonder if perhaps there was not more behind it all. We learnt over many years of propaganda in Rhodesia to ignore what the government said about there being a communist behind every tree, but it is strange that this blatant shooting should come at that time when Rhodesia's economy was benefiting so much from its bountiful tourism. It would have been easy to organise - and why were so many hours of firing ignored so successfully by the Zambian dictators of policy, when Livingstone, a major town, was only twelve miles away? Rumour had it that Zambian troops had been ordered to "shoot anything that moves" near the gorges to create seeming tension for the visit of the UN Secretary General.

At 10am the tardy assurance of non-interference with rescue operations was given by the Zambian authorities, but the general feeling among the rescuers was one of disbelief.

The day had already warmed up to 27°C when the helicopter made its first ferrying trip from the improvised landing pad by the tennis courts of the Victoria Falls Hotel. The tourists continued to play tennis there throughout the day, and two hundred metres away were swimming and sunbathing at the pool.

The rescue team and armed escort struggled for four-and-a-half hours to bring Christine's body in and to search for Marjan. Two days had now elapsed since the shooting. Most of the time the teams was in open range of mortars, light machine guns and rifles which could be seen half concealed in the bushes on the opposite side of the gorge.

Not a murmur had yet been raised overseas in the talking shops of the United Nations and the rest. To us in Rhodesia this was unreal.

The helicopter continually swooped in and out and it was extremely dusty, with leaves and twigs whizzing about like homemade dust devils. I had really no idea what I was supposed to do - I'd never been involved in a major news story before, so I tried to keep up with the rest. They always seemed to keep together like a flock of guinea fowl. I suppose that way they were sure not to miss out on anything the rest were told.

The presenter from the South African Broadcasting Corporation went part-way down the gorges with the police and a handful of braver reporters. He was then out of message range, so I was told to relay rather inconsequential messages on the rescue progress for the Rhodesian and South African mediums. Late in the afternoon I sent in a voice report for both countries. It was fortunately my day off from work.

In spite of my worst fears, I couldn't have done too badly because I got a very pleasant letter afterwards from the Head of Radio News thanking me for my assistance (I was a "tower of strength" apparently, "in a reporting operation which kept the RBC/SABC team in the vanguard of world news coverage." He hoped I would co-operate with them at other times, and sent a nice fat cheque.)

Next day the papers were full of pictures of the rescue, almost filling the front pages of our national newspapers. Inches away from the passport photographs of the Canadian girls which were reproduced, was a report of an instruction made by Dr Kurt Waldheim, then Secretary-General on the UN Economic and Social Council, to "mobilise with immediate effect all forms of financial, technical and material assistance to Zambia" following the closure of the border with Rhodesia. The report went on: "Dr Waldheim's representative in charge of the aid programme, Sir Robert Jackson, newly returned from Lusaka, told council yesterday that the determination of the Zambian Government and people to help themselves was 'very, very impressive'."

We in Rhodesia felt just a little bit bitter about this.

Later Dr Kaunda, President of Zambia, burst into tears when confronted by Marjan's father at the terrible tragedy of the girls' deaths. No doubt Sir Robert Jackson would have found this very, very impressive too.

Christine's body was flown back to Ontario, where her father was a Presbyterian minister. Marjan's father was a retired schoolmaster. From good revolutionary stock these two lasses - Zambia would have been hard pressed to have found two more patently harmless people to murder in their fight for freedom than these two girls.

CID investigators with the rescue team found evidence of forty-eight shots in the rocks near the murders. The search went on by spotter plane and on foot for Marjan or her body.

Some days later Zambia admitted the murders. They said one lone sentry shot "because they appeared to be on their way to attack a vital Zambian power station". The three had "started swimming across the Zambezi from Rhodesia and were in Zambian waters when they were shot". The sentry was "defending the power station". They did not add "from girls in shorts and suntops".

(These rapids through the gorges are popular nowadays for whitewater rafting. People are regularly thrown from the inflatable rafts - Paula was ejected from the boat when she went. It is all part of the fun, they say. Most are rescued.)

Rhodesia needed sympathy but got little, although in Britain the Telegraph laid it out clearly: "Zambia is responsible for appalling cold-blooded murder...whichever way you look at it. The Zambian Government's tardy explanation is weak and does not fit the facts. It also leaves it clear that the Zambian troops either are given far too bloodthirsty orders or they themselves act irresponsibly.

"The only argument to which Zambia and her supporters can fall back is the familiar, although dangerous and utterly invalid one, that tyranny in Rhodesia is so monstrous that any violations of international law by her neighbours, however murderous, is justified. But this is the very opposite of the standards that are accepted elsewhere."

And the Guardian deplored the lack of international interest: "But, except in Canada, the incident is now regarded as over and done with. This is a disgrace."

A day or so after the shooting, Martin was walking beside the falls with a party of American tourists when they heard more brief bursts of automatic firing coming from the near the bridge. They had reached what was called "danger point", because of its geographical position extending on to a rocky point over the chasm. They were not more than two hundred metres from Zambia, not far from the armed Zambian soldiers on the bridge.

Martin swears to this day they were firing at him. He used to wear a big straw hat that everyone at Vic Falls knew him by. He reckons he went near to, or on to, the bridge so often the Zambians knew he would be with tourists, and decided this was a good way to pick tourists out - and off.

Zambia dismissed the latest shots as "a despicable lie". They went on to attack Rhodesia in words that were now sounding like an old record: "The existence of the rebel regime is sustained by a compound of arrogant deceit and reckless disregard for human life."

We hardly recognised ourselves, and hardly agreed with Robert Burns when he said:

"O wad some Pow'r the giftie gie us
To see oursels as others see us!"

TWELVE

A week after the shooting, Marjan's parents arrived in Rhodesia from Canada, their trip paid for by an unnamed South African. They said they were convinced their daughter was still alive.

The Drijbers were unassuming, pleasant and "good" people. Because they were in the news, some accused them of seeking it. But this was not true. They were solely anxious to know about their daughter's fate, and then when they became resigned to her death, they wanted not vengeance or recompense, but for the truth to be made known to the world.

When Oscar Drijber was invited to go and see Dr Kaunda in Lusaka, he refused to fly there, or travel via Kazangula, through Botswana; so for the first time in five months someone was allowed to enter Zambia directly from Rhodesia across the Victoria Falls bridge.

There were six of us on the bridge. I think the Press of the world was late because apart from Mr and Mrs Drijber and two plain-clothes policemen, there was only Dave, the local photographer who did reports for American magazines, and me. It was half-past-seven in the morning and the cool air rose from the gorge beneath us. It was very pretty. Mrs Drijber remarked to me how beautiful the falls looked. I would have thought she would hate the falls and these gorges for their terrible associations.

I asked her why she was not going with her husband to see Dr Kaunda.

"We want to make sure that one of us is here to carry on our plans," she said quietly. "In case something should happen to Oscar."

Her voice was almost inaudible above the sound of the falls.

I asked her if she had found much fresh evidence.

"Enough," she said

We waited in the middle of the bridge by the yellow and white lines. There was no one else in sight. That bridge scares me at the best of times. After five minutes two paramilitary policemen armed with the customary automatic rifles strolled across from the Zambian side of the line.

"Good morning, how are things in Rhodesia?" one of them asked in English. They were polite. We were polite. They had the guns. They said they did not know there was anyone due to cross that morning. I think they were telling the truth. There was little communication between departments.

We waited. We shuffled. The photographer, Dave, took pictures and one of the Zambian policemen got a little irritated and asked him not to do it. He put his camera away for a few minutes. No one crossed the no-man's land between the yellow and white lines, a few metres apart.

A small party of baboons offered us some slight diversion as they walked hand-over-hand along the guardrails of the railway line. They decided we were harmless and hopped around making a great deal of noise on the trucks of the train, which was waiting to be taken over.

The Zambian paramilitary policemen were scruffy, as they slouched with their hands in their pockets, but they were nothing compared with the ordinary policeman who next approached. He was dressed in an almost ankle-length black gabardine raincoat, which he obviously made a habit of sleeping in at night. He had no laces in his boots and his hat was battered and dirty.

He didn't know anything about the crossing either.

I began to look around for a quick avenue of escape if necessary. I asked one of our plain-clothes policemen how long he thought it would take to vault over the rails and beneath the trucks. He seemed to think we'd be surprisingly fast. I hadn't vaulted over anything for twenty-five years, and then I'd broken my arm doing it.

Our policemen were talking about one of them going back to the Falls village to phone Livingstone. (It is a strange twist that all through the troubles we could phone Livingstone and the Zambian border post from Victoria Falls, speak to the chief immigration officer, what you would, as long as we knew the number.)

If they had concealed pistols I hoped he wouldn't go, making us one defender less. The Drijbers showed no impatience.

At exactly eight o'clock a car drew up at the gate on the Zambian side of the bridge. Two Africans in smart, dark, civilian suits got out and walked across the bridge towards us. They spoke sharply in vernacular to the policemen, who retreated a step or two.

One of them shook hands with Oscar Drijber and said he was from "State House" in Lusaka.

"He is quite safe with us," he assured us politely, and with a pleasant smile.

Mr Drijber kissed his wife and gave her a reassuring hug, then turned away from us across the bridge to Zambia, a brave man. He said he expected to come back the next day.

We walked back over the bridge to where the Rhodesian newspapermen and some others representing various agencies were standing, their telescopic lenses trained on the bridge. I couldn't understand why they hadn't gone on the bridge, even though they had arrived late. I supposed they didn't need to be there at the event: they'd seen so many similar occasions, they'd pretty-well got the story made up the night before. Unless the Zambians had shot us all, and then they would have had a better story and have it all on film. Could they have been scared?

I drove back to the Falls Hotel to see Martin. As I got into the foyer my knees began to shake and my teeth were chattering. It must have been the cold atmosphere of the big entrance hall.

Oscar Drijber returned over the bridge two days later. I don't know how many times I'd driven down to the bridge and up to the police station (so they almost thought I lived there), and then I missed his return

I missed a scoop, but left a troubled man in peace.

By this time, many of us at the Falls were feeling pretty low and upset. I had an easy job, working morning or afternoon-evening shifts, so I had part of most days off for my news investigations, and my boss would stand in for me if I was really in a fix, as long as I told him the news first, he said, but I didn't like to abandon my family entirely. Paula and Martin appeared to be living on snacks and cokes by the hotel swimming pools, though I could see it was nice for Martin with all the girls in bikinis there.

By this time I was doing reports for the Bulawayo and Salisbury national newspapers, though I wasn't supposed to be working for both as they appeared to be bitterly opposed. I was running with the hares and the hounds and exhausting myself.

When life appeared to settle down, one of them would have me haring or hounding down on some (may I introduce yet another hunted creature?) wild goose chase.

When I suggested they already had their Iana reporter there they would retort sharply: "We want our own version. They sometimes keep the best bits to themselves, and we want to be first." Best bits of what, first with what? Were there two-toed African tribes here too?

I began to think they weren't paying this penny-a-liner too much either, for all the hours I spent chasing rainbows, though I've always liked rainbows, as well as hares and hounds and wild geese.

Yes, and I thought I was going crazy.

In June, when things had quietened down a bit, Oscar Drijber returned to the Falls and followed the path his daughter and her friends had taken down the gorges. Walking around the hot, life-denuded gorges seemed to be all anyone could do now, but they fairly kept their secrets and remained the same, except for the bullet holes. He saw the torrent where no one could enter and survive, unless they were equipped for shooting rapids, and even then they could float only when and where the rapids let them. When he came back he said he was more sorry for Zambia than before.

His idea was to present all his evidence to the Canadian Government, the UN and the International Court of Justice, and anyone else who would listen. At the time he rejected Zambia's offer of compensation. "All the money in the world wouldn't pay for her. All the compensation I expect and demand is the truth and justice." I wondered where in the world he'd find that. Certainly not in Africa.

147

A year later he was pressured by the Canadian Government to accept fifty thousand Canadian dollars from the Zambian Government as compensation, not for the loss of his daughter, but for expenses incurred on his visits to Rhodesia and Zambia. Mr Trudeau's government told him that to refuse would be "tantamount to an insult by the Canadian people to the Zambian Government". Zambia was receiving the equivalent of over sixty-two million Rhodesian dollars in aid from Canada at the time. One insult more or less should have made little difference.

But Oscar Drijber refused to touch any of the money or any interest from it for his own benefit. He said all his expenses had been paid for by the Rhodesian Government and outside donations. He said he intended to use the gift for purposes he knew his daughter would have approved, but he refused to specify these.

On the anniversary of his daughter's death, the Drijbers brought their two sons with them to Rhodesia. A small stone plaque was laid in a garden at the Falls: "The Lord is my helper, I will not be afraid; what can man do to me?"

Man, on the other hand was doing a lot to Rhodesia and the Victoria Falls. The tourists were staying away.

"Tourists, don't be scared: PM", said the headlines.

But who could blame them? Even the waterfalls were letting us down, and were running drier than ever before in living memory, according to many old residents. We pointed out to tourists how dramatic the bare basalt cliffs looked, but the few Americans that were around told us with some forthrightness they had not come eight thousand miles to see a lot of bare black rocks. The couriers were really fed up with the daily hot walk through the parched Rain Forest with thirty disgruntled and sweating tourists in tow.

In 1974 South Africa's white, ruling party, the Nats, were sitting safely, and perhaps a little smugly, behind the Limpopo, with buffer states Rhodesia and Portuguese-governed Angola and Mozambique between them and black Africa. It is an unenviable position, being a buffer state, even though we were being actively assisted by South Africa, who quite openly admitted they preferred to keep their front line on the Zambezi rather than the Limpopo.

In March 1974, the war was brought home to South Africans when five South African policemen returning from patrol were shot by terrorists beside the Zambezi River.

The shooting coincided, perhaps deliberately, with the opening of a swimming pool at the Falls SA Police camp by the South African Minister of Police, Dr Helgaard Muller. The pool had been donated by the Vic Falls residents as a thank-you gesture for helping defend us.

The attack was made at a fishing camp right near the small island of Kandahar, in the middle of the river, where our launches disembarked passengers for tea twice a day.

It was inhabited permanently only by monkeys, and temporarily by waterbuck, hippo and elephant, that swam across from the Zambian side, or waded across the rapids from the Falls Game Reserve in the dry season.

No one would admit how close the fishing camp was to the island. We all told deliberate lies about where the shooting had taken place. The boats stopped operating for one afternoon and evening only (engine trouble, we said), and then continued to ply their way up to the island next morning.

"Oh, no, it happened much further up the river, right on the Botswana border."

Meanwhile we stood on Kandahar and looked out over the fishing camp (bearing the same name, which the smarter visitors picked out), where the South African policemen had been relaxing after their hot patrol to the west and south. Reaching the fishing camp, they decided that all was safe - a reasonable supposition, but I suppose unforgivable for policemen on the border - took off their clothes, washed in the river, swam a little, and left no-one on guard. The terrorists were waiting for them, marched them into the bush and shot them.

The Sunday papers arrived at the hotel full of the screaming horror headlines and a large map right across the top of the front page with a fat arrow pointing to the fishing camp next to the falls and village. Many visitors were waiting in the foyer ready to go on their tours of the falls and to board the bus for the launch cruises, so Martin deftly took the papers off the van and stuck them away out of sight in a back room. I think you could call this suppression of the news.

It shows how desperate we were to keep everything appearing normal.

The South African papers had a ball, with reports of road blocks all around the area, with tourist cars being searched, even turned back, massive "seek and destroy" operations near tourist areas, and Zambian troop movements to the borders. Little of it was true but we saw very few South African cars now.

That beautiful stretch of river in the game reserve with its sandy bays, rapids and picnic spots beneath the high vine-covered trees became even more "closed to the public" than it had been for the previous fifteen months. We despaired of it ever being opened again.

Nevertheless, everyone in the Rhodesian travel industry went up in flames when the editor of a South African travel magazine urged the Association of SA Travel Agents not to hold their conference at the Falls as planned, in case the Zambians started taking pot-shots at them as they sat on the Falls Hotel terrace in their coffee breaks and sundowners.

"Et tu, Brute!" we cried in disbelief to these, our sometime friends, who were entrusted with the task of selling our attractions to the South African traveller.

"Suicidal" was the word the magazine used, and we looked at ourselves and thought of the boats sailing three times a day up to Kandahar, and passing less than a hundred metres from the Zambian bank. But we saw nothing to dismay our passengers, as long as we hid the newspapers.

Looking back at this now in 2005, and the present troubles in Zimbabwe, we can read reports of ex-Rhodesians again demonstrating their amazing skill at seeing only what they want to see and waiting, forever waiting, sure only of one thing that kept the farmers going from one drought year to the next and kept Rhodesia running through many years of sanctions; then with a black government having their farms taken away from them – sure that "next year will be better".

THIRTEEN

People who have taken to living at the falls throughout the ages have really not been good at war. The Tongas who lived in the valley in the 1500-1700s were a peace-loving people and allowed themselves to be overrun and raided by successions of Makololo, Lozi and Nbebele conquerors. Then came the Leya tribe, which means, "to keep out of troubles", and they mixed successfully with the Tongas.

The Boer War and the Matabele rebellions of the late 1900s did not reach their way through desert and swamp to the falls area. And Victoria Falls' contribution to modern world wars was the sighting of a "mysterious aeroplane" in 1915. According to the newspaper of the time, the locals conjectured if this meant German troops would be marched that way, though "no force of any magnitude could be moved across the desert country between Grootfontein and the terminus of the German SW Railway to the Zambezi without having transport." It was five hundred miles and would take six weeks "therefore ample warning will be received, and troops would be carried over the Union Railways and massed against invading forces in a few days." (It is a long time since the days of German West Africa, and most of us have forgotten about it or never knew.)

The falls area of today is always being overrun by people of many nations (called tourists), but no-one yet has tried to capture it, although many Rhodesians began to wonder, when the Russian President Podgorny was taken to look out over the gorges in March 1977 and came out with the enigmatic pronouncement: "Ah!"

He also said the Zambezi river was the dividing line between freedom and slavery. We didn't argue - he wasn't there for long. But which side had which?

As we were so overrun by reasonably friendly foreigners and far away from the rest of the world, it was mooted at times that the area should be made an international area as far as trade was concerned. This would have been marvellous for us Falls residents, with duty-free liquor - but no-one else in Rhodesia and the world could be made to enthuse. Just dog-in-the-manger attitude, or sour grapes, which was it?

It was among the scares and the evil portents that tourism was being killed off by the threat of terrorism that we set up our own tour agency at the Falls. We weren't going to run our own tours initially (transport was unobtainable anyway), and Martin carried on working for the touring company and at the African Dancing evening.

It was a little shop that the touring company had found uneconomical to run; they in turn had obtained it from a small firm that had gone broke. We called the agency the Rain Forest and had real water streaming down the window to represent the falls, and a miniature Rain Forest of palm trees, creepers, ferns, lichen-covered branches and even a tiny stuffed crocodile. The insects and toads loved it and volunteered to join in the atmosphere, and I had a free-ranging cricket that sang to me when things were quiet.

It looked pretty good, and people naturally stopped often to stare at the water on the window, even if they didn't come in to buy a tour.

We had bought a garden fountain pump in Durban while on holiday - such luxuries were unobtainable in Rhodesia in 1970. I left Peter's Motel, as after a year or so working anywhere I would grow restless. (Women of my age had no chance of promotion and people changed their jobs regularly then.)

I wasn't as happy as I should have been in our little shop. I was plainly trying to do too much and, well, blame my age. Our shop didn't close at the weekends, and as it wasn't yet on its feet, we weren't justified in employing help while I had a break. For a few days every month I had a contract to take round small groups of people on an exclusive personalised touring basis. Sometimes more than one group would arrive at the same time, and I was kept running for a week. Martin stood in for me at the shop and wangled his days off to achieve this, or we'd ask one of the couriers.

I was still doing the RBC correspondent bit, and stringing for the national newspapers that continued to be extremely demanding, but for little pay.

Also I had just finished writing the Falls and Wankie district chapter for a guide book brought out by the Tourist Board and the AA, and as always, they had required this in a hurry; and every week someone would suggest I write an article for some publication or even for the Falls Publicity Association advertising programme. I knew nothing about advertising, but it cost them nothing as I was on the committee. I would even do odd tours of the falls or up the river for the touring company when Martin was really stuck for someone.

The heat was "something else" (Rhodesian for unbearable), and by the time I got home I was utterly finished. But every evening I would go down to the river with our dog, Hayley, and try and unwind. I remember once I suggested to an American at a loose end: "Go for a walk by the river. It restores your soul." He said he hadn't a soul to restore, which rather left nothing else to say.

Martin seemed to survive better than I did, though he was working far longer hours, and he had given up smoking. I don't know how he managed it. We should have called "Halt!" but it was all so interesting it was difficult to know where to start giving up. This went on for a year, and I think on the whole I got quite good at concealing my inner strange feelings. The strained look, if only people knew, was only there because of my trying to exert self-control over my natural desires to fly up to the ceiling, hammer my painful head on the door jamb, sit on the floor and moan, scream back at them like a fiend or collapse in a heap, while still attempting to smile and give good advice and sales talk. I'm sure that many of you, if you have read this far, will know what I mean. I seemed to be past bursting into tears. I wondered if a physical illness wouldn't be preferable to the way I felt right then.

At this time in the 1970s many doctors gave out tranquillisers as if they were sweets. I was given several sorts at different times and they all made me feel even worse.

We were given the chance of moving to the Zimbabwe Ruins branch near Fort Victoria (now called Masvingo). It was a quiet branch of the touring company, 450 miles away, and we were both relieved at the prospect. It would be much cooler, among other advantages. Martin would be his own boss - he would be manager with two African drivers. The idea was to try and build up the area as a tourist attraction. It was also nearer to the rest of Rhodesia and to our daughters.

Just before he was offered the transfer, Martin had got himself a job as manager of the new Wimpy Bar at the Falls - a really suitable occupation for me, the vegetarian, to help him at. Paula was disgusted. She doubted the status of the job, though we could see nothing wrong with that part of it. Sometimes, for long after, Martin told people how he should not have turned down the job in favour of going to the Zimbabwe Ruins. If he'd taken it he would be rich now, he says. And both of us nervous wrecks, I says, and certainly not together.

When Martin had decided to give up smoking the year before, it had been hell. He had been trying for years, but this time the health warnings would not be ignored.

So one day he said: "I'm not going to smoke any more," and didn't.

He sucked sweets, ate chocolate and biscuits, and large meals, and at last put on weight for the first time in his life. He also wanted to gnaw the walls and chew the carpets, and generally behaved as they say is cold turkey. I've never smoked, so I could only imagine the torment he felt. For sure, it has to be your own idea. According to Martin you also have to wait for the day when you start feeling so grim with each cigarette, that you see you're signing your own death warrant. The only part I could play was to resist saying: "Oh, go on, have a cigarette," at the height of the strange withdrawal symptoms.

In those days there were no pills or nicotine replacement therapies to help the poor sufferer, or, at least, none that we knew of.

While I was working at Peter's Motel I had been over to England, mainly to see my mother. I went for the month of October and I must admit by the time I left England I was feeling the cold badly. I seemed to have enjoyed this visit to England less than I had any other time on holiday in England, even though my close relatives went out of their way to make me feel welcome, and they turned down their television sets, and even turned them off, to talk to me. But I am a poor letter-writer and I had lost touch with nearly all my old friends. Everyone was getting old.

Here in the midst of such an interesting, restless world, my former associates were entangled in their own small webs. They were really not at all interested in my way of life. With few exceptions, they had no conception of what was happening in Africa, or, indeed, where Rhodesia was.

In Rhodesia we were too fully, if not accurately, informed about Britain, from government reports, newspapers, broadcasts and individuals who loved to dwell on Britain's troubles with strikes, the Irish problem, devaluation and hooliganism. Whenever I'd visited England I'd always found it a tremendous place, even after more than twenty years' absence in Africa. I was always overwhelmed by all the things there were to DO in England and places to visit and the nearness of towns.

There were endless societies, many of which I would have liked to take part if I lived there (or so I thought): the writers' club, Vegetarian Society, anti-vivisectionist league, Beauty without Cruelty Society, the RSPCA, the ramblers' association, the ancient monuments association, the history club, the local dramatic society. I felt I would not have time to attend all the evening classes I would like, to take literature and language courses I had in mind, and the degrees and diplomas I would have stringing after my name. But people sat at home and grumbled.

Out there were the museums and art galleries and beautiful old churches and halls, shows and theatres and plays and exhibitions, and the forests and woods and moors, and the sea, all kinds of sea, breaking on windstrewn rocks, sliding along the yellow sands. And there's the north and the south, and the west and the east of it, and all so different, so filled with complex people and villages and interesting activities, and accessible.

In Rhodesia to go a journey was to get there - the journey and the passing through were tedious.

But if you were a woman travelling alone at that time (as I was), enjoying any of these things, you became so self-conscious, the enjoyment was torn away. I always used to think that one of the advantages of getting older would be that men allowed you to go places by yourself. Why wouldn't they? I suppose that is one thing that women have achieved for the twenty-first century - to be allowed to go it alone. At least the women of some nations have.

On the way home to Rhodesia from that last October visit we were fogbound at Heathrow. We sat in the jumbo for a long time, hopefully. We were off-loaded with our hand luggage. We ground our way in buses through yellow and unmoving fog. The Rhodesians on the bus began to see why they stuck it out in Rhodesia. We drove in gasping double-decker buses, and if the driver could see anything he must have been a Martian.

I was amazed at the speed and efficiency those thousands of people were handled and given food and rooms. Twenty planes were grounded, and a good proportion of these were jumbos. I was sorry for the young parents with babies trying to manage with hand luggage. Some people had been delayed for twenty-four hours already on troubled Middle East and Greek routes. It is odd that such predicaments, which we would talk about to friends and wonder at then, are now accepted if not acceptable as normal travel, and it really isn't so long ago.

Next morning we were fast becoming a crowd of grubbily attired but well-acquainted friends. We all enjoyed the same queues together, and were almost swapping addresses and invitations. Many of the men were unshaven. We watched the mist-enshrouded buildings on the other side of the runway disappearing in the grey swells of fog, and we sighed.

But at 10.30am, with cheers from three hundred, we set off, to land a few hours later on Ilho do Sal, in the Atlantic. Planes to Rhodesia were not allowed to fly over many African territories, so here we were, refuelling on the excruciatingly ugly Isle of Salt.

We arrived at Salisbury at 3.30 in the morning, seventeen hours late, and were awaited by a group of weary but relieved and noble relatives and friends (Martin among them), and by grumpy immigration and customs officials who had been called back on duty. Planes did not normally land in Salisbury at such hours of the night. Then off to the Falls in a brave little Viscount; a small fleet of them kept flying all the fifteen years of Rhodesia's sanctions and isolation from the world.

One holiday Martin and I did manage to take together while we were working at the Falls was on a Union Castle ship from Durban to East London, Port Elizabeth and Cape Town, then after a few days back again on another ship to Durban. More than anything we enjoyed the English idea of service. Many South Africans could not stand the English stewards, but after the African servility of that time, we found it a very refreshing attitude they adopted. We generally cleaned our own cabin and made our own beds and even replaced our own light bulb, and we got our own drinks at the bar, but this is the way we preferred things.

The waitress at our table told us all about her troublesome love life, but she dished us up smartly with some really great food at the same time. English-flavoured food, English draught beer - it was as good as a trip to dear old blighty itself.

Table Mountain showed off its tablecloth to us magnificently while we were there, and the cable car was horrifying and an experience not to be forgotten by a coward like me, and never to be repeated if I can help it.

Paula was cross we did not take her with us on this holiday. She was at an age when nothing "old" pleased her at all. We'd told her a little unkindly that if she came with us we wouldn't enjoy the trip, and neither would she. So we sent her off to the Polytechnic in Bulawayo to learn the wonders of shorthand, typing, book-keeping and French. It was the first holiday we had spent together without the children since our short honeymoon at Rhodes Hotel in Inyanga. We were surprised how well we got on. If we didn't feel like it we didn't have to sit on the beach for hours, and if we wanted to "waste" our time looking round the shops (as we hadn't seen any big shops for a long time), then who cared? Who cared if we dawdled for hours over coffee by the beach front, or a beer on a lively hotel verandah. We knew we were acting middle-aged and we didn't care.

Paula had earlier applied to Air Rhodesia for a job in reservations, which Martin felt would be a good foundation for becoming a travel agent, her main interest then. She was told there were no vacancies, but she would be contacted. She hadn't much faith in this, but she was proved wrong. In March she heaved a great sigh of relief, lost her shorthand, book-keeping and French books, picked up her grandfather's old typewriter and departed to Salisbury and Air Rhodesia.

When it seemed certain we were leaving the Falls for the south of the country, Martin booked himself on a ten-day trip into the Okovanga Swamps in Botswana. This isolated region had always fascinated him ever since he had discovered it on school atlases: tufty bits of grass scattered across the middle of Africa, and rivers meandering into pans and depressions with no outlet to the sea. There were probably crocodiles and hippos drawn in the spaces, too, as on such beautiful old maps.

At the time I hadn't the energy to make the trip. There were six men in the party and two driver-guides, travelling in two Land Rovers. They got lost several times and camped in some pretty bleak spots with the regular campsites a foot deep in good African dust. They saw herds of animals that probably spoilt them for the rest of their game-viewing lives. And they got stuck in sand in the middle of the main street of Maun, a town glorying in large letters on the map. They spent the last two days sitting by the side of the swimming pool of the "touristy" hotel on the border of Rhodesia, washing the dust out of their throats and the cracks in their skin. Even then I have never seen such filthy people in my life as the apparitions that returned - and hungry.

They had done all the things Martin had always wanted to do, including travelling the swamps in a flat-bottomed boat and camping out in a remote mosquito-infested island.

It was all boys' adventure-story stuff come true.

FOURTEEN

This time our move was orderly. We had a proper furniture van, and the car was reasonably empty but for suitcases - and Vicky.

Vicky was the latest in our line of Alsatian bitches. Fuji had died of old age, Pixie (the cat) of enteritis, and Hayley of a tick-borne fever. We so hated the heartbreak of losing them that we had decided not to have another animal, and certainly not another big dog. After a month without a dog, I had taken the last Alsatian puppy of the litter at Peter's Motel, after having studiously avoided even going to look at them. Vicky was eighteen months old when we moved. She was named after the falls.

It was afternoon before we managed to get off, so we stopped overnight at a small hotel near the Wankie Game Reserve. We swept past the hill where the car had broken down on the move up to the falls while towing the overloaded caravan. I suppose this easier way was how normal people moved.

Our African maid, Emily, who came in the mornings to clean and wash - she was the nicest woman you could hope to meet - thought Christmas had come. She suffered from high blood pressure and would sometimes turn up to work in the morning with her ankles and legs abominably swollen. Her husband knocked her around and would often steal her money so she could not afford to buy her pills. In the end he left her, so she sent her children off to her mother in the tribal trust lands, found herself a boyfriend and was much happier than I had ever known her, taking her pills and attending the clinic regularly for check-ups.

I like to think she retired from work and went on a long holiday to her mother and children on the proceeds of our move.

Before Emily, I had been gifted with two women fast on each other who, my neighbour told me, were prostitutes in the township. They were pleasant and didn't steal. They washed and ironed reasonably, but didn't like cleaning up. This was well before Aids became commonplace in Africa.

It was always so hot at Vic Falls that the breaks between servants were a trial. I tried everything, even getting up at 5.30am, which went completely against my nature. Martin was better at housework than I was (if asked he'd say he was better at anything than I was), and had the art of making the place appear clean, even if the corners gathered spiders. (I'm pleased to relate that living servantless in Britain now, he's aware of corners, and who cares anyway – it's generally too dark to see.)

On Rhodesian farms in those days, some people, and not necessarily the richest, went in for a retinue of servants in the house and garden, rather like, I imagine, the old days of the Indian frontier. Each servant had a lesser servant to assist, a *piccanin* as he was generally called in Rhodesia. The word has been lost now, with political correctness, but only means "small" or "a child". Families who could hardly afford to feed their own children would have an ill-clothed, largely unwashed young African boy to run after their every whim: "Sweep up, Yottam, clean up the baby's sick, Yottam, find the piccanin boss (the son of the house), iron the boss's shirt, find the piccanin madam's hat (the daughter of the house), take the baby for a walk in the pushchair, give the dogs their *skoff* (food), water lo flowers *lapa side.*"

Lapa side means over there, over here, the other side of the room, the other side of the garden, the farm, the world. It was part of *Chilapalapa* or (dare the word be uttered these days?) Kitchen Kaffir that everyone spoke in the early days of Central Africa, and still do if truth were known, though perhaps with a new name. True, it can cause a confusion of meaning when giving an order: *"Aikona faka lapa, faka lapa."* Quite plainly it means "Don't put it here, put it there." Or, on the other hand: "Don't put it there, put it here." It is the accompanying gesture that makes the difference. Confused? .

A true African language was on the whole of little use to the European settler - if he moved to a different region he encountered a different language or dialect, so he rarely bothered to learn any thoroughly. Kitchen Kaffir served very well. It was a combination

162

of basic Bantu, English and Afrikaans, with a vocabulary of only a few hundred words and a grammar so simple an uneducated tribesman or a small child could grasp it quickly. Every noun was preceded by *lo*, which meant this, that, a, the, and gave a certain lilt to the conversation. If you said *lo* you could follow it by any made-up, bastardised noun, or leave the noun out altogether as understood. *Yena lo*, that's it, you've got it!

There were no refinements: a fine day was *mushe sterik*, a good tobacco plant *mushe sterik*, a well child was *mushe sterik*, or everything was a *shupa maningi*, a headache, a barn of tobacco that wouldn't get its temperature up, a late bus, a tractor that wouldn't start, an employer who expected too much of his workers.

In South Africa now there are eleven official languages. *Shupa maningi!*

The trouble with Rhodesian gardens is that they need watering every day for a major part of the year. And when it rains the weeds grow so thick and fast that keeping the grass from taking over the house is even more trouble than the watering. Then on the farm there was the wood to chop for the "Rhodesian boiler", that miracle invention for heating bath water for houses in the bush. It was simply a 44-gallon drum set on its side over a boiler fire near the back of the bathroom or kitchen, with pipes leading directly to the hot taps. Stoking this was the gardener's cherished task because he could roast *mealies* (maize cobs) and sweet potatoes and cook hard mealie meal biscuits *(potehai)* on it, and stand around it on cold or wet mornings.

So water was invariably boiling hot, yellow, frothy and mixed with deposits from the inside of the drum. It was no good trying to change it - the water was heated in the method that suited the gardener's cooking arrangements, otherwise the fire was allowed to go out and cold baths for all. The rubbish was burnt there, but the waste of fuel and trees cut down was enough to make an ecologist or economist cry.

On farms and in town a male servant was the norm. In town he lived in a tiny house out at the back of the property and he would linger around the house all day and evening till the supper dishes were washed and put away. These servants were not allowed to have their family living with them, and were lucky if they saw their wives and children on Sunday. With many, their families still lived in the tribal lands with grand-parents, and sometimes many days' journey away, and they would sometimes see them only on their annual leaves, or in times of family bereavement, when they would go away for a week to attend a funeral of a brother or uncle. They had large extended families and "brothers" didn't always have the close relationship we were led to believe.

When we went to visit Martin's parents after the farm had been leased, we were amazed at the feudal set-up of their household. They still had a retinue of eight servants, most of them retired farm labourers with nowhere else to go.

There were two servants in the house, three or four in the garden and the rest odd-job men or drivers. By the house was a vegetable garden large enough to support a big hotel, and all for two elderly people who ate few vegetables anyway. For myself I can never relax and enjoy being at home while I have a servant around. The thought of eight makes me want to hide away in a dark corner.

When we arrived at Zimbabwe Ruins our house wasn't finished, so I led the life of a lady, living in the hotel for a month, while we egged on the slowest builders on earth to build enough of our house to make it habitable. (When we moved to Kintyre in Scotland twenty-five years later, we found their equals in speed.)

After the years of over-activity at the Falls, I was bored stiff at Zimbabwe. I sewed curtains and read desultorily, but I was too unsettled to write. My reference books were packed away so I couldn't even rustle up an article or two, and not one fiction story could I dream up. I hung around the place all day, feeling useless. I was a nuisance to Martin.

It was not a good introduction to a new home, or to my newfound freedom from the small rat race I had devised for myself at the Falls. I imagine I felt like a man feels when he first retires from his job, and I'm sorry for him. I saw my Dad experience the same. I did not have enough sympathy for him at the time.

The Zimbabwe Ruins are the largest man-made constructions in Africa south of the Sahara. Today they are a maze of walls, some finely built and in good repair, and others stretching down the Zimbabwe valley and up the hill, their granite blocks crumbling apart, or sometimes rebuilt by later tribes.

Zimbabwe is generally accepted to mean "great houses of stone", though some translate it as "the graves of the chiefs". The Africans of today regard it as their ancestral heritage, and the country of Rhodesia became Zimbabwe in 1980, after independence from Britain with an elected black government.

The main temple lies in a shallow valley overlooked by the hill ruin that is known as the Acropolis. Zimbabwe was a great centre for gold trading and the Arab trade route ran south-eastwards to Sofala on the Indian Ocean. Gold was traded for porcelain beads and ornaments which came by way of Arab dhows from India, China, the Middle East and Egypt, until Zimbabwe became the richest town in southern Africa, with a population of 10,000. It reached its peak in the fifteenth century when the finest walls were built.

Near one end of the temple is a solid conical tower twelve metres high. No-one can explain satisfactorily what purpose it served there.

Zimbabwe lies in a wet valley, and at any time of the year can be enveloped in a soft mist or plain cold, driving drizzle. In former centuries it was even wetter, and was a favourite spot for rainmaking ceremonies, particularly on the Acropolis.

All the walls are built of large carefully selected granite blocks, some of which were so large it is difficult to see how they were carried there. Particularly for the later walls, when the nearby stone outcrops had run short of exfoliated material, the stones were brought several miles without mechanical means. Like the dry-stone walls of Scotland and northern England (including my native Derbyshire), the walls had no bonding, and it was perhaps this which has kept the walls standing fairly in tact through centuries of temperature and moisture changes and despite subsidence.

No stories have been passed down from father to son about the builders of Zimbabwe; these tribes disappeared without trace in the sixteenth century.

When Karl Mauch, the German-American explorer, who first publicised the existence of the ruins to the outside world, asked a Makaranga tribesman he met there in 1871 about the builders, he was told: "They were built when the stones were soft, or they would not have been made so square."

"When the stones were soft" is a popular way with many Africans for expressing a very long time ago.

There are innumerable stories about who built Zimbabwe. Very few people thought primitive Africans of any known tribe at that time had the wit or will to build so much and so well. Even those who feel it must have been done by tribesmen, either in slavery or religiously inspired, say it was directed by outsiders from Asia. In 1973 a beautifully illustrated book ("Great Zimbabwe" by Peter Garlake) was published, which expounded the theory that Arabs, using the trade winds and monsoons, were responsible, not only for the richness through trading, but for the building of Zimbabwe. Without doubt the Arabs were connected with trade in gold, ivory and slaves here, but historians say the Chinese pottery and Indian goods found buried in the ruins were only trade goods, not evidence of Arab settlement.

An official tourist board poster inviting people to come to Zimbabwe Ruins in the 1930s illustrated a ghostly Queen of Sheba fanned by a ghostly palm leaf receiving an offering of gold from a black servant or slave among the fallen walls. It is certainly romantic to think of this as the lost King Solomon's Mines, the lost empire of Prestor John, or southern Africa's link with the ancient Phoenicians. It was good for the tourist trade to encourage people to believe the ruins date back before Christ, and that they were likely to meet the Queen of Sheba wandering around the moonlit grey-stone passages.

Frederick Courteney Selous, the great hunter and explorer in

Africa at the end of the nineteenth century, dismissed them as "comparatively modern", the grave of a Mashona chief. On the other hand, Cecil Rhodes, after a brief visit, described them as an old Phoenician residence, and the district the Ophir of the Bible.

Such building in stone is completely alien to normal African styles, and much superior to any other stone building found in central Africa. They stood entirely alone at the time they were built, though others followed after Zimbabwe was abandoned.

Any historian or archaeologist at the end of the nineteenth century, and even into the 1970s, who dared voice the opinion that Zimbabwe was of African origin was promptly squashed by those in authority.

Mention the ruins to any group of people in Rhodesia and someone would start getting hot under the collar.

In 1969, questions were asked in the Rhodesian parliament about the Bantu theories being put forward by the employees of the Ancient Monuments' Commission. They warned their employees to be "absolutely impartial" when presenting theories. So, no matter how conclusively they backed their arguments with carbon dating and historical investigation of artefacts buried, they were not permitted to express their conclusions in Rhodesia. Official guidebooks brought out in 1976 made no suggestion at all about who built Zimbabwe.

But Africans in Rhodesia were in no doubt, and before fuel-rationing became too strict, many parties of African schoolchildren visited the ruins. They looked smart but rather out-of-place in their English-type school uniforms, with wool trousers or skirts, white shirts and ties, blazers and felt or straw hats. They were earnest and well behaved, each with notebook and pen. Such uniforms reflected an oddly colonial custom when worn by people searching for freedom.

The ruins are marked on Portuguese maps of the sixteenth century, and a Portuguese writer, Joao de Barros, told how Swahili traders had seen an inscription over one of the openings in the wall, which learned Moorish merchants could not read well enough to decipher it, or ascertain the language. This was the only reference to any writing or inscription at Zimbabwe, so if we discount this one account, we may assume whoever built the walls was illiterate.

And no ancient graves were found nearby.

We were hoping when Erich von Daniken, author of "The Chariot of the Gods" and books on visitations to Earth from space, came to Zimbabwe, he would evolve for us some new and exciting theory about who built it. But he was only interested in the shape of the temple and the placing of the conical towers, which seemed similar to the orbits of two stars (one of which is visible only once every fifty years), which are known to a remote African tribe in Central Africa.

We found this rather involved and not easily explained to visitors on a casual morning tour.

Why couldn't he, I wondered, have backed what was shown in the film made around his theories, that this valley was a landing-ground for space ships like those of Nazca in Peru, and the temple and the conical tower were landing indications? That would have been a real help to emblazoning the ruins. I was beginning to feel like Martin - as long as it was a good story, it didn't have to be the absolute truth.

Mr von Daniken gave Martin a miniature bottle of whisky, such as airline passengers are given free, to thank him for several days of his time, free accommodation at the hotel, free transport, many drinks and loan of books about Zimbabwe. We didn't bother to buy his next book.

When we arrived at Zimbabwe and found there was no simple guide book, Martin wrote one - a guide-yourself book containing the spiel he told visitors on his tours every day, with a diagram of where to walk, where to stop and what to look at there. He had it printed on the only available paper, newsprint, with a rough pasteboard cover. In spite of these utilities it sold very well, and at least offered some explanations what the ruins might be about, and how best to see them.

But the most fantastic and romantic explanation for Zimbabwe is found in a book "Psychic Episodes of Great Zimbabwe", which was written in the 1930s by H.Clarkson Fletcher, following a series of séances by Bulawayo spiritualists in the temple of Zimbabwe. At the time I thought it was one of the most unusual and affecting stories I had ever read - when I managed to cut my way through a great swirl of confusing mists.

The spirit that appeared was a Queen Ulali, who said she was the last of the superior race that had lived on the Acropolis and in the temple. The tribe were busy building, smelting gold and manufacturing ornaments, and worshipping their gods. She painted a vivid picture of the sufferings of the black tribes, who worked for them, enduring fevers, starvation and rampaging wild animals which growled and shrieked nightly at the stockades, their howls mixing with the groans and screams of suffering from the workers in the valley.

The women and young children of this elite tribe were kept prisoner on the Acropolis, except for occasional journeys down the hillside into the temple, when the priests ceremoniously raped women. She spoke of hidden tunnels and caves in the hillside. (These have never been discovered, as far as I know.)

When everything started to go wrong in the land, the women were sacrificed one by one on the altars until Queen Ulali was the only one left. She hid in a cave and when they came to fetch her there was a great landslide, and she is buried there, never to be found.

Another report of the evil of Zimbabwe is found in a book published in 1966 by a Zulu writer, V.C.Mutwa, "Indaba My Children". He reports that Zimbabwe means "Fort of Infamy", and was built on lust, greed, gold and the slave trade. After a terrible battle, thousands of elders stood in the ruins of Zimbabwe and promised "that such a thing as Zima-Mbje was never built again in their lands - that the infamies of this cruel place would be recounted in order to discourage future generations..." Lastly the grey-haired elders placed a curse on Zima-Mbje. "They cursed it to be desolate, lonely, lost to mankind until the end of time."

I have walked round Zimbabwe Ruins scores of times and I have never once felt any evil emanating from the old walls. On the contrary, they smell good, of herbs, wood-smoke and mustiness, and even a vague smell like incense. You rarely see a snake, but squirrels hop along the top of the temple walls, beautiful red-winged, purple-crested louries scream from the trees that grow inside the temple, and the velvet-eyed dassies sit among the great boulders of the Acropolis.

People on Martin's tours who claimed to possess extra-sensory powers said they "felt" things in the ruins. One woman in his group felt so ill she had to be taken, shaken and pale, back to the cafe near the ruins. She said she felt dreadful evil around her. (I am unwilling to discount her anguish. I felt the same in the Coliseum in Rome.)

If we had visitors staying with us, a favourite jaunt at full moon was to walk around the ruins looking for spooks (we waited till we had company because we didn't quite like going alone). We never saw the faintest wisp of a ghost. We heard baboons, who were as scared as we were and even more vociferous, and an odd jackal and owl, and scratchings and twitterings in the trees and rocks. Once we met an American woman tourist casually strolling by herself on the top of the Acropolis. She was a brave woman and surely had few fears of the next world, or this. Or perhaps she was the reincarnation of the Queen of Sheba, or Queen Ulali.

At the end of the nineteenth century, thanks to the Victorians' infinite skill in destroying history, anyone could buy a share in the Rhodesian Ancient Ruins Co. Ltd., and dig up any ruin that took their fancy, taking any treasures for himself. It sounds daringly exciting, but hardly in accordance with any ideas of preservation.

A highly qualified South African conservationist, van Riet, had made a survey in 1975 to advise on the preservation of the ruins. This was the man who had made the unpopular survey of the Rain Forest at Victoria Falls. At the Ruins he advised nothing modern should be allowed within sight of them. Once again nearly all his recommendations were very unpopular with local residents and anyone trying to carry on any tourism business. But as soon as they started to be implemented, the war hotted up and Rhodesia found herself with more urgent things to do with any available money than engage on a vast new programme of rebuilding the amenities of the reputed ancestral home of the Bantu people.

And then in 1976, there wasn't enough money even to cut the grass, let alone remove the rest camp and restaurant, or dig up the golf course, restore it to nature and build a new one as planned. So the jackals were allowed to roam free.

No-one ever went round the golf course without losing three or four balls in the termite holes, easily a metre deep in places, or buried in the grass on the fairways, where the grass was almost as high as the holes were deep during the rains.

At last we were able to move into our cottage.

It was very pretty - delightful with wood beams and a wall and fireplace of dark stone, and with real stone floors. It was sweet with new thatch and soon had bougainvilleas, if not roses, round the door. And the mountain mists swept over the Acropolis and the fresh winds swept up the valley. Sometimes they met and swirled before our front door.

In Rhodesia we called the cold mist *guti*. For eighteen months it seemed to us it rarely ceased to blow and drizzle, though it can't be true because I remember several fine days when we even went for a swim in the hotel pool.

The next year was a drought, and it was so hot we remembered Vic Falls and perversely wished for the *guti* again; it suited the old stone walls and mossy vegetation much better. Martin found, when it was dry and hot, his tourists just didn't like the Ruins. If they stood in their borrowed raincoats with rain dripping off the ends of their noses all morning, tramping the ancient stones with heads down, they were much more likely to say how they had enjoyed their morning than when they spent the morning scurrying from shade spot to shade, half listening to what Martin had to say, wondering when they'd have a chance to get a cool drink.

Martin tried to take all the tours himself (some people won't

171

delegate), which meant he climbed the 120-metre-high Acropolis most mornings and was quite fit. Even when he got tired of saying the same old things day after day, a few days off (only when there was no tour, naturally,) would resuscitate him and he'd be away again in true form.

Tourists would often say afterwards: "You must love the Ruins!" He always appeared to be enthralled by them. It was odd how he managed it because I know at heart he didn't like the Ruins at all. To him, more than to his most disinterested visitors, they were nothing but a pile of stones.

As the hills of Zimbabwe region got nearly twice as much rain as the flatter cattle-ranching lands of Fort Victoria, only twelve miles away, the change in vegetation as you drove out there was quite noticeable. Candelabra trees, a sort of euphorbia, stood out on the granite hillside among the grey rocks that were covered with red and orange lichens. Many hundred years before, the little Bushmen used to combine the milky sap of these same candelabras with pigments obtained from ores in the rocks and soil to make their wall paintings of stick-men, cattle and wild animals. These may still be found under overhanging rocks and caves.

The bush trees are covered with trailing grey-green veils of parasitic growth that looks like weed in a fast-flowing stream. The barks of the trees are matted with moss and grey and orange lichens and bear orchids in the crooks of their branches. When the sun comes out the growth shrivels and the region looks unremarkable.

The Makaranga have lived in the area since the eighteenth century. Many maintain they are the leading tribe of this part of Africa. Their traditional chiefs' name around Zimbabwe is Mugabe, and the bodies of two of their chiefs were found buried in caves on the Acropolis. A Mugabe was at Geneva in 1976 to lead a faction in the abortive political talks there. He was the one who shouted most about killing off all the white men. He was to become President Robert Mugabe.

The Makaranga tribe has been shut away in the misty valleys for so many years that they have difficulty understanding variations of their mother tongue, Shona. (But perhaps it is no worse than the Welshmen from the valleys trying to understand the Cockney of sixty years ago.)

Men of their tribe have a particular and peculiar roundabout reasoning, we found - in the old days we used to smile at their odd expressions and logic, but then we became dignified and proper (and ulcers took over), and they lost a chance to smile with us.

Our cottage stood in the hotel grounds, and I was in the hotel reception one afternoon in time to hear the Makaranga handyman talking to the white girl receptionist:

"There is trouble with the boiler."

Groan from the receptionist. "Oh, no, what is it?"

"It is that I cannot light the boiler. Someone - I cannot say who it is - has let the fire under the small tank die because there are not many people in the hotel and the boss will not let the garden boys get the wood and has given many of them the sack, but it does not matter as there are no people staying in the rooms near the piccanin boiler that has no fire."

The receptionist was lost. "I thought you said it was the main oil-fired boiler that was wrong?"

"Yes, I cannot light the oil boiler from the wood fire as there is no fire because there is no wood in the fire and it has gone out."

"Why can't you light the boiler with a match?"

"I cannot light the fire with a match because there is no matches."

This was getting more hole-in-the-bucket all the time and I followed the build-up eagerly.

"Get some matches from the bar then."

Handyman disappeared for ten minutes to return with a bar chit for two cents to be signed.

The handyman took the chit back to the barman, and it was duly put through all the books. The trouble was solved and the hotel guests were once again able to have hot baths, and the handyman had the box of matches that he wanted, and everyone was happy.

173

Perhaps in other circumstances, if the manager had been away, the fire would not have been lit for days, and overseas visitors would have been irritated, but not one of them would have questioned that there was indeed some trouble with the boiler.

FIFTEEN

Travelling fast and travelling alone cannot be achieved on African buses. You may travel fast in sharp bursts, or even experience the additional excitement of an occasional race along country roads with another bus - the driver unable to resist any longer the urgings of his often drunken passengers. But you may also arrive two hours late, or a day, or a week - who cares?

Bus companies were often owned by astute African businessmen; one of these companies in the Fort Victoria district, which ran buses in the tribal areas and African-purchase farms, ran fifty buses, was reputed to be worth half a million dollars, and employed at least two white men always as mechanic and accountant. African businessmen often employed Europeans though many qualified Africans were looking for jobs.

On the top of country buses is everything - bicycles, furniture, baskets, cases, bundles, and chickens - inside is everything else including the goat.

The buses were magnificently old, with hard, upright and surely indestructible seats, with the world squeezed in knee to seat. They charged, belching, over stones, ruts, and narrow bridges, through soft sand, and for a few cents the province was yours. From the windows were tossed maize cobs in the spring, mango pips in the summer, orange and naartje (tangerine) rinds in the winter, and beer cartons all the year round. They moved over the countryside in a pall of self-made diesel smoke and dust. It was impossible to follow close in a car and live, but when risking overtaking, it was likely a box would slip from the roof rack on to your neat, smooth bonnet. The passing of the non-returnable dumpy beer bottle was a blessing. (At risk of being a misery, friends in Zimbabwe tell me the fares on these buses are so high now, many town employees can no longer afford to travel to their kraals and families regularly.)

The drivers worked really hard: they controlled noisy, complaining and often inebriated passengers, collected fares, and still managed to keep the cumbersome, heavy load on a fairly straight course, without any of the aids of modern vehicles.

The drivers of the green buses on the Zimbabwe road would even watch the back mirror and allow cars to overtake on the narrow tar, somehow edging their buses out of the way. When the blue colours of another bus company hove into view, it was wise to park well out of the way in some accommodating ditch until the happy wanderers had roared past.

Africans from the tribal lands were then still unsophisticated enough to look upon a visit to Fort Victoria, with its population of 3000 white and 11000 blacks as an outing to be talked about for weeks. They generally visited the Pakistani-owned shops where goods were cheap and bright, and they could meet their friends while being entertained with loud music from the transistor radios that were for sale.

Up the road from Zimbabwe along a dirt road that wound through lichen-covered rocks and deep forests of overhanging trees was a Dutch Reformed Church Mission, Morgenster, which incorporated a school for the deaf and dumb, hospital, church, post office and a printing press for Shona language school books. The population of the mission was more than that of many villages in Rhodesia.

We used to drive out sometimes on Sunday to the bare stone hills and barely populated valleys. It was best after a rainy spell, when streams ran down the rocks and the resurrection plants and ferns turned to green. The resurrection plants were fascinating - visitors would pick a sprig, carry it around in their suitcases, forget it at home for weeks and then, when they finally got around to putting it into water, the woody dark stem would spring into bright green leaves and flowers.

As we passed through the homesteads of the mission on the way to the hill, all the windows and doors were firmly shut, and curtains drawn to contain Sunday. But at least their religion meant their gardeners had Sunday off, which was not generally the rule in Rhodesia.

Later, when I was working in the police offices in Fort Victoria, I read a report from an African informant about Morgenster Mission: "There is no trouble there with the Dutches because they are not interested to talk about politics only about the Bibles." But when the troublemakers went on the rampage, it was this sort of philanthropic people who often suffered most. I wish someone would explain to me why students, when angry, burn their colleges and libraries, workers raid their clinics and hospitals, and tribesmen destroy their schools and cattle dips.

During the 1976 "troubles", Fort Victoria really began to live up to its name and became a fortress. By July there were more defence vehicles on the road than there were civilians, and in the streets camouflage uniform was normal wear. Suddenly, a country where, earlier, new vehicles had been unobtainable, now it came out in a rash of new lorries and Land Rovers. It was difficult to see who was paying for them.

Income tax was not high compared with many other countries, but we were now living with a ten-per-cent sales tax, which grew to fifteen per cent a year later. So practically all goods bought in shops, or meals in restaurants, had this added on afterwards. As far as I was concerned, it gave a feeling of distrust to simple buying. And one of the best things about going to South Africa or Europe then, was to go into a shop, see the price marked, and fish around in your purse for the cash, feeling assured you had not been diddled. (South Africa later adopted the same sales tax system.)

When Paula went off to England and Germany on holiday, staying mainly with relatives, we fervently hoped she would say how wonderful it was and that she'd like to live in Europe. By 1976, it was becoming clear that we would have to go and find somewhere else to live outside Rhodesia, and, if wise, outside Africa. Paula took to her relatives very well, and they liked her a lot, and Martin and I were gratified. She loved London and spent a lot of time walking around looking at the shops, seeing the sights, finding her way on buses and tubes and trains, things entirely alien to her life before. She had not been to Europe since she was five.

But Rhodesia was best, she said, when she returned.

Martin and I felt this attitude, which reflected the feelings of most young people in Rhodesia, distressingly shortsighted. It took a long time, a generation for most, before they were proved wrong, but like many friends of our generation, or older, we could see no way for Europeans living there but to once more uproot and try again. The elderly were prepared to stay for the rest of their lives. We felt it might be possible, with Martin's parents for instance, as they were opposed to leaving, to shut themselves away in a little pocket somewhere, let the storm blow over, and emerge to hope what was left was not too great a ruin, but even Kenya failed.

We felt the Rhodesian Government had left it too late to achieve this. If the attempt at partnership had been carried on after the Federation with Nyasaland and Northern Rhodesia broke up in 1963, then there would have been a chance, and Rhodesia might well have been a prosperous country. But white Rhodesians had hated the uneasy relationship then, which embraced so much patronage.

But for those who had to emerge into the world to earn a living, we felt life would be startlingly different in a short time, in spite of Britain and the West's hopes that Europeans would stay to help administer a new country.

When I thought of living in a black country, I could not help but think of Zambia, and the stories of repression of freedom for people who lived there. More than many things I revere freedom of speech, and this had been proved impossible in any black country yet.

In African countries, including Rhodesia, the four freedoms evaluated by Franklin D. Roosevelt were now moving into extinction. Freedom of speech, freedom of worship, freedom from want and, perhaps never found in Africa since time began, freedom from fear. Once they had been repressed here, could they ever be revived? Or would they go now like the wild species of animals and birds that were being poached and slaughtered in the north, to be lost forever?

Those with patience who are willing to teach would feel it their duty to stay. I am impatient of ignorance and cannot teach. The same gems of wisdom said over and over again soon appear to me to be platitudes, and I long to say something outrageous just for a change. Even as a child I hated to hear the same story more than once, or to hear a phrase repeated several times in a sentence as in many fairy stories (and with lesser politicians). When I have read a newspaper thoroughly once, I dislike going back to it.

The national newspapers, The Rhodesia Herald and the Bulawayo Chronicle, believed without doubt in the freedom of speech. They reported the news honestly, but when it was too disagreeable to the government or thought to be a danger to security, the censor would chop out whole paragraphs, even whole columns, leaving large white spaces on the pages, and often most of the front pages.

I was spare-time correspondent for the Fort Victoria area for these newspapers, as I had been at Victoria Falls. I liked the odd jobs that took me out, but I couldn't cook up interest in the parochial goings-on of Fort Victoria. It was partly because I wasn't actually living in the town, and calling on anyone meant spending a whole afternoon in town. But it was mainly the fault of my intolerant personality - I condemned the population of Fort Victoria in one fell blow. After Victoria Falls, they seemed to be staid, unimaginative and self-satisfied.

Fort Victoria was the first town to be founded in Rhodesia by the pioneers who came up from the southwest in 1890: hence its name. Martin once suggested to the Fort Victoria Publicity Association, who were debating how they could attract more visitors to the district, that they would never get anywhere until the association changed its name to Zimbabwe Ruins. It is true Queen Victoria or Queen Wilhelmina still seemed to reign over the town's main street, which was too wide but without lanes for modern traffic, though wide enough to turn an ox cart. When a black government came to power it was renamed Masvingo, but I can't see that did much for a battered tourist trade.

The town was a centre for cattle ranching, and many of the inhabitants were the sons and daughters of pioneer Boer families, who had trekked north from South Africa in ox wagons, facing tremendous dangers and privations. Boers, or Afrikaans people of today, have many qualities, but among them is not, generally, the ability to view the wide world from anything but a very biased viewpoint. They extol the virtues of a language that is spoken only in South Africa, while international English clamours unheeded in their midst to be given the star place for understanding and communication.

But South Africa itself was a terrific place for a holiday, and sometimes I felt I wouldn't mind living there, if they'd have us. While at Zimbabwe Ruins we had three weeks leave and toured the mountains and the Natal coast. Now without our caravan, we stayed all the way in holiday cottages and rest camps.

Once again we found the abundance of food in the large supermarkets amazing and we were happy to get our own meals rather than face the expense of restaurants. Instant food - the large variety of frozen foods (that weren't "off"), ready-mixes, vegetarian foods for me, white rolls (not grey like at home), beautiful imported cheeses, lovely, lovely wines, and cheap. I remember being fascinated by dried potato flakes - I can't now think for the life of me why. And after there were Black Magic and Quality Street chocolates, and pure instant coffee. And I got fat in three weeks.

We'd go out for sundowners and sit on the verandah on the main street or on an esplanade and watch that altogether strange world go by. How my heart ached for the world since we went to Fort Victoria! More than ever before I found in myself the need to go, go, go. To go to "Go", as Paula also needed.

It's no good asking people where they want to go, when they feel like this; they don't know where Go is, only that it isn't where they are, and some places are less like Go than others.

Of all the foolish things to buy and cart back so far, was a fish tank, which Martin bought, at my request, for my birthday present. It came complete with thermostat, pump and heater, but wasn't slopping tropical fish all the way back as some of our friends wondered. It was empty. It had started off empty. And when we got back to Rhodesia we couldn't get tropical fish any more in the pet shops. We should have guessed. But, nevertheless, we persevered and managed to find some fish in the end. It was as entertaining as the TV, which, I agree, wasn't saying much. We could watch the fish going by, even if we couldn't watch the world.

Looking after Susie's fishes on the farm while she was at school had taught us the rudiments. I remember the first time one of Susie's fishes died, and the general upset, and when they started killing and eating each other I could have slung the fierce swordtails out. (I know now we shouldn't have kept them with the other fish, yes.)

It was like playing God - trying to create a happy world, while the occupants are only interested in killing each other off.

It was obviously time to stop playing God and get myself a job.

When Martin's tourists had spent the morning at the ruins, they had nearly always seen enough of grey stone walls, so in the afternoon they were taken down to the nearby dam, Lake Kyle, which was Rhodesia's second-largest dam after Kariba, and sometimes taken over the ferry to a game park which was the home of many white rhinoceros. (These white rhino had been so well protected in Umfolozi Game Reserve in Natal that they could now safely be exported to the rest of Africa.) Trophy hunters had eliminated rhinos from their natural regions in Rhodesia over seventy years before.

We bought a dinghy and used to enjoy tying up to the small islands in Kyle and having a picnic at the weekend, when no tourist planes arrived. But Martin didn't like to fish, and I would have been extremely unhappy if he had, so when we had exhausted all the rocky islands and inlets (there was very little bird life), we lost interest and sold the boat. Martin liked sailing, but displayed no interest in sailing on Kyle. He liked wind and space.

I don't know what was wrong with Kyle. It was a pretty enough place, yet it never caught on as a tourist attraction. You could pull the fish out of the water and watch the scenery, though, as it rained so much, holidaymakers wouldn't even do that for very long. Kyle was boring. I'd rather stay at home trying to write, or read a book, or even cook the lunch and do the washing-up.

Yet a few kilometres down the road Rhodesia's first President, Clifford Dupont, who had recently retired, was drawing on Kyle for the quiet inspiration needed to write his memoirs. Mr Dupont, a small man of gentle aspect, who had taken on a very difficult job in 1970 after UDI, often used to come down to the lake when he was in office, to fish and get away from his worries, and to recover from his health problems. Sometimes, poor old gentleman, he could barely walk when he arrived. He hardly ate anything and sometimes, except for his fiery eyes, looked piteously weak. But everyone liked him.

When Martin had a car accident I passed without stopping. We had gone into Fort Victoria in separate cars that morning, which was part of our complicated transport arrangements because we operated car hires and tours from both Zimbabwe and Fort Victoria. I saw two cars smashed up at the side of the road but there were lots of other cars and people around, including an army Land Rover and a caravan, which almost blocked the road. I was already late for work as usual. Rather than cause congestion, I drove on through the small lane still open. The road was slippery after heavy rain and I had to concentrate on getting through the narrow space. There was another car impatiently at my back (when isn't there?).

It never occurred to me it might be Martin involved in the accident till I arrived at the Police Station where I worked. One of the young policemen came out: "We heard you'd had an accident," he said "I'm just going out to attend it. No-one's hurt badly."

I drove quickly back into town to where the drivers kept the company vehicles. I felt cold, and not sure what I was doing. The Zimbabwe Hotel had that moment telephoned the drivers to go and pick up the people from the airport without Martin, as he'd had an accident. I rang the hotel quickly. There I received assurance that Martin was all right, though suffering from shock. The owner of the hotel was right now driving him into the doctor's surgery. No one else was hurt beyond a few bruises.

I found him eventually in hospital. He was suffering from concussion and shock, and talking nonsense. I wept, and perhaps not entirely for his sake. I thought I was married forever to an idiot. He kept asking me the same questions over and over again, worrying about his visitors for that day and what was happening to them. Nothing I could say would make him quieten his foolishness.

The nurse insisted on giving me a couple of tranquillisers, but I didn't take them, though I told her I had. I had all Martin's work to see to somehow. Martin's was a one-man job; come hell or high water his tourists would not stop arriving and be required to be shown and transported around. Others would require their self-drive cars neat and clean and waiting for them whenever they arrived. His diary was a mass of hieroglyphics, and I was the only one who had any chance of deciphering the instructions it held. My boss sympathetically gave me time off from my job till my life sorted itself out.

It was one of the luckiest (for me) coincidences that Susie and her husband, Peter, were staying with us on their way back from holiday in South Africa. Without them I, too, would have started talking nonsense.

"What are you doing here?" Martin said to them when we went to see him in his hospital bed. (They had arrived the day before and we'd had a very happy afternoon and evening altogether.)

Susie rarely cried, even as a child, but she was crying at the bedside now. Peter and I were vainly trying not to let Susie get too upset as she was seven months pregnant. The nurses at the hospital were more interested asking her when her baby was due and how she was feeling, and if her baby was kicking well, than in her apparently idiotic father's condition.

Martin did recover, quite quickly, but has never fully regained his memory of the accident or the time after it. One day, months after, he suddenly said, as he was sitting back in his chair: "I've remembered something. I remember an amazing silence and sitting in the car thinking how beautiful and quiet it was, and someone trying to persuade me to get out of the car while I was saying: 'It's all right, leave me, I'll be all right. Let me stay here.' The silence was beautiful."

The accident was proved not to be his fault; the other car had gone out of control on the muddy road and driven right into him head on. Martin had driven as far to his side of the road as he could and had virtually stopped when the crash happened, but he still remembers nothing of this. It took him a long time to get his driving confidence back.

Paula came down from Bulawayo, where she was working for Air Rhodesia, on a week's leave, and did the tours round the ruins for her Dad. What she didn't know about the ruins she made up for in charm (I think) and pleasant conversation, and everyone seemed quite happy with her guiding. At least she had a pretty sound knowledge of Rhodesia's history and geography, which was more than most of the foreign couriers at Victoria Falls had been able to offer.

*   *   *

During our two years at the ruins, one of the most exciting thing we did was to ride through the game reserve on horseback. All around us herds of buck moved across the plain by the lake as though they had wings. The white rhino did not even look up from grazing.

It was an altogether different feeling from viewing game from a car. We were part of the wildlife and felt part of it. We were of the sounds and smells, the scrunch of grass, the bird twittering for dear life in the thorn tree, the hammer of the hooves on the hard ground as a herd of sable antelope fled. The animals there were not so wary of the horses as of a car and they lingered, watching, till we were close. The nosey warthog skittered around near the horses completely without fear - on their part at least. We saw zebra eye to eye with our horses, giraffe like trees, inquisitive kudu that

184

merely stared, ears big, eyes pensive, and tsessebe that ran so fast with shoulders hunched. It was one of the most tremendous experiences in life.

Later that year Fair Lady magazine in South Africa sent me back one of my stories with the drawings that had already been made. Months before they had paid more than I'd ever been paid for a story from a once-sale. The editor wrote: "Bad news... Because of the way things are at the moment we've decided not to use any fiction that could cause offence to black people... We personally don't feel it could upset anyone but we are not prepared to take a chance." I felt it could not cause offence either - it was written as the situation was in a farming community fourteen years before. And now that situation could cause offence. I had drawn no conclusions on the situation. I was so disappointed I shoved the large envelope away in a cupboard and left it there.

At least it proved one thing - I did not write for money, because I had already been paid well, and I could sell it again if I was able, if I had the heart. When you try writing, disappointments come thick and fast. Why do it? Why does anyone do anything like this: flower arranging, amateur acting, dog breeding, being a courier?

I think everyone likes a pat on the back sometimes, and you never know when you might get one.

SIXTEEN

Since UDI, shortages had got worse, insinuating themselves into our lives until we began to wonder if we were living a full life in this modern world.

Petrol rationing hit the worst. There were few regular buses, even connecting the tree-lined suburbs to town centres. Rhodesians hate walking. It is often very hot or very wet, and at lunchtime or five o'clock, when workers were leaving offices and shops, the sky would open with violent thunder, and drains would become two-metre wide streams in ten minutes. Unlike the Englishman of that time, the Rhodesian resident did not carry his raincoat or umbrella; nothing could protect him from the summer rains if he was caught.

The petrol rationing that re-started in 1975 gave everyone enough petrol on a ration card to get to work and back in his or her particular car, and that was it. We had been subject before to petrol rationing, just after UDI. Now there was no petrol to go and see "auntie", and the Afrikaans, in particular, do love visiting within their generally large families.

No petrol for the rugged Rhodesian male to go fishing, play or watch sport, or for anyone to go to the city for shopping. The way to a life-long friendship was a gift of a 25-litre petrol coupon.

Each family was given an allocation for an annual holiday, which the government, like all hard-pressed governments, hoped they would take within the country, but not actually at home, because the holiday hotels and tourist attractions on the borders or near trouble spots were going broke. This included nearly all the tourist spots by the end of 1976 - Victoria Falls, Wankie, Kariba, the Eastern Mountains, and Fort Victoria.

Visitors to the country could get as much petrol as they required, but the price of 23 cents a litre in 1977 - more expensive even than

186

in Britain - was a deterrent in itself. The Rhodesian dollar was then on a par with the pound. The police were too busy to enforce the nominal speed limit, to save fuel, of 100 kilometres an hour. Drivers went as fast as they could afford. There was only one automatic speed-monitoring machine in the whole country. For a while South Africans used to love zooming up the main roads - their speed limit of 80 kilometres an hour (later raised to 90 after protests) was strictly enforced. "Come to Rhodesia and try out your new Mercedes", we should have advertised. We thought it must be odd to buy a car like that and never be allowed to "send it". Later: "Shoot up the roads and get shot at" seemed more apt.

The limits had a reverse effect on Rhodesian drivers who would carry on driving as they were accustomed to while on holiday in South Africa, and subsequently received in the post numerous speeding fine notices when they got home. They didn't pay them, and then were afraid to return south of the border for a long time.

South Africa, when later they suffered sanctions because of their apartheid policies, did not ration petrol, but closed their petrol stations from midday on Friday until Monday morning every week. (No-one likes working weekends anyway, do they?)

We wondered how Britain managed during the Second World War, when all oil was imported through perilous seas, and planes were still kept roaring in the skies. To us, in our different war, it was fantastic to see programmes like "The World at War" on TV. What we would have done for a squadron of Spits or a few Churchill tanks thirty years later!

One noticeable characteristic of our war machines was their shape. The enemy wasn't in the skies, but underground - with the instrument of the coward, we said - the landmine. Vehicles and trailers were inverted pyramids. The first time we saw a "hyena", which was used by police support units at Victoria Falls, people turned out in the streets to stare. It rose off its point on high wheels to a crown of bulletproof glass. They were said to be practically indestructible by terrorist weapons. The glass itself cost R$1000.

And after the hyenas came the leopards and the rhinos, and

heavy mine-proofed Land Rovers, which gobbled precious petrol faster than a heavy lorry. Even civilians and government employees were using them to inspect the schools and visit clinics, mend the telephones and build bridges in the danger areas, which embraced a lot of the country. One car hire firm even advertised a mine-proof vehicle for hire.

Mine-exploding vehicles were improvised, as no mine detectors were at first available. We would see great, unwieldy apparitions with 44-gallon drums strapped all around them and straddled-out wheels blundering down the main road into the Victoria Falls village. It added up to a space-vehicle effect. We found it interesting, but, like the four voices of Grand Opera, the Publicity Association, Town Council, Tourist Board and Chamber of Commerce screamed out loud in unison – "What will the tourists think?" So the war machines were diverted to the side roads and it appeared safer.

The day four South African motorcyclists were shot at by terrorists during the Easter weekend, on the main road from South Africa to Fort Victoria and Salisbury, it marked the end of the tourist trade in Fort Victoria. Three died, and the young girl in the party escaped. The pattern was familiar. We knew the lingering deaths of hotels, restaurants and stores would follow as inevitably as night followed day.

At the same time, yet another rancher in the district was ambushed on his farm road, while going about his normal work. Quite naturally, I thought, some ranchers' wives began to turn to thoughts of South Africa, where they were most likely born and brought up, and to emigration, in a desire to protect their children, even if their husbands obdurately refused to budge.

I was sent off by the newspaper to get an interview with the injured rancher in hospital. "I am staying," he said, which is what everyone wanted him to say, so got reported.

But the convoys that were instituted after the shooting were quite fun, if you weren't in a hurry. There was a great togetherness in Rhodesia sometimes, portrayed especially by the few South

African visitors, who were more pro-Rhodesia than the Rhodesians. And the convoys made life easier for the hitchhikers.

The first convoy was started at the end of April, right when we were setting off on our holiday "down south". They left twice a day.

But we decided to go through Bulawayo and see the family and so miss the convoys. There were no convoys along the Bulawayo to South Africa road because no one had been shot on that road as yet, though there weren't many miles between the almost parallel roads.

On the way back from our holiday, when we were seventy miles north of the border at Beit Bridge, Martin drew up in a lay-by.

"Let's eat lunch," he said.

I looked around. There was Rhodesia all around us. Trees, bush, the road, the lay-by, the litterbin, and nothing.

"What, here?" I asked, firm as a sack of mealies in my seat.

"Yes, why not?"

"We'll get shot."

"Oh, rubbish." He got out of the car and started to get drinks from the cold box.

"I'm not getting out of the car - it's an ideal spot for terrs."

I had been working for the police for a year and caution had rubbed off. I like to think of it as caution and not cowardice.

We drove on. I refused to stop anywhere and we ate our bread rolls as we drove.

Two hours later someone <u>was</u> shot on that road, and not far from the spot we had thought to stop.

After that, convoys were started on the Bulawayo to Beit Bridge road.

No one was obliged to travel by convoy, but they must travel in the morning or early afternoon. They were warned of the dangers at roadblocks and then it was up to them. Most people did take the independent way - Rhodesians and South Africans are like that - but nearly everyone carried firearms in their car when they undertook a journey. Even policemen admitted it was probably safer to take firearms and travel alone - that way you had a chance of getting past any ambush by travelling fast (forget the 100kms an hour rubbish).

The next girl the freedom fighters managed to kill on the roads was eight years old, and it happened thirty miles from Fort Victoria. At work I was shown the bullet that had been taken out of her chest, now on its way to the lab.

What do you think when you see such a disquieting object? It was clean and looked like any other spent bullet. Yet surely, like the stains on Lady Macbeth's hands, it could never be cleaned off. If it were given to a spiritualist medium, would they see anything about it?

It was like a length of tree-bark rope that had lain around the office, generally on the floor, for a week. Some poor African in his twenties had strung himself from a tree half a metre from the ground and killed himself by it. Poor instruments, both of them, with which to end a young life.

Around this time we were constantly being exhorted by politicians and the RBC and RTV to perform contortions like shoulders to the wheel, noses to the grindstone, tightening our belts with our best foot forward and our heels dug well in, while getting our teeth into the problems, having bitten more off than we could chew presumably. We knew we had our backs to the wall. But in the bars and club verandahs, it was still bottoms-up as the Castle and Lion lagers flowed freely, or at least cheaply.

Scotch whisky was practically unobtainable now, except in tot form in hotels, and then was very expensive. The black market price was R$10 a bottle, which was a lot of money for then, for us. (By the early 2000s it would cost tens of thousands of Zimbabwe dollars, should it be obtainable, or out of this world on the black market – better to make your own.) Rhodesia was by the 1970s making its own, and it was becoming less harsh. It was distilled - dare I say it, as I live in Scotland? - from sugar cane. Cane spirit was the fighting spirit of Rhodesia, we were told.

For a few months something went wrong with the allocations for imported brandy extract and there was uproar. Local brandy is the *dop* that South African and Rhodesian pioneers built the country on - take our whisky, take our butter, take our sons, but never take our brandy, man. So South African exchange monies were found and joy returned, preferably mixed with ginger ale.

But joy did not return to the smokers. At the end of 1975 the great tobacco country of Rhodesia, whose main export had been tobacco, and whose farmers and tobacco processors were renowned until UDI as producing some of the best and cheapest tobacco in the world, started to manufacture abominable cigarettes.

The number of brands was cut down to nine types, which we were told would satisfy everyone. You've guessed it - they satisfied no one. To save a million dollars a year on packaging material, the cigarettes arrived in the shops in homemade pasteboard, and the cigarettes were wrapped in the ubiquitous newsprint (unwritten on). It really took us back twenty years to when Martin, out of cigarettes on the farm, would buy a packet of eight "Star" smokes for a tickey (a silver threepenny piece). They were made from loosely- packed sweepings and tobacco scrap.

The new austerity cigarettes were dry, without flavour, and many people gave up smoking on the spot. There was a great outcry, and surprisingly, outcry won and after a few months the same utility types were slightly better packaged in foil.

The cigarettes were still dry and unsatisfying, but people got used to them.

At the beginning of the contretemps, the well-known firms of Rothmans and BAT had removed their brand names. I don't smoke, but I noticed people eulogising about South African cigarettes they'd bought on holiday. A change from the old days when overseas visitors loved the quality - and price - of Rhodesian cigarettes, and South Africans took home 30-packs (the boxes with plain white bases ideal for scribbling notes on), together with the copper-ware, skin wallets, native carvings and elephant-hair bracelets.

About this time the bakers' prayers became: "Forgive us our

daily bread," and conscientious housewives rushed off to their kitchens grasping cake flour and mealie meal and grandma's fifty-year-old recipes for baking bread. White flour was only allowed for confectionery. We had the National Loaf. The promises of Lord Graham, Minister of Agriculture at UDI, that we would eat sadza (the national maize porridge of Africa) before we surrendered, were coming true.

To save foreign currency, flour was being extracted from locally grown wheat up to 86% for bread making. We were told it was better for us. But was it edible? It was grey and soggy. In the larger towns the bakers seemed to make a better job of it than in smaller bakeries. Don't get me wrong: I prefer wholemeal bread, when it isn't a rock on top and a bog at the base, as in Fort Victoria.

But once again we were told there was a war on. Many of us felt it was the Rhodesian Front, who made up the government, who had caused the war, and as we had always opposed the Rhodesian Front, we were aggrieved at our deteriorating standards.

It made us sorry for the Continental countries during the Hitler war with their black bread. I can't remember England's wartime bread being so unpalatable.

"A Jug of Wine, a Loaf of Bread – and Thou".

We were told Rhodesian wine would improve. In fifty years it could be as good as South African, and in the meantime one of the characteristics of the pleasant little wines of Rhodesia was the terrific hangover that followed. Two Saturday night glasses of wine could well still be making me feel ill on Monday. But people said they got used to it. To promote sales of Rhodesian wines the price of South African wines rocketed, which made the few South African visitors upset, as they were fast developing a taste for wine. It was said that one of the troubles with Rhodesian wine was that the grapes did not get enough sun at the right time - and this was Rhodesia, our Land of Sunshine and Opportunity.

But the Rhodesian cheeses that went with the wine at parties popular then were good. They compared favourably with English, Australian and New Zealand cheeses, and won most of the prizes at the Rand Easter Show in Johannesburg. Cheese became so good, in fact, that we exported it all to South Africa, and one summer we were rationed to one small packet a family. Losing money, dairy farmers had cut back their herds. Being lacto-vegetarians, this hit our family below the belt, as well as making us tighten our belts as exhorted.

Rhodesian and South Africans love steak to the point of worship. The place where they prefer to cook it, that smelly, grubby, ash-ridden hole, the *braai*, is where all the noblest aspirations were sounded and resounded. With Castle in hand, feet bare, grubby shorts and shirt a-flap, they extolled the virtues of Rhodesia, mainly, as far as I could gather, because there was cheap steak and beer. Steak in Britain probably cost four or five times as much, in South Africa perhaps half as much again. Rhodesia's economy must be sound...

So I am biased because I don't eat steak. But I found it tiring every time I met a tourist who was visiting friends in Rhodesia and was well indoctrinated to reply to any remark about the poor quality of, say, coffee, or the lack of variety in the shops with: "But your steak is so cheap!"

But throughout all the sanctions there were always plenty of most essential goods in the shops. Over the twelve or so years, Rhodesian manufacturers became clever at imitations and substitutions. Many people who found their way to Rhodesia in the thirty years after 1945 were often resourceful, had powers of leadership, and had a fund of initiative and inventiveness. In contrast, the main stream of second and third generation Rhodesians were quite often content to sit and enjoy what had been made for them by their pioneering forefathers. When the terrorist war came, they preferred to fight to cling on to what they had rather than to go out and try to make something better, both within and outside their country.

Rhodesian-produced clothes were reasonable and inexpensive, even though some materials were imported. Not the height of fashion, and we all thought Marks and Spencer the tops then.

As all kinds of engines and machinery were chronically in short supply, everyone was a mechanic, and all parts and cars and machines had to last forever. We went one better than: "Give us the tools, and we will finish the job", and the motto became: "We will make the tools and finish the job". It was brave, ambitious, admirable, and a dreadful waste of intelligence and ingenuity, and a man's time, which was fast becoming a great consideration with more and more military call-ups hovering over firms like a giant albatross of ill fortune.

When Frelimo (in Mozambique) closed the border with Rhodesia, a surprising thing happened - we started wrapping our goods in plastic and paper bags again. Obviously the Frelimo and Mozambique had no longer any use for our exports of packaging in their present life-style. What did they wrap their piri piri chicken in now, we wondered.

We had thought the whole world was no longer using plastic and paper bags. We believed we were doing our bit to preserve Mother Earth. Instead, by our plastic exports, we were encouraging the people of Mozambique to make one vast rubbish dump of their erstwhile beautiful beaches. Shame on Rhodesian exporters! Rhodesians were no longer holidaying in Beira, so we hadn't seen. Before the Portuguese gave up on Mozambique, signs in many car windows had appeared: *"Obrigado Mozambique"*.

Thank you. But no longer…

(In 2002 South African supermarkets stopped liberally giving away plastic bags because the roadsides and parks were taking on the appearance of rubbish dumps.)

At this time we were allowed to burn our newspapers. Not a ceremonial affair or in spite, but rather a gentle lighting of the evening fires in the lounges. Boy Scouts no longer headed the drive to collect waste paper (most of it had stood out in the rain for months before being collected and proved useless to anyone). Now we were told the whole process of recycling it was too expensive. It didn't feel right at first carelessly tossing away my papers in the bin, and in fireless summers the storeroom got full and spilt out.

Yet the Brutus-dealt blow to any sense of righteousness of our present life was dealt by the honourable men of the propaganda agencies. Rhodesian radio and television programmes told us endlessly that we were fighting a psychological war. There was a communist behind every tree.

We heard of the witch-hunts that went on in America and South Africa and others, and now, we were told six times a day on radio and television how good, without reservation, the Government of Rhodesia and all its followers were, and how blatantly wicked was the rest of the world, with the possible exception of South Africa. I listened but could not believe. Gradually intensifying over the fourteen years since the Rhodesian Front assumed government, these politicians did protest too much, me-thought. There was none of the finesse of propaganda levied by the British during Hitler's war. If it were aimed at a less sophisticated population, why were the more sophisticated mediums of television and English-speaking radio used? I have seen normal overseas visitors transfixed, staring at the box during these programmes in utter disbelief that a reasonably advanced community could resort to such twisting and hypocrisies.

You can always turn it off, as we did. Many Rhodesians swallowed it whole.

As soon as we came back from leave, the African woman who came to clean the house and do the washing in the morning announced she was going off on a month's leave. She had been looking after the house while Martin's relief had been living in it.

It may be hard for someone out of Africa to believe, but in my soft way of living, I had never before had to do all my own housework for as long as a month.

So I spent my first month's salary after returning home, on a second-hand and old but apparently sturdy washing machine: the first washing machine I had owned in twenty-two years of married life.

Like kids, Martin and I vied with each other who should do the washing. (Now do you believe what a simple life we led?) When our daily help returned, somewhat to my surprise, and I was relieved of normal housework, I had so much leftover energy I washed all the blankets and curtains in this sturdy Volvo of a machine, and we were cleaner than clean. Maybe it still runs.

The police station at Fort Victoria where I worked in the mornings, served the districts outside the town. It got me away from the small community of Zimbabwe Ruins and provided money for holidays.

I liked my job. I was working among young people, and I think parents miss that relentless energy and youth of their children when they have left home, after they've got over glorying in the peace. For some months before, I had been working in Fort Victoria for a homeopath and osteopath, but the house where he practised was dark, like many old houses in southern Africa, and I was on my own most of the time, which wasn't the best environment for my recovery from the low mental state I'd brought on myself.

(One good thing about Fort Victoria was the doctor who made time to sit and listen to me and talked me out of the tranquillisers I'd been prescribed at Victoria Falls. I am eternally grateful to him.)

The policemen really did get younger in Rhodesia - it wasn't imagination. For fourteen years there had been National Service call-ups for eighteen-year-olds to serve, at first six months, then later on for a year. In 1976 this was extended to eighteen months, or to "indefinite" call-up in some cases. So that young men between sixteen and thirty-eight could not avoid call-up, a law was brought in that forbade any man of these ages from leaving the country without permission. This applied to white races only.

Conscripts could volunteer to do their time in the police or the Internal Affairs Department, when they worked with District Commissioners in the border regions where the tribesmen were being harassed by the terrorists.

This seemed to me to be the most thankless job, though on the face of it seemed a soft option, as there was no actual combat fighting involved. They were often blown up by landmines on the remote roads and they were sitting ducks for terrorists' pot shots and ambushes. The only company they had for months on end were unsophisticated tribesmen and any patrolling army personnel.

They were there to help the tribesmen to a better life, but who has hope enough for the future with mortars whizzing overhead and the risk of abduction whenever they set foot out of the fenced area? Better to join the infantry and blindly set yourself to shoot anything that moves after curfew or sunset.

On the whole the National Service policeman was a more intelligent lad than the regular. He had two months training as opposed to the normal six months, but apart from some sketchiness over the elusive "documentation", they appeared to do their job as well, if not better, than the regulars. If they liked the life, they were invited to sign on as a career policeman, but after four months those I met were, without exception, counting the months to their release.

My work covered all the odd clerical jobs that were not directly connected with crime. I had a lot to do with documents market "Confidential " and "Secret", (I didn't progress to "Top Secret"), and it constantly amazed me how uninteresting were secret documents. They mainly concerned Africans with long, unpronounceable names, mostly beginning with "M", who performed such subversive acts as not paying their sheep-dip fees, or calling Ian Smith rude names. As the war progressed, some tribesmen were being "persuaded" by wandering bands of terrs to steal cattle from white-owned farms and rob neighbourhood stores. When these secret subversive acts increased, a regular policeman was put on the job of recording them.

Other secret documents concerned matters that, I felt, it would make little difference if the whole country knew about them, and in some cases would be better for everyone to know. It made me lose faith in secrets. But burning papers was a real thrill. I wanted to fill in a requisition in sextuple to order a posh incinerator so I could burn them as with authority. Instead I had to do them out the back in an old dustbin, where the wind whipped round and sent the pieces dancing to oblivion.

Our buildings were old government offices, long ago abandoned

197

by every other department, a collection of small buildings, two rooms to each, dotted around the camp at random. It was difficult to imagine why they had been put in these particular places. To get a new pencil from the stationery cupboard you twisted your ankle along a seemingly endless and uneven stone path, to get from one office to another, you trod in puddles and tripped over innumerable dogs. We had mid-morning tea under a tree. It was very informal, and the local dogs, temporarily bereft of their working families, loved our reassuring company, biscuits and saucers of milk. Sometimes we counted a dozen, and they ranged from Great Danes through Alsatians and boxers to terriers and a miniature Pekinese.

Those waiting to pay fines, make statements or complaints, and bear witness, sat huddled on benches, on the ground, or in small round shelters. This was the tradition of the British South Africa Police for nearly ninety years being carried on. It is like the revered name they still kept, though they were neither British nor South African.

I don't know how superior new stations in town got on without the facilities of large grounds, with taps, benches for the elderly, shade for the mothers to breast-feed their babies, and sun for warmth for all.

Questioning an African from the remote areas, whether he was a complainant, a witness or an accused was a lengthy task. This was the way they were - with little continuity of thought, precision, or much regard for the whole truth. Their logic was quite different from the white man's and I defy any man who was not brought up in Africa to start to understand. On the whole, I think they believed themselves to be honest and truthful. They just lost their way.

Today in 2005, reading reports of the Mugabe government and elections, it is evident that many Makarangas have surely lost their way.

SEVENTEEN

The war really started in the second half of 1976, and a great change came over the way of life of white Rhodesians. Now the pattern of life for all young men was to go out into the bush, shoot terrorists, come back, drink beer and find a girl, then off to shoot some more, or be blown up by a landmine.

As the terrorist incursion increased, so did the talking. Politicians talked a lot, nationalist leaders talked a lot, and nothing was achieved, so the young men carried on shooting and getting shot. One day they shot thirty-one terrorists. There were still a lot more.

Everyone talked so much about how Rhodesia should be governed and who by, that most of us felt there was nothing else to say; but after the Unilateral Declaration of Independence on the 11th November 1965, so many emissaries had come and gone, so many conferences were held on boats, on bridges, among the frozen Swiss mountains, among the South African jacarandas, in government offices in heat waves, in African villages under trees in the rains, that surely they were only discussing the weather or the scenery.

Ian Smith described his own UDI as a "three-day wonder", and Harold Wilson said the rebels would be brought to heel "within weeks rather than months". In case we didn't recognise ourselves as rebels, he meant us whites - we were all lumped together no matter what our opinions. Eleven years later the Americans sent in the "flying doctor" Henry Kissinger, on a diplomatic shuffle round Africa. Mr Smith temporarily withdrew his head from the sand, and to everyone's amazement he accepted the package deal he was presented with, and then Dr Kissinger flew off again to help lose the US election. Which left the Rhodesian Government confused and holding a time bomb, which was majority rule in two years.

Twelve years after UDI innumerable white Rhodesians were still determined to fight it out to the last man if they had to. They believed Rhodesia could go on as a civilised, white-man's country forever. They could hardly be blamed: we had been given so many "last chances" by British diplomats and politicians who flitted across our front-page headlines and were now names we barely remembered. Who were Herbert Bowen and Sir Morrice James (first final offer 1966), Lord Alport (late final offer 1967), George Thomson, James Bottomley (late night special offer 1968)?

It was like the evening papers running out of superlatives for late editions, but with us it had ten more years to run, or so it proved.

What did the Pearce Commission of 1972 discover that the Whaley Commission of 1968 hadn't? What was said on HMS Fearless at Gibraltar in 1968 that wasn't said already on HMS Tiger at Malta two years before? What was said at Geneva in 1976 that wasn't said on the White Train on Victoria Falls Bridge the year before?

The truth was there was nothing more to be said. Everyone wanted a share in the pie - and in Rhodesia there was only one white man to twenty-four blacks.

It looked as though the cartoonist's conception of Ian Smith as a latter-day island Japanese fighter emerging from the forests in a thousand years to surrender was not far from the mark.

Rhodesia's recorded history starts in 1890, when it was administered by the British South Africa Company formed by Cecil Rhodes, who had accumulated a vast amount of wealth on the South African Rand gold mines and in Kimberley diamonds. Eight years later a Legislative Council was elected, and in 1923 Southern Rhodesia became a self-governing colony, with a Legislative Assembly being elected from the country's "more substantial property owners and salary earners".

It is odd that in the Second World War less Europeans served on Britain's side than during the First World War, though the European population had increased from 24,000 to over 61,000 in the intervening years.

Ian Douglas Smith (later the Prime Minister of Rhodesia) was one of those who fought on Britain's side as a fighter pilot in the Second World War. The slightly hooded appearance of his right eye is caused by an accident when taking off at night at Alexandria in 1943, when he was given up for dead.

In 1953 Southern Rhodesia formed the Federation with Northern Rhodesia and Nyasaland, which lasted for ten years under the leadership of Sir Godfrey Huggins and Sir Roy Welensky. This was a wealthy time for Southern Rhodesia: Kariba was built and many trunk roads constructed across the country. Southern Rhodesia also made its first uneasy attempts at multi-racialism (as far as Governor General's cocktail parties went, at least).

When Federation broke up, Northern Rhodesia was granted independence and called itself Zambia, so Rhodesia's "Southern" prefix was dropped. Rather forced attempts to mix races socially were also dropped, with a sigh of relief in most people's opinion - black, white or brown.

Rhodesia declared itself independent two years later - UDI.

When, after a referendum of the predominately white electorate, the Rhodesian Government declared the country a Republic in 1970, many of those who had voted "yes" felt they had been duped. The referendum had been concerned with black and white voters' rolls, but had been taken as a vote of confidence for the Rhodesian Front Party to go ahead cutting off our last ties with Britain.

Then in September 1976 came the big surprise. Mr Smith announced on television in his dry, flat voice that a settlement had been reached and in two years there would be majority rule. On the whole we cheered and clapped. It seemed the end of uncertainty, the end of the war, the end of sanctions. I cried. It meant the end of life as we knew it in Rhodesia. We would not stay.

Martin was cross with me. "You've always hated Rhodesia," he said. "You can't cry now because you're going to leave it."

But it wasn't true, and he knew it, you can cry when you leave a life you have known for twenty-four years, and, anyway, my "hates" were the heat, and the flies and the dust...

I think I wasn't alone in my weeping, at least among the older folk. Once more the young refused to accept it.

It was only our idea we would have to leave. The white man would be invited to stay and carry on living and working under a black government. I felt this would be impossible, at least in the beginning, until the black politicians settled down to their responsibilities. We'd be near enough fifty years old by then, so could we wait that long? (We were wrong, as it proved - it took twenty or more years for anarchy to overcome the country and for the population to come to starvation.)

There would be an interim government, half-white, half-black, Mr Smith said, until an election could be held, when a black government would be certain to be elected within two years.

Everyone was amazed - it was unbelievable and a complete round about face from all that the Government had been saying for the last eleven years, and indeed for eighty years. What was even more surprising was the talk of compensation for those who wished to leave the country. A few months before, when this had been mooted, Britain and America had been accused of asking Rhodesians to sell their birthright for a mess of pottage.

For ten years we had put aside any hope of getting anything from our farm. It's value on paper was R$90,000, its debts amounted to R$25,000, which left what seemed to me to be a fortune divided between Martin and his father. The thought of being allowed to take even a portion of this out of the country to start a new life was unbelievably elating.

We were right not to believe.

Now came Geneva.

It was a farce. By now Black Nationalist leaders had become so accustomed to flitting around the world (we could only speculate who was paying) that they were probably more at home in Europe than Mr Smith was. Just everyone wanted to be in on Geneva, which they thought would be the grand finale: four different creeds of nationalists, all our neighbouring countries' representatives, men of trade, farming, commerce and mining, preachers, opposition politicians, reporters and cameramen.

Everyone talked (except perhaps the cameramen), no one said anything, and it was an expensive disaster. Some hotels were charging £50 a night, a fortune then. The price of steaks was often quoted, and all the poor relations were fast looking for cheaper accommodation and places to eat.

The conference was late even getting started. After a fortnight it still hadn't really got off the ground, so Mr Smith announced he was going back to Rhodesia: "I have a country with peculiar problems - such as terrorism and sanctions - to run and we must go back and get on with the job."

Before Christmas the conference adjourned, never to be reconvened.

Ivor Richard, the Chairman, tried a Kissinger shuffle through Africa. He seemed a reasonable man, and clever. Someone should have told him the problems were insoluble. Ian Smith had told him in his down-to-earth fashion (African earth, too), that it was "like feeding crocodiles. The more you give the more they want."

So Rhodesia got down to fighting again. At the beginning of 1977 the Minister of Defence, Reg Cowper, proposed call-ups should be extended to fifty-year-olds, and for longer spells, with less recourse to exemption for everyone. Mr Cowper resigned soon after, about the same time that the British Foreign Secretary, Anthony Crosland, died of a heart attack while studying papers on the Rhodesian issue. But the drive to get the twelve thousand uninvolved men in this age group into the war continued.

Martin was one of these. He had not volunteered, and for this received a lot of indirect criticism. He would not volunteer, he said, to fight for a cause he did not believe in and which was plainly a lost cause. He was perhaps one of the few men who had seen war action - in the Royal Artillery in Korea twenty-seven years before, presumably in a fight in which he believed.

Susie's husband was in a special unit, "SWAT", like the black-uniformed American unit then starring in a show on television. Designed to combat urban terrorism, they were all excellent shots and trained in abseiling down high buildings, breaking through windows, being dropped from helicopters on to roofs, bursting into locked rooms wearing bullet-proof jackets, all the exciting stuff kids dream about.

Another young friend spent his time speeding up and down hillsides and through ditches and streams on a small high-powered motorbike, in a special unit designed to get over rough country fast.

I suppose unless men get it out of their systems, they are still looking for exciting deeds of fiction heroes when they are fifty, like most of the volunteers in Rhodesia were, at first.

Africans were not conscripted. No one said why. Perhaps too many of them had their sympathies with the enemy. If sufficiently educated and fit, they could volunteer for the police, army or police reserve.

Every day, as I went to the Police Station to work, about sixty or seventy of these police reservists would be seen marching up and down the parade ground, still without uniforms. As far as I could see they received very sketchy instruction and were then given rifles, a blue overall uniform, and sent off to the tribal areas to keep law and order. It seemed a very dangerous situation to me, and I watched with misgiving as they increased in numbers. But, fortunately, I wasn't being asked for my opinion.

At first lots of older volunteers enjoyed the war. They leapt around like overgrown cadets in their ill-fitting camouflage uniforms, waving rifles: "Just let me get at them!"

As the war progressed in time and intensity, and their service commitments increased, some of them stood back and began to ask: "What are we fighting for?" They watched their businesses and farms, which had taken their lifetimes to build up, decline through lack of attention. Many had to leave their wives and children alone on isolated farms while they themselves went off to "Bright Light": to guard other farms. Their wives became nervous and strung-up at being on their own and trying to look after the work of the farm and the children, supervising large gangs of African labourers who believed women of any colour were lower-grade creatures. And at night an attack on their homestead was not unlikely. Their children's schoolwork declined, and the older children became uppity with mom - dad was in the bush.

I saw one toddler in the supermarket - she couldn't have been older than three - with Mom and a smaller child riding in the trolley, pull at her mother's jeans, pointing to the small packets of sweets. It was not for herself, it appeared, because Mom replied: "No, darling, I've got Daddy's things already for the bush."

By the time that child was five and ready for school, what sort of havoc would there be in this country that her Daddy was again preparing to fight for? Would this child have to take her seat in a grossly overcrowded school with twenty black children to every one white? Would all those children be sufficiently advanced in English for a class to even get under way? Or if the class should be conducted in Shona, would this child learn enough to be able to compete in the world outside, as her background and hereditary would require of her?

Or is this an over-simplification of the state of affairs?

In July 1976, the defence budget jumped by 40% to R$84 million, and in February 1977 to R$98M, not including R$47M for the police vote. The money had to come from somewhere, so sales tax on all articles and foodstuffs, with one or two exceptions, went up to 15%, and income tax bore a 10% surcharge once more, though we were assured it wasn't half as bad as Europe, or most other countries.

And a new language grew up. A Rhodesian accent is different from most South African accents, if you know what to listen for. The guttural Dutch influence is less pronounced, but the thinning of the vowels and loss of diphthongs is there. Rhodesian men talk in their throats, women in a high voice without using any of their facial or nasal resonators. In moderation, when the tone of the voice is good, it is not an unpleasant accent.

But most Rhodesians' vocabularies (and more so South Africans') are painfully small, in men for decent words at least. This was remedied to their satisfaction at least when a new war slang grew up, a language centred round brown jobs (soldiers), blue jobs (airmen), and the fuzz. Then there were floppies (terrorists - they flopped down when shot), flat dogs (crocodiles), graze and *chibuli* (food and beer), and invariably *lekker* chicks (the desirable sort men in the bush dream about).

When Rhodesia started to manufacture its own firearms, it hit the front page (no censorship, no!). Variations of the Israeli-manufactured Uzi, a semi-automatic rifle that could be fired from hip or shoulder, were designed and manufactured by different firms around the country.

Once again Rhodesia was proving its skill and ingenuity. It was a pity this pride could not have been used to manufacture articles to build a nation .It would have been a fine nation.

As expected with so many firearms around, armed robbery increased: a crime that had hardly been known before in Rhodesia. Policemen still did not carry side arms, but by 1976 rifles and Uzis were carried as a matter of course when going to rural areas or to known "situations" in African townships, for instance.

So to be in the swing (as we lived on the edge of the bush) we got back from the farm our pistol and 303 rifle, (dated by our son-in-law at 1890 or so, and surely used in the Matabele Wars). We had bought the pistol years before, while on the farm, about the time of the Battle of Sinoia; the rifle we had taken over as part of the farm. If we went into town for a big night out on Saturday night, perhaps dinner and a visit to a drive-in cinema in Fort Victoria, we took the pistol. If we ventured to Bulawayo to see the children we took both pistol and rifle. It was not a pleasant way to take an evening out or to travel. We had target practice, and I was a better shot than you would think.

It was not only the Israeli rifles Rhodesians admired, it was their raids that won our hearts. After the raid on Entebbe, Rhodesia decided to try the same. Sick of terrorist attacks from Mozambique, Rhodesian commandos struck by helicopter and by road into this neighbouring territory, at a terrorist base camp seven miles from Umtali and the border. They destroyed the camp, killed three or four hundred terrorists and Tanzanian troops, and knocked out the border post. They returned after a few hours "having suffered only a few minor injuries".

Mozambique, with the United Nations and Britain held firmly by the nose, said the raid had been on a defenceless refugee camp. But I don't think anyone in the world believed them, including the Russians, who were allegedly sponsoring the war from the east.

Rhodesia maintained that hot pursuit was not the same as invasion, and that we were only following in the footsteps of Sir Francis Drake when he "singed the King of Spain's beard" four hundred years before.

When the Portuguese retired from Mozambique and Angola in 1974, the borders began to close in on Rhodesia. Umtali was a pretty town a few kilometres from the Mozambique border (you will have trouble finding it on the map now - look for Mutare).

Although it was the third largest town in Rhodesia, and indeed one of the four cities of the country, it kept its small-town atmosphere, with flamboyant trees, low buildings, large gardens and one main street.

In the good old days of Beira holidays all Rhodesia was a little envious of Umtali, the nearest place to the sea. The townsfolk would nip over the border often and bring back seafoods and demijohns of Portuguese wine, and have their tanks filled with off-ration petrol.

But suddenly Umtali was on the forefront of the war, and came under rocket and mortar attack at 4 o'clock one morning. Roofs were burst in, windows broken, furniture destroyed and cars damaged. No one was hurt, but everyone got into a dither about the safety of their children and a great patriotic fervour swept through town. Five hundred pupils from the girls' high school marched through the main street singing "Rhodesians never die":

"For we are all Rhodesians,
And we'll fight through thick and thin."

Their song was repeated six times the next day over the radio. They carried posters: "Nothing will scare us away", "We have faith in our soldiers", "Rhodesia is super", "Umtali can take it".

There was a special poignancy in the high school girls and their marching song as three months before three of their schoolmates had been blown up by a landmine when visiting their friends on a farm nearby. One was killed and another had to have both legs amputated.

A titled elderly woman (her name, oddly enough, was Lady Wilson) said she was "bloody angry" when her farm was fired upon. It was only three hundred metres from the border. She had sent two armed Frelimo fighters packing a few months before when Umtali was shelled: "Shoo! Go over your side of the border. You can't come into Rhodesia like this," she told them as they walked along a border road to her farm.

Britain said: "We deplore all violence." They said also: "We cannot recognise the right of hot pursuit across international borders exists". No wonder Rhodesians could never understand British reasoning

It is tremendous country up there on the border mountains, high and cool, with mists. Cecil Rhodes planted oak trees and apple, peach, apricot, plum and pear orchards. Later, tea and coffee estates provided for Rhodesia during sanctions, with some over for export. Green peas and fresh vegetables grew more flavoursome and less "strung out" in these mountains than on the hotter, lower farms, and this was where most of the frozen and canned vegetables were grown and manufactured. The roads to the farms were often mined, shelled and fired upon, and the farm homesteads were attacked at night. The African workers were abducted and their children prevented from going to school.

Every time something happened, the newspapers would send a photographer and reporter to see them, sure to come back with the residents' message: "We're staying. Nothing will move us."

World War II safety tactics were now needed. After more shelling of Umtali three hundred bomb shelters were built by people living on the "bad" side of the steep hill that rises above the town.

Cecil Rhodes had once moved the whole town in the 1890s across this pass and into the valley facing Mozambique, because the railway could not be taken over the steep hill. It was called Christmas Pass by the pioneers. Corrugated- iron and board houses, furniture, goods, all had been taken over the hill on ox wagons. In those days it was the lions that used to roam the streets of Old Umtali that people feared most, these and malaria and black-water fever.

In April 1976, the terror war was increased and spread distrust and fear around the land. Men, women and children of all races, in all places, of all walks of life, were attacked apparently indiscriminately anywhere the attackers were likely to get away with it.

Middle-aged people were attacked in daytime as they served in their stores in remote areas, or on the edges of townships; the incapacitated elderly were murdered in their beds; young girls were shot in ambushes while being driven from school, at road blocks on the Botswana border when they were eight or ten or eleven and staying with their grandparents; tourists were shot at while travelling on main roads or making ferry trips on Lake Kariba.

Farmers were beginning to regard ambushes and mines as occupational hazards: they were fired on as they sat down to dinner, as they walked to their barns and stores, as they drove to dip their neighbour's cattle while he was away on police reserve duties, as they shut their kitchen doors in the evenings, as they locked up their security fences in the afternoon, even as they drank their beer at the local club. They took to flying in their own small planes to avoid the hazards of the roads, and were fired on as they got into their aircraft. They went fishing in the Zambezi and were fired on from the opposite bank. After a while the terrorists established themselves in the African farming areas and tribal lands, so the interior of the country was no longer relatively safe. Sometimes African beer halls in townships adjoining the cities were shot up, and grenades were thrown into nightclubs in the centre of Salisbury. A lone terrorist shot two Indians as they fished in a small dam in a weekend picnic spot near Bulawayo. It was difficult to see what they were aiming to do.

If I'd still been at Victoria Falls and working for the newspaper, my telephone would never have stopped ringing as terrorism reached a climax in November and December of 1976. Goods trains and bridges were blown up; the farmer living very near Shangaan Musha, where the tribal dancing Martin presented took place, was shot in his house, and one of the dancers was shot while the troupe was returning to the village in the back of an open vehicle. Peter's Motel was attacked and an ex-colleague (by coincidence a Canadian again) from the touring company was shot dead in the reception office where I had worked.

The police captured the terrorist, who confessed to all the Victoria Falls murders, landmine detonations, shootings in Bulawayo, and to one of the most shocking murders of the sickening fight, that of a bishop, a priest and a nun, half-way along the road to Bulawayo from the Falls. Then he escaped while being held at the Falls in the small prison at the police station. The hunt went on for weeks in the uninhabited country along the Zambezi, but he wasn't recaptured. He might have crossed the river into Zambia, or the border to northern Botswana. We heard very little about how he managed to get away in the first place, and often wondered who were our friends and who supported the side that paid best, promised most, or threatened worst.

This bishop and his party had been stopped on an isolated dirt road, ordered to get out of the car and were shot down in cold blood. One nun escaped with a bullet in her leg by crawling under the car. But the worst atrocity against the missionaries in 1977 was against seven priests and nuns who were hauled out of their mission building, walked down the road, and once more shot down apparently without a second thought. A priest, who lay still and feigned dead, lived - heaped over by the bodies of his fellow-workers for Christ and the African people. One elderly nun with arthritis, who fell over before she reached the killing ground was also spared.

Missionaries were the most affected of the white population, as they did not arm themselves, and they lived in isolated areas where police and army personnel travelled only in mine proof vehicles. Some were abducted while travelling isolated roads on foot or by car, and were never heard of again.

But the African tribesmen were as usual the most vulnerable and therefore the most oppressed. There were innumerable stories of abduction, murder, mutilation and rape that rank in horror with stories of Nazi oppression. An African worked in Fort Victoria who had part of his lips and ears cut off by "Freedom Fighters". His wife was obliged to fry and eat them.

Twenty or thirty terrorists marched into an Eastern Districts tea estate, robbed all the African families present, then gunned down all the twenty-seven men whom they had grouped together, within sight of their wives and children. I suppose their crime was that they worked for the white man.

Many hundreds of African boys and girls walked more or less willingly over into Mozambique and Botswana from their schools on the borders. From there they were taken to training camps in Zambia and Tanzania to become guerrillas or prostitutes.

From one school alone four hundred children aged twelve to eighteen were abducted in one night by two terrorists. A few escaped, and after deputations and personal appeals from parents, who hired buses to go and see them being kept in Francistown Police Station (Botswana), fifty more returned. Many were afraid to go back to their homes. Three hundred of them were taken to Zambia. A few weeks later it was reported that fifteen of these had been shot for refusing to join a particular political group.

Their parents were normal well-meaning Africans, schoolteachers, farmers, storeowners and small businessmen. Were their children so bored they would do anything for excitement, or did they really hate the white man so much?

Surely no end can justify these means. In the slaughter the end was being lost sight of.

So for their protection, and to try and stop those who were in

211

sympathy or from fear aiding the terrorists, the Africans in the border areas were moved into "protected villages", something quite out of keeping with their way of life.

Normally they lived in small, scattered kraals with their relatives only, among their own tribe, each cultivating a patch of land near the kraal. They did not steal each other's crops, and being nearby, could protect them from buck and pig and baboon. They surrounded themselves with their cattle, goats and chickens, and their children went out every morning to take their father's cattle or their mother's goats to graze in the grasslands nearby.

In the protected villages there were too many strangers, living too close together. They had to walk too far to their fields and could not guard them at night when shut away in the security of the fenced village. They were told how good the villages were, with hospitals, schools and a good clean water supply and sanitation. But they missed washing their clothes in the rivers, and Saturday night beer drinks at neighbouring kraals.

The District Commissioners said, quite rightly I'm sure, better these hardships than suffering terrorists' atrocities. But still they threw food over the fences to the terrorists, and smuggled it under their clothes (producing a lot of "pregnant" women), as they went out each morning to their fields past the guards at the gate.

Overseas correspondents said with some truth that these villages bore a nasty resemblance to concentration camps.

EIGHTEEN

In the middle of it all Britt Ekland arrived like a Scandinavian spring flower.   When she arrived at Zimbabwe Ruins it was probably one of the most exciting things that had happened since the Queen of Sheba left.   A German film company spent several months in the area (fortunately during our historic heat-wave), making a fiction film about the nineteenth-century slave trade in Nyasaland.

It was the sort of film that would never pass the film censors in Rhodesia, but it was really tremendously exciting for us simple souls.   We could look out of the bedroom window at the sheikh's tent on a rocky outcrop thirty metres away.   It took months to design, manufacture and erect this monstrous tent out of heavy canvas painted to look like skins.   It was used for one day's shooting.   But when it was finished, the interior was a place of glory, with gold foil on floors and pillars, gold silk curtains, gold-painted seats and low tables, and above all exquisite large brass urns and ornaments.

Our dog, Vicky, found the filming and general activity great fun. They were shooting one sequence at the sheikh's tent over and over again.   Cameron Mitchell rode up over the rocks, pulled up his horse (generally), and after preliminary greetings said to Ray Milland, who played the sheikh in white robes and ornamental black cape: "When da Silva gives his word, he gives his goddam word." He then dismounted and followed the sheikh into the tent.

It seemed a relatively simple two-minute shot.   We watched them act it out twenty times or more, while we clutched on to Vicky's collar – so near was excitement and running horses.   She managed to get away once and it meant another retake, but they all took it philosophically.   I suppose you can't really have a sequence of a large Alsatian running on the heels of a Portuguese prospector in wild Africa.   But she took such an interest in the filming I'm sure that she can be found tucked away unnoticed in one of the shots.

213

She loved the German cameramen and production assistants, and they played with her to while away the endless waiting that seemed such a major part of filmmaking. Being a German shepherd dog she naturally had an affinity for Germans, and had learnt their language from a neighbour and visitors at the Falls.

Stars, actors, technicians and production staff spent hours waiting around in the heat; the actors often dressed in cumbersome and ornate Victorian garments, and with faces made up with false beards and melting paint. The slaves had the advantage at this stage.

But after the stunt man nearly fell off his horse twice as it stumbled on the rocks, Ray Milland dried up on his lines (how he could I don't know because we ourselves knew them by now), and the horse put its head in the wrong position, a car started up at the hotel, a plane flew over, an African gardener burst into song, a child in the watching group cried, and a lesser sheikh forgot to come out of the tent in time, then, finally, the action was complete and they moved on to another ninety-second sequence to the sighs of relief from the gathered audience.

We were further relieved when Cameron Mitchell abandoned his horse for the next shot and stood on a box while he talked about da Silva's word, and the audience focused on Sheikh Milland.

They stripped the tent down at the end of a long day. When the film came back from being developed a few days later, the editor found a flicker in the film caused by some electrical fault. So they rebuilt the tent interior and patched up the outside (it had rained heavily in between), and started again.

Cameron Mitchell had already left the country, so the action was changed a little and included only the back view of the stunt man dressed in his clothes.

So that the schedule would not be put out, some of the interior scenes were re-filmed at night. In their harum-scarum rush they drove over the standpipe at the back of our house, so we had a fresh-water stream but no water in the house. Martin put in a temporary joint by the light of the sheikh's tent. This rush, rush,

rush, then wait, wait, wait was worse than trying to get somewhere by plane during the early hours of the morning.

Each of the stars had his own way of passing the time: Ron Ely, with sixty-four Tarzan TV hours to his credit, went for a run round the golf course every day and ate a lot of yoghurt; Trevor Howard sat around a lot and talked to anyone who showed interest; Ray Milland sat in the verandah by his room and read or chatted; Cameron Mitchell's voice could always be heard - he liked to be in a group, got bored and flew off to Salisbury or wherever he could; Britt Ekland hid herself away, though occasionally she would sunbathe by the pool if no-one was around, or she would be driven down to the garden cafe by the ruins (in the smartest car Martin could provide for hire, which wasn't saying much, though he personally and reverently polished the seat every day). She would sit reading in the quiet shade, a little lonely, never wanting to talk to anyone except perhaps Joan, who owned the cafe and had a warm heart, or to Vicky, or to Rod Stewart in California daily. This was quite an achievement on our bush phones and when she talked in private from Martin's office it gave him another seat to polish.

Many thought her insignificant, dressed in cheesecloth and big hats, and a little dull, but when she gave an interview on our television, she came to life as she talked and charmed everyone, and we could see why she was a star. I was naturally on her side when criticism was made - she liked my dog.

In a pretty creek of Lake Kyle a mock river-station was constructed. What seemed to us to be a magnificent structure appeared on the rocks, to represent a two-storey hotel of wood, thatch, stone and kaolite, which was carved and painted to look like stone. We wandered around it with its wide steps and thick rough timbers above the large hall-lounge, and thought we wouldn't mind living in it. A big open fireplace lay in the centre beneath a hole in the roof for the smoke. Beside the creek was a landing stage built of rough logs, which looked better than most of the permanent ones around the boat sites of Kyle.

But most magnificent was a fifteen-metre-long paddle steamer:

the "Southern Cross". The paddle wheels were driven round by the water as it moved along with the help of a concealed outboard motor, and the smoke that belched out of the big funnel emanated from tyres burnt directly underneath. It was destined to be blown up in the final scenes.

Some filming was done on a small island in the lake, and while constructing a hut, labourers accidentally dug up two African graves. The remains were buried in another part of the island, but from then on things started to go wrong. In the large cast of "slaves", who were being played by Africans from local tribal lands, superstition was rife.

Their fears were proved right when the lake ferry hired for the day sank 150 metres from the shore while carrying thirty-five African extras, staff and technicians. It was loaded with a quarter of a million dollars-worth of cameras, sound equipment and vehicles. Five people were drowned and all the equipment sank to the muddy bottom of the lake.

There were choppy waves on the lake and a heavy mist. No-one on the bank saw the ferry sink, and the alarm wasn't raised until one of the technicians swam ashore. Then the "Southern Cross" with funnel askew and broken deck and paddles flying round went steaming out like some wounded hero, and did the bulk of the rescue.

Next day the police sub-aqua team arrived from Salisbury. They recovered the bodies and floated the vehicles and equipment up to the surface by balloons. Nearly all the film taken that day, including the "blowing up" of the paddle steamer "Southern Cross" could still be used. This was fortunate as many of the scenes featured Britt Ekland, who had already left Rhodesia.

One scene featured a pool in the rocks where "slave" extras would be shown bathing. As no suitable pool could be found, one was blasted in the rocks right by the hotel. The few visitors we had in the area were fascinated, and all the neighbouring farmers thought the war had arrived in their backyard.

While the extras bathed, actors and actresses dresses as wealthy nineteenth-century Portuguese drank champagne on the rocks, cheering on a sheikh while he took pot shots at the naked swimmers. One sequence showed an African with his head just above the water. Before he had gone in we had seen wires along his head, invisible a couple of metres away. Suddenly, as the shots were being fired, his head appeared to split open, revealing "bones and tissue" while "blood" poured down his face. The poor man could hardly have expected it by the look of horror on his face, which must surely have come over as the finest piece of acting in the film.

"Right!" the Director said, this time after the first take, "we certainly can't retake that, right or wrong."

Later in the story crocodiles were introduced to the same pool from the nearby game ranch. I hate to think what their part in the story was.

I suppose in the flow of the story these scenes would not appear too horrific, but it is easy to see one reason above all why the film could never be shown uncensored in southern Africa: one scene featured Britt Ekland (it was her stand-in) being raped by a black slave.

Gradually they all departed and left us very quiet again. The next door hotel started to rebuild the bar after it had been turned into some Zanzibar-looking den for the film; Martin and the other car-hire firms took their battered cars and trucks to the panel beaters, and replaced misused engines and tyres; the ferry owner inspected his wreckage on a deserted grassy bank; and the hotel receptionist went to live in Germany with one of the film production men.

Lake Kyle, it seemed, would never be the same again.

There had been a lot of ill feeling among the local residents about the fraternisation that had gone on between the black and white members of the film retinue. This was a few months before we were told officially we must all be brothers (and sisters presumably).

It came as a shock to us in our sheltered existence to see white

217

men playing chase with Zulu girls around the hotel grounds in full view, and full disapproval, of the respectable and conservative black hotel staff. There were audible sighs of relief when the crew packed up and left.

Yet, after a few months, our hotel owner couldn't stand the quiet and went off to Switzerland (he wasn't allowed into Germany with his Rhodesian passport), to see if he could persuade anyone to make another film at the Ruins. But they would only come, they said, when there was a settlement and an end to terrorism, which, it seemed, they were almost as weary of waiting for as we were.

Tourism was going through an extremely bad time. Zimbabwe Ruins had always been the quietest branch, but, before the latest terrorism attacks, had been building up numbers happily. German and American tour companies stopped coming, and the independent visitors who flew into Fort Victoria for one or two days of touring, dropped to half a dozen or less a day. Oddly enough, young women still came on their own – mostly English, South African and Australian. And we saw more Australians suddenly than any other nationality. Perhaps with the girls it was a risky business their travelling on their own anyway, so the additional hazards meant little.

The hotels suffered because Rhodesians and South Africans would no longer travel by road for fear of being ambushed. The largest hotel group in the country reckoned they lost a million dollars in six months, after losing a million over the twelve months before.

The Safari Hotel near the Ruins had a fire in its thatched dining room, probably caused by a lightning flash, and it was virtually closed for rebuilding. The owner of the Zimbabwe Ruins Hotel, from which Martin operated, managed to peg along on its good reputation with the locals and the army - he served good food and often had a party going on.

The tourist board brought out a scheme where you could travel from almost anywhere in Rhodesia for four dollars on a tour bus, as long as you stayed a few nights in affected hotels. Even then, city people were wary, and only a trickle took advantage of the Zimbabwe Ruins bus from Salisbury every weekend. Call-ups were also affecting prospective holidaymakers. After months in the Rhodesian bush young guys, and now older men, no longer wanted to spend their holidays out in the bundu once more.

Every month another hotel closed. The farmers in one isolated area in the Eastern Highlands clubbed together to run the abandoned hotel. The remaining civilians needed somewhere to go. Rhodesia was shrinking, and its facilities with it.

The National Tourist Board and Air Rhodesia had beautiful offices in the major cities of South Africa and were constantly running promotional campaigns. The offices sat clean and empty with few enquiries. So they employed more girls to go out to the supermarkets and shopping centres and to tea parties to convince the South Africans how safe it was.

The tourist board said it was essential to keep these offices going so that when the great settlement arrived, the wheels would be oiled and ready to be set in motion, ready for the great boom. Paula was now working in Johannesburg (had she got to "Go" at last?), for the tourist board, and we heard she was a great persuader when it came to convincing people how super Rhodesia was, at least at Victoria Falls.

I suppose this was the same reason we stayed at Zimbabwe Ruins for so long - we half agreed with the forecast of prosperous times beyond out wildest dreams, for at least a few years after a settlement.

Press censorship successfully prevented us from finding out many troubles that were happening in the country, but it was clear that law and order was breaking down in African tribal trust areas. Cattle rustling was becoming so rampant that a mandatory sentence of nine years was placed on a conviction. This was an appalling state of affairs and harked back to the dark ages, but the worst of it was that the thieving still went on. Sometimes the guilty were given eighteen years, and even pregnant women and girls were sentenced to nine years.

219

One very large ranch not far from Fort Victoria, which was completely surrounded by tribal areas, lost cattle worth a quarter of a million dollars in less than a year. The tribesmen were utterly cruel in their captures, and would hack off the back legs of a cow to keep the meat fresh. The cow took a week or so to die. (This goes one worse than the live cattle export trade in Britain and Ireland.)

Gangs of juveniles systematically worked their way through the stores that served the tribal communities, stealing what took their fancy, or sometimes clearing out the whole stock. Every day when I worked at the Police Station, groups of these stock thieves and store breakers would be brought in on the backs of lorries: we didn't run to black Marias. The police hadn't enough manpower to cope, the courts hadn't time, magistrates, staff or space to try them all, and the prisons room enough to put them in.

As one young policeman remarked, he didn't know which would happen first: whether there'd be no cattle and stores left in Victoria, or there'd be no tribesmen left in the villages. On this I was willing to agree with Ian Smith that it was all a communist plot. It would appear to be working, though at great cost to the innocent once more. The villages got the worst of it from both sides.

As the strain on the Police Force increased, so did the brutality of the questioning. Time was short and confessions essential to prevent long-drawn-out harangues in court. And the easiest and quickest way to get confessions through the ages has been to knock the accused man or woman around and threaten them. We all knew when the black man took over he would have little compunction how he treated his fellow men in similar circumstances. (Have you read the news lately? Weren't we right?) But as far as I am concerned nothing condones cruelty.

Not that Rhodesia was alone in this respect either. In February 1977 Britain itself admitted charges of "torture and inhumane treatment" against Irish terror suspects. This probably made inquisitors of the world feel better, but it should have made them weep even more bitter tears. How low can a man stoop before he admits that it must be the principles he is upholding that are wrong?

But life in the cities carried on apparently little changed except that women began to come into their own at last in commerce and even on farms, and jobs were actually advertised for men over fifty, as they were unlikely to be called up. Ian Smith said Rhodesia had enough chromites to last us for a thousand years and it did not matter a jot that America preferred to import theirs from Russia. Salisbury's First Street was being turned into a mall with continental-style cafes. At lunchtime the low walls containing the flowerbeds were filled buttock-to-buttock with African workers from the stores and offices, with their wives and children. It makes one wonder where they spent lunchtime before.

Twenty thousand African squatters did threaten the smooth life of the Salisbury townsman once, but they were successfully and peaceably moved away to quickly erected accommodation - we'd never seen a municipality move so fast. They even overcame their inbred horror of traditional-style pole and daga and thatch houses and allowed these to be built on approved land on the other side of town.

Eleven years after UDI, Rhodesia minted coins without the King or Queen of England's head for the first time. Africa's only bagpipe maker died, a crocodile took over the pool at the fourteenth hole of the Victoria Falls golf course, and dassie (rock rabbit) droppings were found to make excellent gunpowder. And 2,500 elephants "had to be shot" in the south-east Rhodesian game reserve of Gonare-Zhou . Wild animals were being squeezed out of Africa.

It was said that Rhodesia had the second highest divorce rate in the world. Too many girls in Rhodesia fixed their sites on marriage as soon as possible after leaving school, and would not be put off by the distressing number of teenage marriages that ended in divorce. These were the days in Rhodesia when many girls were still making "bottom drawers" or at least kists, preparatory to the great day of their wedding, and each young bride-to-be looked no further than the day when she would be a star in a long white dress and veil.

The road accidents per capita were among the world's worst.

Yet still Rhodesia was a wonderful place to live; every visitor said how they loved to come to Rhodesia, how they loved the people and their friendliness and hospitality and helpfulness. South Africans, particularly, loved Rhodesia, and many said they would come and settle in the country if times were better.

There was space, ease and a wonderful climate. Rhodesia took no part in the rat race. When Africans took over there would still be the same of these, yet nearly 15,000 out of the population of 250,000 white people looked in 1976 for another place to go. So there was something else required from life, even by the most simple-minded of us.

But the basic fact that put most people off was that each family wishing to emigrate was allowed to take with them only a thousand dollars (about £900.) plus personal belongings. In August 1976 Ian Smith urged people not to leave: "I say that with evidence I have before me, I have every confidence in the future of Rhodesia. I would urge those planning to leave to think seriously before running." Rhodesians even scoffed at those who decided to move south, "taking the chicken run".

The world was wrong, said Mr Smith. He did not think blacks should necessarily be allowed to run countries and make a mess of them just because they were black, he told Australian television viewers.

Some decided to stay until the beer ran out. As there were only 365 days in 1977 as opposed to 366 in 1976, one Salisbury columnist suggested next year couldn't be worse.

A far cry from the: "Next year will be better" cry of the farmers when the country was young. Our country had aged and was tired.

After the first surprise of the agreement to majority rule in two years, the next amazing thing that was sprung upon us was the repeal of the Land Tenure Act. This Act had first been introduced to the country in 1931, although it had its beginnings in the setting aside of "native reserves" by the British South Africa Company in 1898.

The Land Tenure Act divided the country half-and-half into

white and black areas. This led to bitterness on the part of the Africans, as there were twenty-six of them to every European then. It wasn't as bad as it seemed on the face of it, because a very large number of Africans earned their livings on white-owned farms and in mines and factories, which produced nearly all the goods exported from the country, and in turn through taxation supported schools, hospitals, roads and communications for all races.

African farming was almost always on a subsistence level. If a farmer was to rise above this, farms had to cover several thousand acres in Rhodesian conditions. On cattle ranches they talked of the number of acres per head of cattle rather than head of cattle per acre, as in Britain. To grow less than a hundred acres of tobacco a season did not pay, and the same lands could not be planted to tobacco again for at least four years because of disease. Much of the land on farms could not be used because of rocky outcrops, kopjes and vleis.

Now the Act proposed that Africans could buy land and trade anywhere except designated urban areas. They could stay in any hotel throughout the country and drink where they liked until normal closing time. To avoid immediate emigration of all whites, most European residential areas were still, for the present, reserved for whites, and government schools and hospitals were still segregated. The tribal trust lands would still be reserved for tribesmen. The Minister of Lands, Mark Partridge, qualifying these reservations, said: "It is felt that to force changes too rapidly would be disruptive, and any changes towards integrated development should be allowed to take place on a phased and unhurried basis."

If only the Land Tenure Act had been repealed at the beginning of negotiations, we would now have had a settlement, in theory the end of terrorism, an elected black government, and our borders open to trade. But we had always been told this Act was the cornerstone of Rhodesian Front policy. We assumed that when the Land Tenure Act went, so would the Rhodesian Front. But it was not like that at all, it appeared.

Putting a good front on it as usual, Mr Partridge told us the reforms were "not only inevitable but progressive". He told the House of Assembly: "We must move with the times. Let us do so cheerfully and intelligently and with good hope for the future." It made one wonder where they had been sleeping all through former negotiations.

The Bill scraped through with the help of wheelchairs for the sick Members and the winning-over of some tribally elected black MPs. Only twelve MPs voted against the Bill, while the African opposition abstained from voting. I suppose they couldn't be seen to vote on the same side as the Rhodesian Front.

The owner of the cafe and curio shop at Zimbabwe Ruins started to knock down part of his shop at the same time as the Land Tenure Act was repealed. It was probably only coincidence. Tourism had dropped so low he was losing money, so his family decided to retreat to their small farm near Fort Victoria while they looked for jobs, maybe overseas.

This change of heart in such a man was astounding. He was the keenest member of the Police Reserve I knew - the sort of man who a year before had talked of fighting it out to the last man. We had thought he would never leave.

Rather than let anyone have anything of his that they were not prepared to pay for (whether they were a quasi-government body or private individuals, black or white), he destroyed the buildings he had put up years before. Many were threatening to adopt a scorched-earth policy, should they have to leave Rhodesia without recompense, but this was the first time we had seen anyone enact it.

Our Zimbabwe Ruins Hotel landlord sold his hotel to the neighbouring Safari Lodge Hotel owner on the day the Act was repealed.

After two years, except for our new landlord, we would soon be the oldest inhabitants of the small community of Zimbabwe Ruins. Martin's overseas holiday bonus - a relic of Colonial days - was due, so we decided to go to Europe on holiday and at the same time look around at the employment situation. Martin had not been to Europe for eighteen years. He really enjoyed his job in tourism, and would have liked to stay in the business. The USA had a great tourist industry, but would they love us with our one thousand Rhodesian dollars? We doubted it.

The Reserve Bank would also only allow us R$250 each for a holiday, but at least the Rhodesian dollar was almost on a par with the English pound. Then, when we appealed, the Bank relented and allowed us to take R$100 each from the next year's allowance. They must have been clever to know what would be happening next year in this uncertain country.

We planned to go for six weeks and hoped our English relatives loved us more than we deserved.

We'd be sure to take our "Rhodesia is Super" T-shirts to complete the picture of a pair of middle-aged homeless hippies. Our Rhodesian newspaper suggested living on nothing overseas was all a question of timing: you get to the Trevi Fountains before the cleaners, and to Trafalgar Square before the pigeons. Whether we left Rhodesia or whether we stayed, we were all as a nation saying now: "Goodbye Rhodesia." Some had the strength of will and minds broad enough to say: "Hail Zimbabwe!"

We returned from our holiday long enough to serve our notices at work, put our furniture and belongings into wooden tobacco crates for shipping to Southampton, send Vicky for the purgatory of six months quarantine kennels in England, persuade Susie to have our cat, Smokey, and arrange to rent a flat for a month in Westbourne Road, London, from a Rhodesian.

The border posts of Rhodesia, where few passed any more, bore their signs still like weekend hostesses: "We hope you have enjoyed your stay."

We had! Twenty-five years. Now: "Goodbye."

EPILOGUE

In 1987 Prime Minister Robert Mugabe first began to show himself as the dictator he intended to become. He brutally, and without mercy, quashed the opposition party, the Zimbabwe African People's Union, led by Joshua Nkomo. This was the political party of the Ndebele people, living in the west and southwest of the country. His storm troops slaughtered 7000 men, women and children, and injured, tortured, raped, imprisoned and maimed many thousands more, burning their houses and destroying crops. Nkomo was exiled, leaving Mugabe in complete control.

Our earlier personal touches with murder, in the fight against the terrorists, were but the run-up to the routing of whites from the country that was Rhodesia. In the year 2000, Mugabe declared on Zimbabwe television, referring to farmers: "Our present state of mind is that you are our enemies, because you have behaved as enemies of Zimbabwe and that we are full of anger."

On Heroes' Day, which used to be Rhodes and Founders weekend, in African Unity Square (that was Cecil Square) in Harare (that was Salisbury), Robert Mugabe promised a surprisingly unenthusiastic audience that he would continue the "noble" seizure of 300 white-owned farms in spite of Britain's "crusade to destroy Zimbabwe". All around him the flowers were blooming in the well-watered beds, which were still laid out in the form of the Union flag of Great Britain.

Before the white man built commercial farms, the country was mostly uninhabited bush. Many of the farmers were ex-soldiers, settled there after the Second World War. The way politics are going in Zimbabwe, the land will soon be back to bush, but not the virgin bush, the *bundu* of Livingstone and Selous - by this time all the animals will be eaten or on the shelves as Chinese medicine. *Ufulu*, this elusive "freedom", is being lived out by starving, unemployed, diseased people in a barren land.

In the middle of the year 2000, the first white farmers to have their farms invaded protested by going on strike, and they even persuaded the police in some areas to restore order. The invasions, which came to be known as the land grab, were pronounced illegal by the Supreme Court of Zimbabwe. But to no avail: the black settlers, chanting: "Forward with Comrade Mugabe, forward with Zanu-PF" seized 50 farms in one weekend, bringing to 300 the farms violently and often murderously overrun.

Having won his re-election in June, though by only a narrow majority, in spite of intimidation and cheating, Comrade Mugabe now had to ensure his position by resettling 500,000 of his supporters on over 3000 of the most highly productive farms in the country. Each of these farms was already housing and supporting several hundred black employees and their families, who would immediately be made jobless and homeless.

But the terror was not confined to the killing of farmers. Black opposition politicians were murdered; women, black and white were raped; and black schoolchildren kidnapped and taken away for "re-education" and training in the army. To oppose the government was only for the "suicidal brave or the completely foolish" according to one leader of the opposition party, the Movement for Democratic Change.

Despite winning every Harare seat in the June 2000 parliamentary election, the MDC could do little to stop the oppression but watch. Now President Mugabe, oddly adopting colonial displays of pageantry, rode in his Rolls-Royce with full military escort, which included 32 mounted policemen dressed in the 1890 uniform of the British South Africa Police, even to the white pith helmets. He was about to open what was described as the most oppressive parliament yet devised in this country's chequered history.

(It could be said Comrade Mugabe has good taste if not plebeian. Before sanctions restricted his visits to Europe, he liked to stay at Claridges or the Hilton when he visited London several times a year to shop at Harrods. Grace Mugabe, his second wife and forty years his junior, loved shopping in Paris, Switzerland, London - she must look her best.)

The rest of the world dithered. Farm widows appealed to Britain, but were told white Zimbabweans would be offered no special help if they fled to England. The foreign office dismissed "wild calls" for sanctions and said Zimbabwe must settle its own internal affairs. South Africa decided on a softly, softly approach in spite of the threats that anarchy in their neighbouring country could pose. Kenyan and South African rebels began to mimic the Zimbabwean example themselves of "settling" farms for themselves.

But in the meantime cricket continued and Zimbabwe was scoring well against South Africa and England.

Not so far away, in African terms, in Swaziland, schoolgirls were banned from wearing mini-skirts, which, it was alleged, contributed to the spread of Aids. This didn't work, so females (it was their fault, of course) were told not to wear trousers either. Still no success - next year a five-year sex ban was imposed on young women. They were forbidden to even shake hands with men, and were bidden to wear woollen tassels to show they were virgins. As many African men believe having sex with a virgin will cure them of Aids, this could create problems.

Back in Zimbabwe in 2001, the land grab worsened. Mugabe applied pressure to win the forthcoming presidential election (as distinct from the parliamentary election two years before). He proved that a successful way to be elected president was to assault opposition MPs and their families, invade any townships that had dared vote against his party, the ZANU-PF, in the parliamentary election, and then indiscriminately beat up civilians. He reinforced his home troops by recalling 5000 troops (half the force) from the Congo, where they were defending his diamond interests. These troops proceeded to break up the opposition election rallies.

In November Mugabe decided to ban election inspectors. His troops set fire to the opposition's headquarters in Bulawayo, and rampaged through the townships. (Bulawayo is the traditional centre of the Ndebele tribe. Mugabe belongs to a branch of the Shonas, and they have warred against each other since the Bantu tribes arrived in this part of central Africa.)

In December a new media law allowed the government to close down local independent newspapers, prevent foreign journalists from entering the country, and severely restrict local journalists by threats of fines and imprisonment.

As early as February 2001, a bomb had badly damaged the printing presses of the Independent Daily News in Harare. A BBC correspondent's home was violated at night after he was ordered to leave the country with his family.

As the year progressed, most British newspaper correspondents were accused of being terrorists, and threatened. This included those from the Mirror, a paper formerly counted as friendly to the ZANU-PF party. Legislation was set up to prevent any meeting where the government was criticised, and for the arrest of anyone attending these.

A good way to enforce your own laws is to sack the Chief Justice and appoint your own. This was achieved with some difficulty, and further forced resignations soon followed. "Nazis" was how the government described Zimbabwe's Supreme Court judges. Now who was calling names?

The land grab and murders continued apace, with farmlands set on fire, and 95% of white-owned lands (5327 farms) gazetted for seizure. But in a land where no law prevails, which ex-terrorist took notice of pieces of paper? Farms were taken over at will and owners ordered to stop farming. Most of the land remains idle and unoccupied to this day.

The drift of refugees, black and white, over the considerably extensive land-borders of Zimbabwe became a torrent: into South Africa, Botswana, Mozambique and Zambia, in many cases increasing the unemployment troubles in those far-from-stable countries. The South African rand weakened as investors watched the pre-election violence in Zimbabwe.

Living in town offered no consolation: the cost of living rose rapidly, even for basic foodstuffs; power cuts were normal; running water occasional. Mobs stormed into the factories, destroyed machinery and assaulted employees. Hwange Colliery (Wankie in our day) gradually limped to a halt as the months went by. There was no foreign currency to buy replacement parts or oil to drive the heavy lifting machinery. It had supplied high-grade coal constantly, not only for internal use, but "secretly" exported it over the Victoria Falls Bridge (in full view of tourists and residents) to the Zambian copper mines, throughout the UDI years of sanctions.

Around 1996, tourism had started to build up again, so that the Zambezi at Victoria Falls was described improbably as "a sort of African Butlin's Holiday Camp" and was said to be disturbing the wildlife. Tourism had been forecast to become the country's biggest earner of foreign currency. By the turn of the century, however, there was no need to worry.

Meikle's Hotel, for 85 years Salisbury's pride, closed 150 rooms. Not that the absence of tourists gave the elephants, hippos and rhinos of the Zambezi and other game reserves any peace. Instead the squatters and poachers moved in. Rhino horns and elephant tusks were far too valuable to be left running around.

We had to read in English newspapers of the news about Sinoia, the small town nearest our old farm, where I had driven every day to take the children to school and buy supplies. The story ran that the trouble started between squatters and a farmer. The farmer radioed his neighbours for help. For once, the police arrived - and arrested the fifteen or so white farmers who had been attacked, and put them in jail. Chaos erupted in the main (and only) street of the *dorp*. African mobs seized the opportunity to attack passer-bys, kicking, beating and stabbing them and stoning cars. White people were warned by the farmers' radio network to stay away.

Six more people were also put into the cells when they went to the police station to take blankets and enquire about their neighbours' welfare. In the end they all spent seventeen nights in jail, cold and hungry, in dreadfully cramped conditions, before they were granted bail.

YEAR 2002

At the beginning of March 2002, Mugabe contrived to win by 56% yet another election – this time for the presidential election. Nothing was free or fair about the election, yet after months of violence and threats once again, he still barely won. The opposition had been assaulted, charged in court with treason, thrown into prison. their houses burnt down , and yet, bravely, they managed to poll nearly half the votes. South Africa was the only country permitted to send any observers.

Tens of thousands of people couldn't vote after waiting all day (in the hot sun, naturally). They were unable to vote after the boxes were closed in districts known to be favourable to the MDC leader, Morgan Tsvangirai. To avoid being beaten up at road blocks MDC voters were advised to buy ZANU-PF cards, and say they were going to vote for Mugabe. In this way, for 25p, with luck, they might ward off the youth militia who were controlling the roads. Worth a try!

Later in March, Zimbabwe was suspended for a year from the Commonwealth. Travel to many European countries and the USA was already restricted for most members of the ZANU-PF government.

Ian Smith, former Prime Minister of Rhodesia, was told he was no longer a citizen of the country of his birth, which, over his lifetime of 83 years, had changed in more than name. (My own daughter was born in Sinoia, Southern Rhodesia, and now there's no such place as either the town or the country.)

Many streets and avenues in Harare had enjoyed for years a sort of dual naming: Jameson Ave became Samora Machel, Stanley became Jason Moyo, and seeking directions was difficult. Schools, in particular, suffered some rough re-namings: Queen Elizabeth gave way to Sally Mugabe for the Girls' High School, Winston Churchill to Joshua Tongogara for the boys, Warren Park to Chenjerai Hitler Hunzvi for primary pupils.

As the year went by, when the meagre amounts of maize grown by squatter subsistence farmers and the few commercial farmers still allowed to farm were used up, starvation spread throughout Zimbabwe. There had been bad rains - which was not a rare occurrence. The poor, as usual, the black poor, were the first to suffer.

So President Mugabe got round his travel restrictions and presented a strange phenomenon by attending the United Nations food summit in Rome. Five million of his people were hungry, in a country formerly described as "the bread basket of central Africa", and it was his lieutenants' doing. By the end of 2002, it was estimated by the UN World Food Programme in Zimbabwe that 6.7 million people would need food aid in the country. There was no foreign exchange to buy food. Anything available (round the back of warehouses) was preposterously priced.

When we had been farming, we had been part of the Lomagundi farming community, seeing the same familiar faces at meetings, sports clubs, tobacco sales, local store and children's birthday parties. Abruptly these familiar families (or their off-springs) were given three months to stop farming and move out, generally with no compensation. They collected bravely enough at sports and social clubs - life in the bush can be lonely places - for last games and get-togethers, sharing their stories of brutality (illustrated with black eyes and bandaged limbs) before splitting up, wherever they could legally go, according to birthrights or finances. Some went to flats in Harare, rented by friends, others, more fortunate, achieved residence permits elsewhere to start from scratch again, in tents in Mozambique, to relatives or jobs in Australia, New Zealand or South Africa

The daughter and son-in-law of one of our ex-neighbours took his twelve elephants with him, too, to South Africa. As calves, (rescued orphans from poaching), these elephants had been trained on the farm to take tourists for safaris-by-elephant at Victoria Falls. They knew their elephants would be killed, if left behind, like all other animals living there, when they were ousted from their farm.

Those hoping to settle in Britain discovered that grannie being British was no longer justification for any claim to settle in Britain. The High Commissioner and staff in Harare were accused of making life even more difficult for refugees who had been forced to relinquish their British passports to become Zimbabwe citizens. They were, even if successful, being charged for passports at the black-market rate of Z$1000 to the pound instead of the official rate of Z$90. Some couldn't afford the price. Those allowed a British passport were permitted to take out £500 to start a new life. (They should have taken it then - it was due to get worse.)

Black Zimbabweans working in Britain were appealed to by the Zimbabwean Finance Minister to send money to their families at home, and for those lucky relatives to refrain from changing such valuable sterling on the black market. I wonder where this minister changed his foreign currency, or if he just stashed away any bribes in an overseas account.

This unwillingness to help refugees rather conflicts with plans drawn up by the British Ministry of Defence to rescue the 20,000 or so British citizens still remaining in Zimbabwe in August 2002, should "the war veterans start to evict farmers and there was mass slaughter of UK nationals". If roads were blocked, the RAF would evacuate them from Harare and other collection points with the aid of the Parachute Regiment. It was only a contingency plan, newspapers reported, though members of the Parachute Regiment were exercising for three months in South Africa at the end of the year. A coincidence, no doubt. Cold comfort.

Meanwhile, consider the Bushmen, who were the original inhabitants of southern Africa, and believed to have been around for more than 20,000 years (some said much longer). They were being ousted from their traditional lands in neighbouring Botswana because of diamond mining interests. They had already been mercilessly killed and driven out of their territories by the Bantu tribes and white and Arab activities (mainly slavery and mining), over hundreds of years. These Bantu are the same people who now claim this land was always theirs.

YEAR 2003

According to articles in the Times in May 2003, the population of Zimbabwe had now returned to the privations of hunter-gatherer living. Power cuts and petrol and coal shortages had brought transport, factories and hospitals to a halt. Walking and wood-gathering was the norm, whether you're black or white. In the bush, because of lack of maize meal and wheat flour, food was that found on the hoof, *nyama*. (This had always been the same word for meat and animals.)

It was reported at this time that the life expectancy at birth in Zimbabwe was 42.9 years, compared with 56.0 in 1975; 11.7% of children were dying before five years old; and 33.7% of adults had HIV/Aids - about 2,300,000 people.

But, apparently, the most interesting question of the day in 2003 was should or shouldn't the English team play cricket in Zimbabwe in February in their World Cup games. Conflicting reports were issued daily. The British Government, Zimbabwe ministers, the England and Wales Cricket Board, the International Cricket Club, South African, Australian and New Zealand cricketers, anti-Mugabe protestors, and the English cricket team lined themselves up on one side or the other (sometimes on both or neither sides, and sometime changing sides), naming morals, politics, safety, finance, sportsmanship, and even the good of cricket, as excuses either to let the games go ahead or to cancel.

While the world vacillated, two young Zimbabwean cricketers, one white, one black, became the heroes of the drama. Andy Flower and Henry Olonga wore black armbands to mourn "the death of democracy in our beloved Zimbabwe", during their first World Cup game in Harare against Namibia. Brave men! They put to shame the wilting arguments of the rest of the world. Both men fled the country while they still had their lives. England did not play in Zimbabwe this time, but by then, it did not matter much, except for their loss of points.

The land grab continued and worsened. Overseas charities were thinking twice about sending in emergency food supplies when it became apparent that anyone thought to have voted for the opposition was denied rations at the distribution points. The small amounts of meal in the shops were too expensive for those most in need.

The opposition leader, Morgan Tsvangirai was tried in secret for treason. He and two others in the MDC were said to have plotted to murder Robert Mugabe. The trial dragged on for a year. They were allowed out on bail, but judgment was not expected for many more months.

By August 2003 many white pensioners, once the professionals and administrators of that pioneering country of Southern Rhodesia, were having to rely completely on charitable organisations for their basic needs. The Times reported their pensions had dropped to a couple of pounds a month - 40p for one old lady. When they had sold all their possessions, charity only remained.

It is not surprising that any remaining animals, farmed or wild, were starving and diseased: foot and mouth disease and anthrax in cattle, rabies in squatters' and land-grab farmers' dogs, which were kept for hunting, and not vaccinated. A wildlife park near Harare was invaded, the owner and his family had to flee with their dogs and a litter of lion cubs. The owners feared those left behind would be killed for meat or allowed to starve.

Already in 2003, the cost of basic foodstuffs is out of this world. The price of a shopping basket of sixteen items such as bread, mealie meal (for porridge), flour, cheese, eggs, potatoes, tea and coffee had risen over 17,000% between 1981 and 2003. Before Mugabe increased his power drives, the rise between 1981 and 1999 had been a "mere" 300%. Now, don't blink, or the rise will be another thousand dollars. (Before Independence a Rhodesian dollar was worth an English pound.) The price for a kilogram of cheese was Z$12,150. If you needed some bread with it, that would set you back another thousand.

On November 11, 2003, just 38 years to the day after the then Prime Minister, Ian Smith, had announced his Unilateral Declaration of Independence, a three-bedroom house in Harare cost Z$300-million, or should you be willing to sacrifice those much-more-amazingly-desirable dollars: US$100,000. I don't imagine there is a rush to buy: you'd probably get it for a lot less if you did have the right sort of dollars.

YEAR 2004

E-mails from friends in 2003/4 were heart breaking. They describe the despair on people's faces in towns, the heart attacks and stress, the worry of day-to-day existence, the fear at night, the robberies with violence, threats from the "vets", (the "veterans" who are really lawless youths), and the complete breakdown of law and order. Police will not (cannot?) attend a crime until supplied with diesel and, even if they come, will do nothing except, perhaps, arrest the victims.

They describe the desperate straits of the Africans: unemployed, starving, sick with Aids; the Aids orphanages full, relying on charity and food from the handful of farmers still permitted to grow crops.

We knew of only one of our ex-neighbours who was still allowed to farm - let's call him Jack. He had no idea why he survived, unless some government ministers were allowing him to grow crops so they could step in and steal the proceeds at the end of the season. Sure enough, towards the end of the year, an African arrived, saying the farm was now his, and set about making an inventory of the farm equipment that he said was also now his. Jack and his wife were ordered to leave the farm "forthwith". Jack had developed the farm for nearly thirty years, so the order was ignored. His farm workers, desperate to keep their homes and jobs, barricaded the entrance gates. Such farm workers were not of the elite, most likely not Shonas, and not entitled to any land.

Jack already had a government-approved contract to grow 70 acres of tobacco for ten years, starting the next season. He badly needed a cash crop for his survival. So he and his wife carried on with the farming, while taking the precaution of packing up their belongings, ready for a quick exit. The new "owner" of the farm started, concurrently, to plough a land for maize with his own tractor. He was a month late for planting, he destroyed the contours, and the land became a bog at the first rains.

Much bureaucracy and High Court proceedings followed the "take-over", but still they stayed on the farm when 95% of the farmers had left. They went into 2005 fulfilling the contract to grow the tobacco for export to China - in itself a questionable moral dilemma, but needs must, with a family to support. It is hard to imagine the stress of such a life: Jack was smoking 60 cigarettes a day and losing weight rapidly. Their families (including children) were by now scattered in South Africa, Australia and New Zealand. E-mails we received from other friends living in town reported it was still necessary for them to continue to go out to work, though they were now over 75 years old - hospital operations, costing three-quarters of a million Zimbabwe dollars for the surgeon, had to be paid for somehow. By this time it was impossible to say what the value of the Zimbabwe dollar was: just a barrow-load required. It changed every day, always down, but a million was a lot in any currency. I can't imagine how they survive at present: waiting, waiting for something to change, unable to leave; nowhere to go, no foreign currency to go with. (We were younger when we left with our precious £900, and we were British citizens.)

So they grow what food they can and rear chickens in their garden, buy other necessities on the black market, queue endlessly for petrol, keep out of trouble, keep their mouths shut, but sometimes see friends, console each other, even have a few beers out on the veranda. It's warm in Zimbabwe, as it was in Rhodesia, which was God's own country, let's not forget.

In June, the government announced all land was now nationalised. This meant little, as most of the countryside was lying fallow anyway. The new "owners" had no knowledge of farming, and the machinery lay broken and rusting. Over 60% of the workforce had left the country by November. Even the original squatters were now being evicted in favour of friends and relatives of Mugabe and his ministers. There were more signs that governments in Namibia, Kenya and even South Africa were about to follow Mugabe's land-grabbing successes.

Mugabe spent most of 2004 making sure he would be elected as president in the following March, by arresting, torturing and imprisoning opposition MPs and party followers. Later it would prove dangerous just to live in a constituency represented in parliament by an MDC member.

In March, Harare became the focus of a plot to oust President Nguema of Equatorial Guinea, when a Boeing 727 landed with the intention of loading up with a consignment of weapons. A total of 67 mercenaries were arrested, together with their British leader, Simon Mann, a former SAS officer. He and his followers were sentenced to prison, though most of the Africans were released after a year. Sir Mark Thatcher, living in South Africa, was later accused of funding part of the plot. He pleaded guilty to hiring a helicopter and paid a fine of a quarter of a million pounds. He received a suspended prison sentence, but was allowed to leave the country. President Mugabe was hailed as the saviour of Equatorial Guinea for preventing the attempted coup. Justice was said to have been done.

But cricket must go on and, in spite of tremendous opposition from many sides, the English team did go to Zimbabwe. At the last minute, English cricket correspondents were allowed accreditation, while the team waited at Johannesburg airport for the decision. England won the tour, but it is doubtful if any of the players went home with any feelings of satisfaction, of a job well done. Finance and threats of penalties were the victors. Sport had little part.

Then there was the matter of shaking hands with President Mugabe. The British foreign minister, Jack Straw, did it in New York in November, and then Prince Charles did it at the Pope's funeral. Next Prince Harry got friendly with a Zimbabwean girl whose father runs hunting safaris under licence from Mugabe, and is becoming very rich with a trophy fee of £5200 for an elephant and £2300 for a lion. (Who "owns" an elephant or a lion?) Her grandfather ran the ferry that sank on Lake Kyle, near Zimbabwe Ruins, during the making of the film "The Slavers" by the German film company, (while we were living there). It is difficult for the young princes, but they did enjoy hunting foxes.

However, it looks as though David Livingstone's statue will be allowed to look over the Devil's Cataract at Victoria Falls for a while longer, even though there are precious few visitors to regard him any more. It appears that, 150 years after the falls were first reported to the world, Zambia, having now captured most of the foreign tourist business, wants the statue of this Scottish missionary to grace their town of Livingstone. Suddenly, after years of neglect and vandalism of the statue, Zimbabwe has discovered visitors value his memory, and say he can't go.

YEAR 2005

On March 31 Zimbabwe went to the polls "in a climate of fear". Every trick was played to ensure the election was not "free and fair". The parliamentary map was revamped to favour Zanu-PF candidates: 3.4 million Zimbabweans living abroad were not allowed to vote; western election inspectors were banned; an estimated one million dead people's names were added to the roll; there were not enough observers to cover the increased numbers of polling stations; and in those stations not supervised, Zanu-PF votes, when results were phoned in, were vastly inflated. By starvation, threats and job losses, murder and beatings, many of the remaining population was cowed into voting for Mugabe's party.

From Condoleezza Rice to the South African press, the election was condemned.

Grimly, President Thabo Mbeki of South Africa remained loyal to his friend. President Mugabe amassed the two-thirds majority he required to change the constitution.

Next to be destroyed were the street markets, which were run, often by women, as the last-ditch hope of any income. Throughout the towns, police wrecked the stalls and scattered an estimated 10,000 street traders with tear gas and batons. These poor souls were responsible for national price rises and shortages, officialdom said. The real reason was probably that they were undercutting the new influx of Chinese shopkeepers, set up as part of the country's policy of looking east for trade.

Next came "Operation Drive Out the Rubbish". Shanty towns and even brick houses "with no planning permission" were bulldozed, "unlicensed" factories were destroyed, temporary clinics for Aids orphans razed, schools closed, 30,000 people arrested and many hundreds of thousands made homeless. Why? Apart from repressing support for any political opposition, the idea was to force these "poorest of the poor" back into the farms and the bush - which now lay parched from drought and barren from lack of management. "The Herald", Harare's daily government mouthpiece, urged the starving Aids-weakened homeless to go "back to the rural home, to reconnect with one's roots and earn an honest living from the soil our government repossessed under the land reform programme." It was mid-winter in Zimbabwe, with night temperatures on zero. A woman opposition MP distributed blankets to the homeless who were sitting by their ruined homes, and nuns tried to gather the sick children and find them temporary shelter. As the clearances increased, the soldiers set fire to the blankets and charitable gifts being left for the homeless. Many were interned in bush camps without sanitation or any amenities.

Mugabe, now 81, drove to parliament in his Rolls Royce to expound on the country's economic recovery, in this year 2005 of economic development.

*　　*　　*　　*　　*

Surely there must be some good news; the sun must still shine (unless you're in prison); the Victoria Falls and the Zambezi River must still be flowing; the "vets" can't have stopped this. But if you want to see them, you'll be advised to go to the north, the Zambian side. It's a shame - the view along the falls on the south side is one of the elevating experiences of life. To walk along the path by the mighty Zambezi restores the soul - every time.

So much is lost, inspirationally, spiritually and practically. When I think of the beauty and terrific experiences of wild Africa that Rhodesia offered, that we were part of, helped to build and loved, it is heart-breaking to see now that all has come to dust. Has it gone forever?